MAKING A WORLD OF DIFFERENCE

MAKING A WORLD OF DIFFERENCE

Inspiring stories of the world's unsung heroes

MILES ROSTON

GOOD TIMES BOOKS PVT. LTD.
New Delhi (India)
www.goodtimesbooks.com

Published by

GOOD TIMES BOOKS PVT. LTD.
H-13, Bali Nagar, New Delhi-110 015 (INDIA)
Phones: +91-11-25913301, 45069086 *Fax:* +91-11-45069086
Email : info@goodtimesbooks.com
Website : www.goodtimesbooks.com

First Good Times Edition 2011
Second Good Times Impression 2013

ISBN-13 : 978-93-806191-4-9

Cataloging in Publication Data--DK
Courtesy: D.K. Agencies (P) Ltd. <docinfo@dkagencies.com>

Roston, Miles.
Making a world of difference : inspiring stories of unsung heroes / Miles Roston.
p. cm.
ISBN 9789380619149 (pbk.)

1. Heroes--Biography. 2. Women heroes--Biography. 3. Philanthropists--Biography. 4. Social action--Case studies. I. Title.

DDC 920.02 22

Published in arrangement with
Exisle Publishing Limited
'Moonrising', Narone Creek Road, Wollombi,
NSW 2325, Australia

Printed in India at
Salasar Imaging Systems

Contents

Introduction

Dreaming of shoes

Some 30 years ago, in Buriram, a province of Thailand, there was a little barefoot girl named Kwansiri Chanakiat, or Siri. She lived in a rice-farming village. On either side of the dirt road were mostly small shacks like the one belonging to her family. There were also a few old raised teak houses where more prosperous people lived. Behind walls, on quiet shaded grounds, rose the Buddhist temple, its patchy red pointed roof tipped with chofahs, thin gold bird-like decorations.

One day, as she trudged along the road, Siri found an old newspaper lying on the ground. She picked it up and sat in the shade of a tree not much bigger than she was. Unable to read, she turned the pages, until she came to a photograph. It showed people wearing beautiful shoes.

The little girl was transfixed.

Siri ran home to her mother and father and begged them to get her shoes. Her parents gently reminded her that they were just poor farmers. They could not afford such things. For now, she would have to continue going barefoot.

But Siri would not let go of her dream of having shoes.

One morning as she was playing out on the road she observed the older children going to school. She followed them past the temple, where those golden chofahs glittered. She noticed that like the people in the picture, the students too were wearing shoes. They were simple, sturdy and black, not so pretty or stylish, but they were shoes nonetheless.

'When I was a child,' Siri says today, 'I didn't know I wanted education. But I knew this: I saw nice shoes in a newspaper and I wanted to wear them too.'

Siri ran home and begged her mother and father to let her go to school. Though her parents were poor, they did support her desire for education. They saved money for the fees, and she finally entered school. When she first began to attend classes, she still had no shoes. 'Then later, when I got mine, I hung them around my neck, because I was afraid they would hurt my feet.' Like the other students, she later began to wear the shoes.

Many years later, at university in Bangkok, a large city with far more footwear, Siri met her future husband. After they graduated as teachers and married, they returned to Siri's home village and began to teach at Singhapittayakom School.

One day, Siri paid special attention to a little girl in the class, Khanangnit. This young one always had a hard time concentrating, but Siri noticed too just how sad she seemed. Perhaps the girl reminded her of herself when very young. But even though she had been as poor as she suspected Khanangnit was, Siri at least had her dream, whereas, she says, 'If a child is unhappy, she won't even have a dream.'

Teaching is difficult enough, but Siri decided to take her work even further and pay a home visit to Khanangnit. When she went to see her in the nearby village, she was shocked at her living conditions. The little girl lived with her grandfather, a gaunt man who suffered from schizophrenia, as her mother was in hospital. There was barely any furniture inside the shack, and it was also missing one wall. When Siri asked why, the grandfather explained that as they owed money for the mother's medical bills, they were selling the house bit by bit. Siri asked where the girl slept, and Khanangnit said in the pavilion near the temple.

Then she asked Khanangnit what they had to eat. The little girl showed her an old sack of rice. Siri asked if there was anything else. 'The girl pointed to a small jar of local Isaan fish soup we call plarah,' Siri says. Plarah is fermented, and has a pungent smell; when left too long, worms also get in. 'There was nothing else. I was embarrassed, as I thought immediately that would not be enough for me, but the girl said she had enough.'

Having come to see the little girl's circumstances, Siri also took a hard look at her own. 'We had more than her. We had much more, but we never *felt* it was enough.

'Seeing this girl was just like a slap in the face. Until then,' she says,

Siri Chanakiat

'I'd believed money was the most important thing. But even having money still hadn't made me happy. And from what she said, I realised that whether one has enough or not is in the heart.'

On her way home, Siri could not help thinking about Khanangnit and weeping. But later, when she was in bed, unable to sleep and staring up at the ceiling, she says she realised that either she could cry – or she could help.

She started by giving Khanangnit and her grandfather some money. She brought some extra clothes from her family, and food from her well-tended garden. She also taught the two how to grow a wider variety of vegetables. She negotiated with the money-lender, and arranged for the missing side of the shack to be rebuilt.

Not only did Khanangnit's home life grow happier, but so did her days at school, and her performance there improved. Feeling better, she was able to dream again. This, most of all, pleased Siri.

Siri began to visit other children in their homes – those she noticed were doing badly in class. Often they were poor, and their families were in distress. With Siri's help, their lives at home and school improved too. Then she began to share her simple and direct method with teachers from other classes and their students.

Over the next ten years, with her husband Teacher Chai, Siri organised 50 schools in the region to work with her, setting up a community-based organisation whose name translates as 'The Network for Local Teachers'. She encouraged the teachers to make home visits, to see directly the situations of the children who lived in poverty. With no government or outside funding, her network helped thousands upon thousands of children, with their own and community contributions of second-hand clothing, food and money. But they also taught families to farm new varieties of crops and become more self-sufficient.

Not only did Siri and her network support the children in their daily lives but, more importantly, they encouraged their dreams, whether they wanted to be rice farmers, teachers, doctors or astronauts. 'I had a dream when I was young that I wanted to have education, so that I could wear shoes,' Siri says. 'It was a child's dream. But this sort of dream is serious for young children. Even though it seemed as if it was nonsense, it served as a drive as well. I want to help every child to have a dream.'

Siri had the courage to want shoes and get them, and that meant going to school. But unlike many who achieve their own personal goals, she has spent a lifetime inspiring other children to fulfil their dreams too. At first, she and the teachers in her network relied only on their own resources. Now the government and outside organisations have begun to notice the extraordinary results they are getting and are bringing their simple method of care to ever more people in other districts of Thailand.

This is a book about Siri, and people like her, who better the lives of others, sometimes in their own communities, and sometimes thousands of miles away. People like a working-class couple who built an animal farm for children in a slum in Amsterdam. Or a renowned architect who builds houses for the wealthy and environmentally responsible resorts in China but who feels his creative challenge is to fix bathrooms for the health of thousands of Aboriginal people in Australia.

There is an event planner from South Africa who organises weddings, corporate events and bar mitzvahs, and feeds homeless and low-income communities with fresh leftovers like fruit and yoghurt, smoked salmon or beluga caviar. And a Catholic priest from Binghamton, New York, who found his joy and calling in easing the way of the dying in a Buddhist hospice in Thailand.

A man in Kenya helps glue-sniffing street children achieve their dreams too, even taking 20 years with one who eventually became a teacher. Another man leaves a job at L'Oréal in Paris to start a restaurant and beauty salon staffed by former street kids, giving them skills so that they can change their lives. And a man in China who helps thousands of children who were orphaned after the government allowed the blood supply to be contaminated with AIDS.

There is an Aboriginal nurse, who ensured the members of her community controlled their own medical clinics. And an African Methodist minister in a devastated section of Pittsburgh, who founded a Montessori preschool for poor children and healthcare centres for their parents. There is also the first sex worker – commonly termed a prostitute – to be the keynote speaker at a major human rights conference in Poland. And a former criminal turned social worker in a Moroccan ghetto in the Netherlands. There is the man in the UK who took his love of football and used it to change the lives of the homeless, worldwide. And an exiled rebel from Darfur who, unlike so many revolutionaries, listened to his people, rather than urging them to listen to him.

This book is not just about what these people and others have done, but what they have learned through improving the lives of their fellow human beings. It is also about what works if one wants to offer help. Although these people come from a wide variety of cultures and countries, they all share certain key principles.

But ultimately the book is about their secret. It is what Siri calls 'the contentment of giving': that helping others gives one's own life happiness and meaning.

It is widely believed that to do good in the world demands suffering and sacrifice, and that the only reward may be in some sort of afterlife, such as heaven or reincarnation. Another myth is that the problems of the world are so insurmountable that anything one does feels futile and in vain.

But what scientists are now starting to learn, through studies in Canada, the US, the UK and other countries, Siri and the others discovered through experience: doing good for others on one's chosen scale, whether for one person or for thousands of people, can do oneself good. Here and now. That by being unselfish each of us can, in a sense selfishly, have a life full of meaning and contentment.

That is the true dream of getting shoes for Siri. To get our own shoes and shoes for those in the world around us.

Chapter 1

No news is good news

In Frank Capra's 1945 film *It's A Wonderful Life*, two angels are stars in the night-time sky. They twinkle energetically as they discuss George Bailey, the troubled hero who has spent his life trying to improve the lives of others.

'A man down on earth needs our help,' flashes the first angel.

'Is he sick?' flickers the second, concerned.

'Worse. He's discouraged!'

'Nulla nuova, buona nuova' goes the old Italian phrase. No news is good news. To appreciate its truth, all you have to do is read the news, any day of the week. Whether transmitted by newspaper, television, the Internet, mobile phone, gossip or carrier pigeon, the reports seem almost always discouraging. They may convey the horrors of war – 'civil', as in Sudan, or invasion, followed by more 'civil' fighting such as in Iraq, Afghanistan or the Congo. A report might present the poverty and increasing fuel and food shortages in the developing world, or even in developed economies like the US and Europe. It could show the corruption of politicians, conflicts associated with immigration and integration, indigenous people's lack of rights, the AIDS epidemic or global warming. At the other end of the scale, the endless gossip about 'celebrities' demonstrates that even the glamorous may lead horribly difficult lives, often exacerbated by a lack of privacy.

To counter such despairing reports, there are clarion calls from former politicians, those same celebrities or others from popular TV shows saying we can solve these problems through debt relief, sanctions, or donations from us, the so-called general population. We send money to rush in help, for example to fight famine in Ethiopia as Live Aid tried over 20 years ago, to fund those affected by the tsunami in 2004, or the tsunami-like Cyclone Nargis that affected Burma in 2008.

Yet even as aid is supposedly given, people's suffering just seems to continue. The news we get is that little difference is made by any of our efforts or donations. Problems just keep arising, often exacerbated or even caused by the very same governments that are supposed to serve their people.

In Burma, it was the country's military government that refused to allow aid to its own populace, leading to the deaths of perhaps a hundred thousand more people. Other international governments stood by, wringing their global hands in despair. In South Africa, where over five million people were HIV-positive, the government remained in denial over the AIDS epidemic. Its president questioned the reality of the disease, and the health minister refused to roll out drugs, instead encouraging the poor population to use olive oil and garlic.

In the context of Africa, international aid from the 1950s onwards involved billions of dollars and now euros. Yet much of the continent continues to be ravaged by poverty, famine, war, the AIDS epidemic and malaria. Many of the countries here and in Asia gained independence in the years after World War II. Yet after the euphoria of achieving nationhood, people became disenchanted. Supported or influenced by either the United States or the Soviet Union during the Cold War, many leaders siphoned off money supposedly apportioned for children, medicine or even water wells. Instead, they filled their personal onshore and offshore reserves.

But you don't have to travel to the developing world to see corruption or inefficiency. One need only look at the flooding caused by Hurricane Katrina in New Orleans, where the United States government let its own people flounder in the muck for months. Ironically, in Africa, specifically Kenya, people in a poor village heard about the horrors of the destruction on the radio and tried to raise money to help victims in the US!

Of course, there are good, well-meaning, intelligent and even extraordinary people working in governments, the United Nations and its agencies, and in large non-governmental organisations such as Plan International, Save the Children, Oxfam, Care and World Vision. Braver than Sisyphus, these individuals push sometimes overwhelming boulders of paperwork uphill and bureaucratic rules aside to solve the stubborn societal ills that will not go away. They may have to spend their careers in lands far from home, trying to create real change for the better. Yet many of them will admit they get frustrated, because the big organisations they work for are just that: big. Because these institutes get so big and so laden with layers of policy, their solutions may not adapt or mutate as quickly as the problems. Locals can also get jealous of what they perceive as very high salaries in comparison to their own wages.

Some of these non-profit organisations have advertised on television for years about children in need, getting viewers to donate out of guilt. In crude industry parlance, some of these commercials are called 'flies in the eyes' ads. Many involve images of starving children, and the promise that change can be made by donating $30 or £30 a month to sponsor one of the said starving young people.

We may even find ourselves reaching for the phone and the credit card to give the money. Then we hear stories of abuse of our trust, or how some of the charities use 80 per cent of what they receive to cover their own administrative costs.

Some say these kinds of approaches even contribute to what can be called 'misery fatigue'. As we repeatedly watch the suffering on television during the course of years, we decide we would rather just focus on our own lives and difficulties, whether big, small or imagined. Eventually, after watching so much discouraging news, followed by the ads, the problems of the world do seem too big – whether it's Sudan, Iraq, the millions of children facing starvation or the certain destruction of the earth. In the face of imminent doom, contributing a tiny amount each month seems quite futile.

To make the problem of global suffering appear more discouraging, those fighting the good fight often seem to suffer even more themselves. That makes the whole state of things seem even more unfair. Legends of people acting for the good of others yet suffering for it are known from all ages; a graphic example is the story of those thrown to the lions during Roman times. Perhaps the most notable 20th-century example would be Mother Teresa.

Although born in Albania, she served the poor and needy in Calcutta, a place thousands of miles from her home, for 40 years. She had pledged her love to her God, taking a vow to Him as to a husband. Though devoted to her Catholic faith, she did her work without what we would normally consider proselytising. She said, 'Of course I convert. I convert you to be a better Hindu or a better Muslim or a better Protestant. Once you've found God, it's up to you to decide how to worship Him.' Her order, started in the late 1940s with only 12 sisters, grew to 4500 in over a hundred countries. Her work was even recognised by the secular community when she was awarded the Nobel Peace Prize in 1979, and she was beatified by the Pope in 2003. Here truly was a woman who epitomised the legend of doing good for others.

Recently, many years after her death, Mother Teresa's diaries were published, under the title *Come Be My Light*. They revealed that while being so admired by others, inwardly she lived a life of despair. She confided in her writings that, though her deep relationship with God inspired her to work with the poor, His presence disappeared soon after her mission in Calcutta began. She fought intense depression, writing: 'Darkness is such that I really do not see – neither with my mind nor with my reason. The place of God in my soul is blank. I just long & long for God ... The torture and pain I can't explain.'

Though she sought solace from father confessors, Mother Teresa only felt His return for one brief five-week respite for the rest of her years. It was as if she felt literally abandoned by Him. Anyone who has ever languished in the absence of his or her lover can relate to that feeling, but her abandonment lasted a lifetime. What kind of reward was that for doing good?

Another hero of the 20th and 21st century would be Nelson Mandela. He is renowned for sacrificing 27 years of his life in prison, and for his part in the fight for the freedom of the people of his nation, all the people. Unlike Mother Teresa, the direct cause of his suffering was his oppressor, South Africa's apartheid government. Yet in addition to Mandela's admirable struggle, he is even more beloved worldwide for his cathartic forgiveness. There is also the lesser praised sacrifice of his wife Winnie Mandela, who raised their children on her own and was later castigated for her activities by the community, and suffered the disintegration of her marriage.

It was only when Nelson Mandela was in his eighties that he began what could be called the semblance of a personal life. I heard him speak at an International AIDS Conference in Bangkok, where he exhorted attendees to solve the crisis themselves, saying that he wanted to finally begin to enjoy his life at the age of 86. 'The fight against AIDS is one of the greatest challenges the world faces at the start of the 21st century,' he said; 'I cannot rest until I'm certain that the global response is sufficient ... The day after tomorrow, the 18th of July, will be the day I turn 86. Allow me to enjoy my retirement by showing that you can rise to the challenge.'

Can one make a difference in the world and enjoy one's life? If not, it is not only the news that seems discouraging but also what happens to those heroes, both famous and unknown, who fight against injustice, and to those of us who admire them and wish to emulate them.

What is rarely shown on the news is how amid tragedy people do live. Our fast-paced news focuses on the tragic big picture but misses the most crucial part: daily life. Because, even in the midst of wars and destitution, people do the best they can, and better. Strangely, many who have had more suffering inflicted on them than we can easily imagine still find happiness and contentment by helping others.

One of my first glimpses of this was when I met a young man in Sierra Leone, just after the country's brutal ten-year civil war. He was wearing a white shirt and khaki pants, and he explained to me how he had been elected the leader of a refugee camp in Freetown, the capital. In the encampment of tin-roofed shacks were people whose limbs had been amputated by rebel soldiers, including a two-year-old girl with only one hand left. Years earlier, rebels had captured this young man near his home. Noting his student ID card, they had chopped his hands off, gloatingly telling him that now he would never be able to study.

Later, however, in the refugee camp, while making sure things ran smoothly and that everyone was fed, he was still determined to go to university. He could no longer write, but he said he would take oral examinations. While we talked, the orphaned little girl stood beside him. He was clearly her role model. After our conversation, I remember watching them walk away side by side, he in his khakis and she in a floral print dress. Her remaining hand held onto his side, and she was skipping. Unlike George Bailey in his moment of despair in *It's A Wonderful Life*, this amputee and student remained encouraged, and encouraging. Or as Siri would call it, inspiring.

Contrary to what one may see in the news, there are many people like that young man. And many who have not had to undergo such suffering to find their happiness. If we have the desire to help people, whether in Africa or in Kalamazoo, Michigan, can we? And have we, like that young man who wanted to get his university degree, the right to our own lives as well?

Yes. According to everyone whose stories I tell in these pages, we can. Like Siri, who takes care of thousands of children, yet cultivates her own family, home and beautiful garden full of all varieties of orchids. While still wearing nice shoes.

The more I got to know people like Siri the more questions were raised. Why help? Is it to put things in a better order? Is it arrogant to think that we can do so in the first place? Why should we believe that someone with no kinship to us has a problem that we can make into *our* problem?

It turns out that the root of the word 'kindness' means to *make* someone kindred, or family. Every one of these people, by kindly reaching out to those who seemingly had nothing to do with them, created an ever-larger family in a sense. And they learned to care for others no matter what situation they were in themselves. Whether their lives are filled with fortune or misfortune, they achieve success in their work with others, as well as in their own careers, and live lives, if not always of joy, certainly of purpose.

So what is it that works when so many billions of dollars, euros, pounds, shillings or baht haven't? Even more importantly, what effect can being 'Good Samaritans' have on us? Could it actually increase our own happiness?

Chapter 2

The goodness gene

It is a bit embarrassing to have been concerned with the human problem all one's life and find at the end that one has no more to offer by way of advice than 'try to be a little kinder'.

Aldous Huxley

In getting to know the people in this book, I allowed myself to put any question to them, no matter how preposterous. If there is a way of helping others that works for you, do you have to be a certain kind of person? Do you have to be predisposed to be happy, even in miserable conditions? Is there something that is common to people who can manage or even thrive in any situation, even a civil war? Do you have to come from a life either of extreme privilege or destitution? Or do you have to come from a warm family, or an upbringing of suffering? Do you have to have a special background or education, say, at Sainthood School? To take it to an even sillier extreme, could these qualities be genetic?

The answer to all of these questions comes down to a simple word: No.

And since not one of the people here would claim to wear a halo, a CV that includes a degree from Sainthood School is obviously irrelevant. One trait that all these people have in common is that they themselves would never take 'No' for an answer, no matter who it came from.

Their backgrounds are far more varied than one could perhaps expect for such a group, if one might call theirs the 'Good Samaritan profession'. A certain upbringing, income, background or class is often expected for those in specific occupations like doctors, lawyers, computer programmers, architects or caterers. But our subjects come from a multitude of professions – and some are rebels.

Many of their lives have had more dramatic ups and downs than a Hollywood film. In retrospect, however, their directions in life seem fated, like ancient Greek myths. But no matter how varied their experiences, upbringing or stories, every one gained the same insights into what works in contributing to a community and to their own well-being. That alone is the uniting factor: they found the same principles, no matter what continent they lived, played or worked on.

And as sceptical as I was, I was surprised to find that by sticking to those principles they each achieved the same result: a life of meaning and contentment.

Some experienced discrimination and racism as they were growing up. But instead of remaining victimised, this led them to fight back on behalf of their wider communities. One example of this is Naomi Mayers, an Aboriginal woman born in 1941. Her country, Australia, is well known for its historical policies against the welfare of the indigenous people. They didn't even get the rights of citizenship until 1967, though they were, as Naomi puts it, the 'original Australians'. A strong woman whose smiling eyes belie her fierce determination, Naomi trained as a nurse and is now CEO of the Aboriginal Medical Service in Redfern, Sydney. This is the first community-controlled medical service in the country. Today she runs it alongside chairman Sol Bellear, himself a fierce activist for the Aboriginal cause, whose background is as a truck driver and union organiser.

Discrimination accounts for the career too of Idris Azraq, a rebel leader from Darfur. In this region of Sudan, a racist genocide is currently taking place. As he says, the Arab-led government is systematically 'Arabicising the country', eradicating and pushing out fellow Muslims because they are black Africans.

Idris is a quiet man in his forties, with a direct and open face, who is always dressed in a jacket and dress shirt. His clothes have seen better days, as has he. He speaks wistfully about growing up in his village of Midob, a life that though poor by Western standards was rich in tradition. Here he had an extended and loving family. Unlike his siblings and peers, he earned the opportunity to gain a higher education and economically improved career in Europe. Yet Idris has devoted his life to the cause of freeing his fellow Darfurians from persecution, whether he is ultimately successful or not.

'I feel I'm one of the few highly educated people not only in Darfur but in my region. So it is my duty to do something for my people. When I was a student and I went to school, the people in my village contributed, giving me ten or fifty pounds, pocket money for transport which I needed. The people there all shared. Now I must do something, to change our lives, the life of our people.'

Idris is a man who now lives on the run, in dedication to his cause and his community while, he says, other countries and the UN negotiate slowly with the very government that is carrying out the atrocities. Yet interestingly, it is education that is Idris's focus. Education allowed him to get to know the 'Other', whether other ethnic groups in Sudan or Europeans. That exposure gave him insight into ways of life other than that of his own people, and freed him, he says, from the closed-mindedness that can result when one has been blinded by the rage of one's oppression too long.

This idea of contact with the Other marks the lives of people such as Father Michael Bassano. Now in his sixties, with gleaming eyes and a strong nose, Father Michael was born into a lower-class immigrant Italian family in Binghamton, New York. At that time, post World War II, his father feared prejudice and recriminations because Italy had sided with Hitler. Father Michael doesn't remember any prejudice against himself, but he does remember how segregated the city was. But unlike many, as a youth he got to know kids from other ethnic groups. That, he feels, is the gift that allowed him to change for the better later in life.

'As a young teenager, I had contact with other people from different parts of the city. I knew African-Americans. I had friends who were Jewish who would invite me to their temple. So I didn't just stay in my Catholic place. I had exposure to people of other faiths and ethnicities. They gave me a broader perspective on ways of looking at things.'

Years later, after a career as a Catholic priest, he left the security of his parish and spent his first ten years abroad working in Chile with the poor communities who resisted the repressive government regime. His next ten years were spent in Thailand, working alongside Buddhists. 'I'm not just from Binghamton, New York now,' he says gratefully. 'I have a wider perspective on the world than just the American point of view. I'm part of a larger picture.'

Another person who could relate to the Other is Paul Pholeros. Now in his fifties, he is a big, gruff man with as big a heart. A renowned architect from Sydney, Paul is one of the founders of the organisation Healthabitat. Beyond his private and corporate clientele, his creative focus is on the glamorous work of fixing bathrooms in Aboriginal communities, where children for years have lost their sight as a result of the shoddy housing conditions. He experienced life as the Other himself, as his father was a Greek immigrant, though his mother was a 'normal' Australian. Paul says that when he was a child no one ever called him 'a wog', a common insult for Greeks and Italians at the time, because he was large even then. But growing up in a household with Greek-speaking grandparents gave him a different perspective that allowed him to be open to experiences with the Aboriginal people.

This was true too of Sandra Meihubers, a dentist. Her family emigrated to Australia from Latvia after the Second World War with little to show for their former upper-middle-class life. 'I've always been Other, and that's a whole conversation there,' Sandra says, laughing. 'But it never worried me. I didn't look different. So I didn't get that visual racism.

'It was only when my family opened their mouths that the accent came out. Or when I opened my lunch at school. I'd have black bread and salami, and everybody else had white bread and tomato sauce. But it was good food.'

As the Other herself, Sandra found working with people outside her own culture more natural and comfortable, whether training people in dentistry in Nepal, or in the Aboriginal community where she originally worked with Naomi Mayers. Or with the man she might even call another kind of Other, her husband Paul Pholeros.

Poverty also prepared some of these people for their future lives, even in developed economies like the Netherlands. One such person is Mustafa, from the Dutch Moroccan community. He dreamed of a career as a soccer player, and had the talent for it too. Yet his poor family were fearful of how his asthma and his sport might endanger him, and feeling isolated from the wider society, in his youth Mustafa became a real 'tough guy' with a notorious gang in Amsterdam West. It was only after the most serious crisis of his life, when he was accused of manslaughter, that he went through his own period of reckoning. He eventually became a social worker, devoting his life to helping other troubled youth avoid the pitfalls he had tumbled into.

Another person from relative poverty is Brenda Gregg, from Pittsburgh in the US. Born when African-Americans couldn't even vote, she felt less racism than some as her community was mixed, due to the multi-racial nature of the steel industry in her hometown. Later the industry's demise turned a thriving city into a ghost town.

What Brenda did have was a family that was poor but hardworking, and still thinking of others. 'I grew up without a lot of money. But I never knew I was poor. My mother went to the thrift shop every Saturday morning. She came home with bags of clothes, and she sewed. We just tried to take what we had and hopefully make a better life for someone else. It was never ever about looking for lots of money. But I always knew what I'd do with lots of money,' she says with a laugh. 'I would build something for poor people.'

From a similar background, but on a continent far away geographically, culturally and economically, is Alphonce Omolu. He grew up in Kenya, in a poor but self-sufficient family, with a few head of cattle and patches of land. After Lake Victoria flooded in 1962, the farming areas around Kisumu became infertile and his father and mother struggled to get by. Yet, he says, his family instilled in him the value of helping others. As a young man he was already volunteering to counsel other youths, especially troubled ones. Years later, when the corruption in his country prevented young people like him from attending university and following their dreams, he was called into his current line of work, helping troubled street children. When the AIDS epidemic hit the country, many children were orphaned and left to fend for themselves. Luckily for some of the 250,000 such kids in Kenya, Alphonce's knowledge and patience also grew.

Someone from a completely contrasting background financially and culturally is Chung To. He comes from a well-to-do family in Asia and the United States. Now in his forties, a modest and quiet man with serene but searching eyes, Chung To was formerly a high-flying investment banker, having studied at Columbia and Harvard, and later working for UBS in New York and then in Hong Kong. But he always remembered the influence of his grandmother, a woman who supported refugees from mainland communist China. She taught him to give, telling him, 'When you are in a position to help others, you *should* help others.' He also credits his Catholic school with fostering his charitable bent, 'as there was a lot of teaching about St Francis'.

It was St Francis who said 'preach the Gospel at all times, and when necessary use words'. Though not a religious man, Chung To seemed to follow this dictum, giving up his lucrative career in finance to devote his life to thousands of children orphaned by AIDS in China.

Yet another person from a middle-class background, albeit a struggling one, is the gregarious Ronni Kahn. A tall redhead in her fifties, like Siri she likes a nice pair of shoes. Ronni was born into a Jewish family in Johannesburg, South Africa. While her parents were not anti-apartheid activists, her neighbours were. They remained the inspiration for Ronni many years later, following a life in Israel, a move to Australia and a divorce after 25 years of marriage. It was a return trip to see those neighbours that set her on a life now dedicated to charity work.

Another mid-career change took place in Amsterdam, beginning in the formerly working-class neighbourhood of Jordaan. This is where Flor was born, a brick-tiler with a thick working-class accent. He married Wilma, a young woman from the more upper-class 'South Side', who worked in a beauty shop. Theirs was still a good life, driving into the countryside on Flor's old motorcycle, or even to France for holidays. That was until Flor found himself working in the poverty-ridden Bijlmer area of Amsterdam, where he met Surinamese kids who didn't even know what a chicken was. 'I started with a few chickens for the children,' he remembers. 'Then there were a lot of children who had never even seen a goat. So I got a goat.' Goat to cow, cow to horse, then horses to llamas, pigs, donkeys and guinea fowl. 'Until eventually it became a farm for us to teach the kids what animals are.' Over the next 30 years Wil and Flor, the urban working-class couple, kept their children's farm growing, literally in the midst of the high-rises.

Then again, there is Siri in Buriram, Thailand. Young and poor, it was her desire for shoes that sent her to school and led to her eventual career as a teacher. But even the way she chose her teaching subject has a fairy-tale quality.

At the age of 18, she was riding in a truck with a young woman who was pregnant. All of a sudden, she saw her companion's face grimace in pain. She yelled at the driver to stop. There was no doctor or midwife available in the rural rice-growing area. She listened to the young woman's breathing grow heavier and heavier, and responded to whatever she wanted, using what knowledge she had to assist the young woman by the side of the road. With patience, she encouraged the woman until the moment the baby was born, keeping on telling her it would be all right. 'I made my decision to study biology, because I delivered the baby in a pick-up truck. I saw during the delivery that this was what life was all about. That was an inspiration,' Siri says today, many years after becoming a biology teacher, then starting her teachers' network, which has helped thousands of babies through their childhood.

She feels she began to learn then what human beings need in times of want. Over time she grew to understand these needs as principles, as did all the other people here, whether from China or the US, France or Kenya, and whether Buddhist, Catholic, Jewish, Muslim, agnostic or atheist.

Their principles might even seem self-evident. Yet strangely enough, in practice they go against what human beings in government and other institutions have done for years.

1. To look: to see the problem or dilemma and allow oneself to experience it.

2. To listen: to hear how the person or community best thinks the problem can be approached, rather than imposing one's own solution.

3. To use what you know: each of us has a skill that can be of help, ranging from dentistry or architecture to what one person calls simply being.

4. To have patience, because short-term change changes back. Unlike politicians' promises to end crime and social injustice overnight, real solutions take time. Even decades.

5. To give encouragement. Even more crucial than throwing money at a problem, though money is necessary too, is to inspire hope and vision, and encourage people to dream.

What each of these people in turn did was to apply these principles to their own lives, which became richer for every single human being they helped. By helping others towards joy, they learned to enjoy their own lives.

And their experience again is being confirmed by science. In March 2008 *Science* magazine reported the results of a study which showed that: 'Spending more of one's income on others predicted greater happiness ... Participants who were randomly assigned to spend money on others experienced greater happiness than those assigned to spend money on themselves.'

For myself, I have my own scientific test that I apply to people, to find out whether their words are just words, or if they walk the talk. My test is to spend time with them, seeing if they make good eating, drinking or simply yakking companions. When someone really likes life, their enjoyment is infectious. Whether at Dunkin Donuts in Bangkok, de Balie in Amsterdam, a Thai restaurant in Sydney, a breakfast corner in Pittsburgh or a lovely garden in Buriram, what I was privileged to get from all these people was a lot of enjoyment and captivating stories.

Chapter 3

Take a look

A man should look for what is,
and not for what he thinks should be.

Albert Einstein

Beside the dusty roads in this Thai village, shimmering in the tropical heat, there is one rice paddy after the other. People have laboured in these fields of luminous green in the same way for centuries. Though it's a way of life that appears peacefully idyllic from afar, it's hard and repetitive work.

Nearby, from the shade of her dark teak veranda, Siri looks out over the small pond in the midst of her lush garden. It's filled with carefully cultivated plants. Unlike the rice paddies, with only one crop, here there is a variety flowers, fruits and vegetables that Siri has spent years learning about. This is a quiet place where she can come to reflect on what she has seen and how she can get others, even the very needy, to see that there are always others still needier.

She tells a story about one 13-year-old boy named Sawarut. A few years ago, the bleakest of futures was awaiting him – life as an orphan responsible for his siblings. At the time Sawarut knew his mother was sick, but he didn't know that she had AIDS. This was before medicines were available, and the disease was a death sentence.

In the eighties, many of the rice farmers of this area could no longer support their families, and numbers of young women moved to the cities to work in prostitution, sending money home. Some of them also brought HIV/AIDS home. Husbands who had gone to work elsewhere brought it back to their wives. In these uneducated and fearful communities, those who got the disease were stigmatised.

If his mother died, Sawarut, as the eldest child, would have to take care of his three younger brothers and sisters. And because of her standing in the community, it fell to Siri to tell him the news. However, she took her time, getting to know him first.

'I wanted him to feel strong, so I didn't tell him immediately about his mother's illness,' she says, pausing for a moment to reflect quietly on Sawarut. 'I paid him several visits, until he became used to me. Until one day it was the right time to tell him.'

First, Siri decided to take him to someone else who was going through their own suffering. 'I asked him to carry some bags of rice, and told him that we would go visit some other people.'

Together, they gave rice to the poorer villagers. 'One of those we went to visit was a girl who lived with a blind grandmother. She had nothing to eat. In their little hut, Sawarut handed out some of the rice to this girl.

'On leaving, I asked him what he thought about the girl he had visited. Having seen the girl with no parents, but only one blind grandmother, Sawarut thought she was much worse off than he was. She had no brothers and sisters, while he had three. And – he still had his mother, even though she was sick.'

It was then that Siri sat him down to tell him about his own mother, because he had seen, directly, the difference between his situation and another's. In comparison to the girl's plight, he felt privileged. And more importantly, he was moved by the predicament of the girl. 'Now I could talk to him like we were two grown-ups. Like he was an adult. Then we could make plans together for his well-being.'

Siri says that seeing like this applies to anyone, whether in the West, Asia or Africa. The only way to understand a situation or to be moved – whether one is Bill Gates or a 13-year-old boy whose mother is dying and who needs to find the strength to carry on – is to look for oneself. 'Just take a look,' she says. 'Not only to speak about it, but to *see*.'

It might seem that in allowing oneself exposure to suffering, poverty or disease, for example, one might become depressed or feel hopeless about the human condition. But Siri's notion of seeing as a liberating experience is borne out by the stories of the couple with a farm in the slum, the architect in Australia, the former heroin addict, and the investment banker in China. Each of these people took a different path to looking at others in distress – a path that could involve happenstance, allowing oneself to be open to it, going through one's own hell, or actually seeking hell out.

Happenstance, and literally taking the bull – or a cow – by the horns, is what happened to Wil and Flor in the Netherlands.

A goat, a cow and a llama in Amsterdam

Wil and Flor

When you treat animals well,
you treat people well.

From the metro platform at Gansenhoef station, a strange sight can be seen in the distance: nestled below stacks of dense high-rises is a small patch of open land and a farmhouse. On one side is an Albert Heijn-chain supermarket, where the primarily poor Surinamese and Ghanaian population shop. On the other side are the dreary and seemingly endless flats. Between the two, an array of animals wander about, as if they are waiting to board Noah's Ark. Walking among the animals, I can see odd friendships. One is between a donkey and a goat, which is literally standing on its companion, defending its privileged perch against all the other goats and sheep.

Children watch fascinated from the safety of the fence, tearing off bits of bread for the goats that bleat and run over to them, forgetting all about the donkey when they see the chance for a snack. Other children wander amid the ducks, turkeys, guinea fowl and sheep, carrying pails and cleaning up after the animals.

This is a 'Kinderboerderij' – the children's farm that Wil and Flor started 30-odd years ago. Only 20 minutes from Amsterdam's Central

Station, from the red-light district and the tourist centre, it is a much longer distance from where this couple began their lives.

Inside a two-storey house, defining the Dutch word 'gezellig' – warm and cosy – Flor and Wilma sit at a table spread with cakes in case the children come inside. Now in his early sixties, with his strong white beard Flor looks like Father Christmas. One might think from his ease of bearing, and his baggy hay-strewn clothes, that he was always a farm boy. But he comes from the old, densely populated Jordaan neighbourhood of Amsterdam.

The Jordaan is an area that hasn't looked like farmland since the 1600s. Now gentrified, and home to a weekly organic market at Nordermarkt, it used to be a very working-class neighbourhood – what might itself have been called a slum. In fact, Flor's accent is very specific to the area – the equivalent of the British Cockney accent.

Flor's wife, Wilma, is thin, almost gaunt, also in her early sixties, and invariably wearing a pale, light sweater. Her heavy-lidded eyes light up whenever a child wanders into the house, and children wander in all the time. That's when she takes a pause from smoking to help them with homework, or to put a young Moroccan boy and a Surinamese boy to sawing, teaching them how to go back and forth as if they were operating a seesaw over a big piece of wood. Or perhaps she will go outside to teach two young boys to collect the animals' 'poop' – a word that sends the boys into paroxysms of giggles.

Now, though, Wilma and Flor take a break from their many chores – which include feeding the pigs, the sheep, the llama, the cows, the turkeys, the guinea fowl, the horses, and the largest pig I've ever seen, which is a huge fan of Flor's.

As Wilma admits, 'We are city people.' Their lives together started when they, like the poop collectors, were children. 'Flor's father was a tailor, and his mother was a housewife. His father made uniforms for the army,' Wilma remembers. She, on the other hand, came from a far more upper-class area than the working-class Jordaaner. She puts on a hoity-toity accent. 'I was from South Amsterdam – the South Side.' Flor laughs.

Though both were city people, there was a slight precedent to this seemingly barmy farm in the midst of the city. 'Flor's grandfather was a crazy guy,' Wilma continues. 'He lived in the Jordaan, in Kinkerstraat.

Flor and Wilma at their urban farm.

But in his backyard, he had all these animals. He had a big pig, in the backyard, as a pet. And chickens and a goat. And a little pony. In the Jordaan!'

She laughs, perhaps a little bitterly, thinking of all the government red tape she and Flor have to go through now to stay ahead of the endless city regulations. 'He had a farm in his backyard, but in those days we didn't have all these laws we have now. Nobody complained about the snoring of the pig. The neighbours next door liked the sound.'

Flor laughs again, as Wilma points outside to the menagerie moving around outside their living room. Then she turns back inside to the dogs asleep on the couch, the box of puppies by the kitchen counter, and to the brown baby goat, which Wilma had taken in after its mother rejected it.

'So Flor gets all this from his grandfather,' she says. 'Yes, he gets it from his grandfather.'

Wilma and Flor have been married a long time, almost forty years. But that figure gets compounded when I learn how they played together as children from the age of three. Wilma's parents had a little wooden house and tent at a campsite in Soest. This wasn't farmland, but forest. Flor's grandfather also had a place there. And that's where the children met every summer.

'We played together at the campsite. We'd go there for three months, and even go to school there. In those days, if you went outside Amsterdam, you had permission from your school to go to school outside the city for three or four months until summer vacation. So we went to school in Soest for three or four months. That was normal. Now it's impossible. Now you can't take the children from the school and put them in another school.'

As they grew up, neither considered going to university. Neither of them even finished formal secondary school.

'I went to household school,' says Wilma, 'to learn to clean the house. But I was seldom in school. I was more on the street. And Flor, he was 14 when he went to work with his first tiler boss.' Flor went to technical school, apprenticed out to learn how to place tiles, in kitchens, bathrooms, fireplaces or anywhere they were needed. Each week, he would go to school one day and work the other four.

They only started a romantic relationship after finishing school. Flor laughs again, his Santa Claus eyes twinkling. He recalls how he showed up at Wilma's house and asked her to come with him; putting on a husky movie star's voice, he tells me, 'I said, "Would you like to take a ride on my motorbike?"'

But she was from – and he now imitates her hoity-toity accent – 'the Souderbuurt'. Her father didn't like him: after all, Flor was from the Jordaan! And when Wilma is asked today if she liked him then, she says point-blank: 'No. But he did have a big motorcycle.'

Wilma went for the ride. When she came back, her father was not pleased. 'I was grounded for two weeks. And I was 19! Still, though my father didn't like Flor then, I think later on he liked him more than me.'

Flor's mother, on the other hand, had mixed feelings toward Wilma. Flor had six siblings, and Wilma says she wanted to keep them all close to her. Nonetheless, Flor wanted Wilma even closer. Four years later, at the age of 23, they married.

So they began living together, having known each other already for 20 years. Wilma worked at a beauty shop. 'It was a big store. I did everything. I bought perfume, colognes. I was something like a little director. I paid the girls. I even did the cleaning.'

Flor continued his trade as a tiler. Wilma proudly boasts that he even built the fireplace in the entrance of the Marriott Hotel. They wanted children, but were unsuccessful in having them then. Still, they enjoyed their life together, in their apartment near de Pijp, and taking trips on that famous motorbike, tooling around the Netherlands or going to France or Germany.

Their life might have continued like that of any normal working-class couple in Amsterdam but for happenstance, when Flor's work took him to the Bijlmer.

Southeast of the old city, this neighbourhood was originally designed as semi-urban living for the middle class, with modernist block-like high-rises in the midst of large bare green areas. But by the time it was developed in the late sixties, the area had lost its allure to its intended market. So, empty, it was used primarily to house the new black population who were immigrating from Surinam, which gained independence from the Netherlands in 1975. Swiftly, the area became an overcrowded slum, similar to housing projects in urban areas of the US or Britain.

Just like these areas, in the 1970s the poverty-ridden community in the dense conditions of the Bijlmer became afflicted with crime, especially relating to drugs. Flor worked in the apartments that were being outfitted for the new arrivals, many of them housing far more people than intended, including undocumented residents and illegal immigrants. But during his lunch breaks, when he would wander freely round the neighbourhood, Flor got to talking with and befriending the migrant children.

A city boy, but with a grandfather who had a pet pig, he was shocked to find that these Surinamese kids from traditionally rural families didn't even know what a chicken was. The only chicken they knew came from the supermarket in a wrapped container, or was the fried drumstick from the corner store. To this day, Flor says he hadn't ever dreamed of following in his grandfather's footsteps, or bettering him. 'It just happened. I was 30. I was working in the flats. And I saw that the children had nothing. In Surinam, they would have had a goat or a chicken on their patch of land. But when they came here, they had nothing, only green and no animals.'

Flor came home every evening disturbed by what he'd seen. The children had been removed from their own culture to a bare inner-city area. They never left, even for a day's outing to see the beauty of the canals of old Amsterdam, or the forest as Wilma and Flor had in Soest. They stayed in a concrete jungle, with parents who felt outside the culture yet were completely reliant on welfare. As he continued to work there over the next three years, the sight of these children was strong enough to move this man from the Jordaan, the former 'slum', to do something.

The first something was simple. Flor went out and bought a chicken – and a rabbit – so that the children would at least know what a real chicken was, and have a rabbit to play with. He made a little coop for the chicken on a bit of derelict land between the buildings, and a little house for the rabbit.

The children were transfixed by the two animals, coming to stare at them for hours and asking Flor endless questions about them. As they talked about animals, he realised that the children also didn't know what a goat was. So he bought a goat. 'The first goat and chicken was only for fun,' says Wil. 'He was working in the flats for three years, so he knew all the children. The other workers knew them too.' His cohorts helped build a fenced-in area for the goat.

Though Wilma supported him, she admits, 'I thought he was a little bit mad in his head, but he couldn't stop. He saw the children were interested in animals. When the children were going to school, they always just looked inside the coops the first time. But the next time they went in and would say to Flor, "Can I feed the animals?" And then slowly, slowly, slowly, the children would come every day. And when he would go home, they would say they wanted to play with the goat.

'And the Surinam grown-ups also felt more at home.'

Then more happenstance. Flor suffered a serious back injury. Though he received disability payments, he could no longer work. Bit by bit, what had begun as a small hobby with the animals became a full-time occupation. Flor just kept coming back to the little plot of land.

'He had the two operations on his back,' Wilma remembers. 'But he's not a person to sit and watch the geraniums. He had to do something.

He came here, and it just grew and grew. Then there were more animals and more animals and more animals,' Wil says, while Flor laughs, stroking his beard.

Where the farm is today was just a little grassy area. Nobody would walk in it then. So Flor put more gates and fences in, for the goat and then – a sheep. The couple laugh as they remember how the children continued to call the goat a cow, because it had black and white stripes. So Flor came home one day and said to Wilma, 'I want to buy a cow.' And her response was, 'You are crazy.'

He promised he would just buy a little calf. When it grew up, he would send it away. So she agreed. 'But then the children asked him, "Where does milk come from? For the cheese?" So of course, then that calf became a cow, and the cow had a calf, and it went on and on and on. And the cow stayed.'

Then a pony came, and then a big horse.

Then other horses arrived. And the turkeys, the guinea fowl, the ducks, the big pig that adores Flor, and even two llamas. 'His father was thrilled with it,' recalls Wilma. 'The grandfather never did get to see it. But he was very proud of Flor.'

All the while, Wilma continued working at her store. But she stood by Flor and his farm adventure. Without her emotional support, both Flor and she agree, the Kinderboerderij would never have been possible.

'I worked a lot,' she recalls. 'Seven days a week in the perfume store. And if I had said it wouldn't be okay that you create the animal farm, it would never have happened. You have to stand together, believing together in what you want. Sometimes he would come home in the evening at ten, but then a wife should not go blah blah blah, ask questions and shout. Because, you know it is fine.'

'I am the motor,' is how Flor puts it, 'and Wil is the fuel. That's how it works.'

Looking through an old photo album, Flor points to a picture of a shed where the first horse and cow were kept. 'It was very small and had only a chair where you could sit for coffee.' He then points at a black-and-white shot of a small building in a state of disrepair, which had been taken over by drug addicts in the neighbourhood. 'Then the addicts started a fire in it. The city wanted to destroy it. We said, "No, stop. Give it to us, and we'll build it up." And the city finally said yes.

'It was all burnt out, all black inside. But we put new walls in it, painted it, and a new floor in it.'

Flor smiles as he recounts how the addicts even helped with the construction. Over time, Wilma and Flor built more and more sheds on the land, and eventually the two-storey farmhouse that they would live in over the next years. Wilma left her job and they moved from their apartment to the centre. Now, in a way immigrants themselves, they became part of the community.

Their biggest – and temporary – stumbling block seemed to be the municipality itself. Finally taking notice of their activities, the government sent a local councillor to ask them what they thought they were doing, building a farm on public land. They hadn't even thought of asking. Finally, with the community insisting that the farm and Wil and Flor stay, they made a deal with the government. They would pay one euro a year rent.

But as Flor points out, this being the Netherlands, they really have to pay that one euro by the due date. Every year. Or else!

They continued the farm, with generation after generation of children coming through, and learning to love animals. Even those who were initially afraid came time after time. 'We have some children here who, for example, are very afraid of dogs,' Wilma says. 'They scream. Then we try to get the children to come near the dog and touch him. And when the fear of the child goes away, you have won something.

'We have a friend who has a very disabled boy. He cannot talk; he cannot sit; he cannot walk. I took his wheelchair, and I took him to the cows. He screamed. That wasn't good. So I took him to the sheep. And finally he smiled. And then we took him inside and let him see the dogs. At first, he was very frightened. But after 15 minutes, he put one in his arms and held it. When you see the twinkle in the eyes of a kid, then you have it.'

When I ask why kids need to see animals, whether it's goats standing on donkeys or just chickens running around, Flor says, 'It's like going to school. You have to see that animals live on this planet. Most importantly, when you treat animals well, you treat people well.

They learn that if you are good to beasts, then you can also be good to people.'

Though childless themselves, Flor and Wilma now seem to have all the neighbourhood's children as their own. Some of them come from very troubled households. But by seeing that the animals need care and nurturing, they begin to see even other children differently.

'You take responsibility for an animal,' Wilma declares. 'That's what we teach the children. An animal is a living creature that you have to respect. And you can see the change in the children. They act differently. They are nicer. They don't beat the animals. So they also learn you cannot beat another person.'

Unlike the big organisations that come from outside, Wil and Flor are part of the community. 'We are closer to the people. Everybody who comes here is treated equally. When a police officer comes, he gets a cup of coffee; when, let's say, the biggest criminal comes, he will also get a cup of coffee.

'We are part of daily life. We don't sit behind a desk and have meetings. And when the people from the big organisations come, we have to tell them to come outside and we show them the problem. To show them the street children; show them kids living in the gutter.

'We are very simple. And when you are a big Stichting [not-for-profit organisation] you have a lot of paper, paper, paper. You sit at a big desk and write blah blah blah blah. And the wanting to help then doesn't come from inside. It has to come from inside. From crazy people like him and me who do it.'

Their lives now are a far cry from where they started, she in the beauty shop and he as a brick-tiler. And they gave up a lot too. They couldn't go on vacation together. Running the farm takes seven days a week, and it's something they have to do together. They've made a meagre living.

They get donations of food, like old bread, from the local supermarket to help feed the animals. They get a small subsidy to cover expenses. And the community helps out, even though they're among the few white Dutch in a mainly black immigrant community. 'We never had a word of "Oh, you are white people." There is no colour here. Around the gates the farm is a special country and village. Everyone who comes here is equal. If you are Surinamese, English, black, yellow, it's all the same. We don't see fat people or small people. They're all the same.'

What Wilma and Flor have always delighted in are those moments of recognition that the children have. That itself is their reward. 'You can see the children like it, and want to touch these animals. That's the reason why we do it. To see that smile on a kid's face, believing finally that he can touch the dog. Or touch the cow.'

Wil points out, admiringly, that Flor didn't ever think twice about this. And that it came purely from his heart. 'It came from inside. He did not go, "Why why why?" He just did it, because he saw the children so enjoyed it. And it gave him a big feeling, to give the children some pleasure. When you see the faces of the children, they give you so much love. And that's the reason – to care about each other, no matter how, or what race or who you look like.'

'Yeah,' Flor agrees. 'That is it.'

That love from the children, no matter what race they are, even changed their own way of seeing themselves. 'When I was younger,' recalls Wilma, 'I thought nobody liked me. And when I grew older, I realised you have to fight to let people see that you always are somebody. I am Wil! And it's in your mind that you have to change.

'I'm now more me than I was 20 years ago. When I was working, I had to paint my nails. I was always very neat and pretty. But now I have to really work. There's no longer nails and make-up. But make-up is a cover, a covering to make you more beautiful than you are. Because when you're not nice, you can put all kinds of things on your face but you're still the same person. Why? Because the nicest things come from inside.'

Thirty years on, Wil and Flor are now retiring, all the way to a real farm in Germany. On one hand, it is a sad thing. However, they are determined to keep the Kinderboerderij and their vision ongoing and intact. The local people agree, and business leaders also see its value in creating a better community.

Because, 30 years on, there are now grown-ups who once were children who visited the farm and value the truly 'nice on the inside' Wil and Flor. Some bring their own children to the farm now. They may not know that if Flor hadn't happened to get a job in this area and seen that children need animals, even the llama that spits at them as they pass, then this Kinderboerderij might never have existed. And all the children and adults might never have learned what Flor learned from his grand-father and his animals: that being good to beasts, one can then be good to people.

'Keep a few bullets for the kangaroo'

Paul Pholeros and Sandra Meihubers

Yami Lester put his arm around my shoulder. He said, 'Brother, you're probably right. Parents should wash their kids. But why don't you take a look at some of their houses anyway?'

Paul is a big, tall man in his fifties, with large, smiling and curious eyes, a thick grey beard and a wild mane of hair. He is a well-known and respected architect, designing inventive and beautiful houses for the well-to-do in Australia, as well as innovative, environmentally responsible resorts in Guatemala and China. He lectures at the University of Sydney. But most importantly, to Paul, he is one of the founders of Healthabitat, an organisation dedicated to environmental health. There are three directors – a doctor, an anthropologist, and Paul – who draw no salaries, though the work takes up three months of their time each year. It is this work that Paul is most proud of, even creatively – that is, having fixed over 5000 bathrooms in Aboriginal people's houses since 1985. It is for this work that he and his team received the inaugural Vassilis Sgoutas Prize from the International Union of Architects, in recognition of their fight against poverty.

But, as Paul says, it was with the help of a blind mentor named Yami Lester that he learned how to see. That was in the central Australian desert near Uluru – formerly called Ayers Rock.

It is a world apart from the suburb of terrace houses in the inner west of Sydney where Paul grew up in the sixties. He was a 'wog', a derogatory term that was sometimes used for people from Italian or Greek backgrounds. 'My dad came from Greece, and worked in an ice cream factory. And my mum was an Aussie mix. A mongrel mix.' So, in effect, Paul was a 'half-wog'.

As his immigrant grandparents lived with the family, he grew up in a house where a second language, Greek, was spoken. That, he says, gave him the notion that there was more than just the one language, English. That understanding would serve his later work well, with the Aboriginal communities having over 250 languages across the country. But for most Australians then, the idea of any other language was decidedly foreign. The food and culture he grew up with were also foreign, but of course to him perfectly natural. 'When you grow up in it, you don't know it's different. I just assumed everyone had three generations in the house, and different languages were spoken.'

But that assumption changed when Paul first went to school. He learned that his background wasn't the same as everyone else's. Luckily, he had 'bona fide Aussie' lunches, thanks to his mother. And the insults he got were few and far between; even then he was big and tall.

Years later, Paul appreciated the difference in his home even more. 'You realise your difference is a great richness. That you know a little bit about the "Other". And that there are other ways to view the world.'

Just as Wil and Flor in Amsterdam had met early in their lives, Paul also met his future wife, Sandra Meihubers, at a young age. After training as a dentist, she would do in the field of dentistry what Paul did in architecture. Now a dental health consultant, Sandra has long worked with Aboriginal communities, as well as creating dental training programmes in Nepal and East Timor. It was she who got Paul to the centre of Australia in the first place.

But as a teenager, she was just a girl he saw but barely spoke to. 'We went to different schools, but there was a train we had to take every day. That's where we first met. It was only seven years later, near the end of university, where we had a different relationship. Where it went from knowing someone exists to then getting together in a more formal sense,' he says, then laughs, 'or informal.'

When Paul was nearing the end of high school, he wasn't sure

Paul Pholeros

what he should do for a career. 'I didn't have a clue. I'd loved to draw from about five. And I was good at mathematics. So someone, I don't remember who, suggested architecture. But I didn't even know what that was. In those days, there was no career guidance. And no one in our family had ever been anywhere near a university.

'In those days, 1971, university was full fees. And my family couldn't have afforded them. But I got a high school certificate mark that allowed me to get a Commonwealth Scholarship. Then the option of going to university all of a sudden was real.'

Paul recounts with a broad smile the conversation he and his Greek immigrant father then had. 'I remember saying to my father, "What do you reckon?"

'And he said, "What do you reckon?"

'I said, "I don't know."

'And he said, "I don't know either."

'It was a great discussion! Then he said, "Well, why not?"

'So I did. And after about the first week of architecture school, I'll always remember thinking, if this is what they reckon is work, I've hit

Sandra Meihubers

the jackpot. From that day on, I don't think I ever considered it work. The entire university course to me was fantastic, doing things I just loved doing. It wasn't planning, skill, intelligence; it was pure luck.'

Like her husband, Sandra's choice of career was somewhat random. Her interest in dentistry, she says, stemmed from her crush on the guy her sister was dating. It can be summed up in one word, she says, laughing: 'Infatuation.'

When we meet, at a Thai restaurant in Bangkok, Sandra has just returned from yet another volunteer trip to Nepal. Like Paul, she spends about 30 per cent of her professional life doing unpaid work.

'There was this guy lusting after my sister,' she says, 'and I was seven years younger, and lusting after him. And he had just completed a dental degree. And I had to fill in an application form to university. I had studied only four subjects for my school leaving – English, maths, science and French – all at reasonably high levels, so there was no clear direction where I was going. So this guy said, "What are you going to do?" I said, "I have no idea." All I knew was I didn't want to do medicine, because at that time everybody thought the idea was that your child would study medicine. So if everybody was doing that, I wouldn't. This guy said, "You'd enjoy dentistry." And the key word he said was: I could be – independent.'

Paul acknowledges that another piece of luck he had at university, which was at least as important as finding himself studying architecture, was to begin a lifelong relationship with Sandra.

Yet another piece of 'luck' was a decision he and two university mates made. In the fourth year of study, it was mandatory for architecture students to take a year out to gain practical experience. However, Paul's group had the idea of outfitting a bus with a show on the environment, and driving it to schools around Australia. They would use what they had learned at university about environmental issues, which even in 1974 were arousing strong interest. While it may sound as if he was already leaning towards altruism, Paul, in his inimitable self-deprecating way, puts it differently. 'It avoided my working in an office for a year,' he says.

So he and his mates worked on their alternative proposal. The reaction of their teachers was mixed. 'Some staff thought our idea was a scam. And some thought it was a radical idea but a good one. So we spent half of our third year thinking how the hell we'd do it. We raised money by going to companies and getting sponsorship to fit the bus out.

'The vehicle was an old 1947 Leyland double-decker with blue and green horizontal stripes, which was being sold off from the transport department in Sydney. We purchased it for the princely sum of $600. It had done two million miles. And we spent our third year every hour out of study hours retrofitting our bus. We put a kitchen in it, a photographic darkroom, and a toilet.

'We left in early 1974 and spent about ten months on the road driving anti-clockwise around the edge of Australia.' They went everywhere except to the centre of the country, where Paul's later work with Healthabitat would begin. They took the show to about 85 schools. But for Paul, the trip offered its own lesson: that one could do anything, if one was willing to put the time in.

'When we first started, people thought it was impossible. Then people thought no one would be interested. All of which was false. So if you have a plan, you just do it. And that's important. That builds into you the fact that you sometimes need a plan that's not mapped out by the university, by the profession or by the powers that be. You've got to make the running yourself and with others that see the problem. The authorities, the bureaucracies, the institutions will never ever make those decisions.'

The trip changed how Paul saw the country. For a middle-class boy who had never been outside Sydney, the variety and immensity of the landscape were stunning. More importantly, it was his first introduction to Aboriginal Australia, because the schools he visited had a high proportion of indigneous children. 'It was only about seven years after the referendum giving Aboriginal people citizenship rights. And it was bleedingly obvious how there was a distinction between that world and the world that we knew. There's a big enough distinction between the country world and the city, but this was yet another division.'

As he would put it, luck stayed on his side, even with Sandra, though they parted on finishing university. Sandra had realised she didn't have the desire to focus solely on making money, so when she saw an opportunity to volunteer in Darwin in her final year, she grabbed at it. 'Within a few days, I was on a small plane heading out to an Aboriginal community with a dentist who had been working for 15 years, with a little kit bag of gear, on the veranda of a Catholic mission hospital.'

This seemed to her fantastic. 'I was thinking, you could do this with dentistry? Now I'm in.'

So, in Paul's words, 'Sandra went her way and I mine. But then I got a grant from the Australian Arts Council to make big sculptures in the outdoors in the top end of Australia. That happened to end in Darwin – only because I was broke and couldn't get back to Sydney. And Sandra had been there for a while. So then we met in Darwin, a key point in the saga.'

Meaning their relationship became once again formal, or informal – however they want to put it. Figuring he should use his architecture degree, Paul got a job in a practice in Darwin as well. This was not long after the cyclone that had hit at the end of 1974. There was plenty of work, not in design per se but in rebuilding people's houses, 'which was a brilliant experience for a young architect, 'cause it meant you were out with the trades all the time. It gave you a fantastic appreciation of just building things. That was a year and a half.

'Then we had to go overseas like you always do; you jump out of Australia. Then got to Greece broke. And figured, how do we get back home? And we thought: England! They speak English.'

Though Sandra differs as to whether or not all their decisions were based on being broke, the two did end up in England. She worked in a dental surgery, and he in a big architectural practice. 'It was a firm with old and conservative directors,' Paul says, 'and I was an upstart colonial from Australia who knew nothing. They weren't into the London fashion statements of the seventies and eighties. They just loved making good solid buildings. I learned a huge amount. They gave me opportunities I would never give to a junior architect in my practice now. I wouldn't be that brave.'

If this were a drama about the hero's journey, this would be Act One, where his skills and experiences were being honed by the fates: taking a bus around the country getting a glimpse of the Aboriginal community, rebuilding houses after the destruction of the cyclone in Darwin, then gaining solid work experience in the UK. Because ingenious practical skills along with understanding of community would be exactly what Yami Lester and his community near Uluru needed.

So Act Two begins. Paul and Sandra went back to Sydney. Ever the iconoclast, Paul decided to start his own private practice. But it wasn't easy to get clients. 'Because I'd been away, I didn't have contacts. And if you're not from a particular social milieu, with parents or friends that are building or renovating houses, there goes your first chance of getting things built. But if you're lucky, you trip over, and you get the first bastard that comes to you.'

Paul did odd jobs to make ends meet. He taught at the university. Using his drawing skills, he did graphics, cartoons and drawings. He even worked on building sites as a labourer, like the fictional non-conformist architect Howard Roark in the novel *The Fountainhead*. 'I did all that so I didn't have to take on shitty architectural work. That was from a teacher of mine. He said, "Try and not do shitty jobs. Because five years after you graduate, whatever work you're doing, that'll be the work you'll be doing for the rest of your life." I was getting close to the five years, and I thought I'd rather dig ditches than do shitty jobs.'

Sandra meanwhile got a job as a dentist at the Aboriginal Medical Service in Sydney's Redfern, working with the Aboriginal leader Naomi Mayers. From that experience, she was offered an opportunity to go to the centre of Australia to work with the Pitjatjantjara people and prepare a report on their dental needs. 'But Sandra adopted the notion,' Paul says with admiration, 'that as well as doing that, you'd do some relief of pain or basic treatment.'

Like Paul, Sandra is filled with enthusiasm; she has piercing yet gentle eyes, and her height is a match for Paul's, making them one tall couple. She also has a pealing laugh as she gives her version of events. 'I went first,' she says. 'I was a dental locum visiting Pinjara land for nine weeks. My assistant was Naomi Mayer's niece. We carried portable dental equipment in a vehicle, and would set up in a small community, 200 to 400 people, for a week or so. Then we'd do the work, seeing the kids, and pack up and go to the next community. I'd been away for a couple of weeks, and then I learned a clinic out there needed renovation.'

'And she had in her chair the chairman of that community,' Paul chips in. 'After he was saying they couldn't get anyone to come out and do this sort of work, she said jokingly, "Oh, my husband's an architect." And this guy said, "Okay, I'll ring him."

'He had two words of English, and I had no words of Pinjara. In those days there were radio phones, which were impossible to hear and took hours to get through. So when this guy rang me, I got every sort of fifteenth word, which was "Okay?" But about a week later, an air ticket arrived. I thought, I don't know what he wants me to do, but I'll grab it anyway.'

'I missed Paul,' says Sandra. 'So we did a deal. He'd come out and do the work, and they'd pay for his airfare. It was a chance of a reunion for a few days.' She laughs. 'It was probably the hormones more than anything.'

By the time Paul got there, Sandra had already moved on to the next community. But their hormones did get a reward, as they managed to see each other in between their jobs. Paul did a sketch design for additions to the clinic, and that began his work 'out bush'. 'The mob on the ground was fantastic. And it all started with Sandra being out there.'

Just as Flor credits Wilma with providing vital support, Paul adds, 'You can only do this when you have a partner that understands the things you do. I couldn't have done what I've done over the years unless I had someone who sympathises with what I'm doing.'

After he designed and built the first clinic, Paul's work in the desert took on its own momentum. 'The mob up the road said, "Well, you did one for them, do one for us." Then the mob at Uluru said, "You did one for them, do one for us."' And contrary to the prejudices of many in the white community at that time, the Aboriginals were excellent clients. 'They did what they said they would do, they were efficient, and they always paid. I always say that, because I couldn't have afforded to do the jobs, if they didn't. They were just good clients.'

It was after he had been working in the centre of Australia for a couple of years that Paul had a meeting with Yami Lester, the leader of the community. When he was a child, the British had tested nuclear bombs out there in the desert. A radioactive cloud had hit Yami and his family, and he had lost his sight. 'But he was a blind man who can see is the way I always put it,' Paul says.

After supervising the building of community-controlled medical clinics and bringing out dedicated doctors, nurses and dentists such as Sandra, Yami saw that medical conditions were still not improving as they should. So he came up with a plan.

'The first time I was formally introduced to Yami Lester was when he put me together with a medical doctor, Paul Torzillo, who'd been out there in the health service, and another guy, Stephan Rainow. He'd trained as an anthropologist but working out there realised that was as much use as an ashtray on a motorbike. So he got into environmental health. He spoke the language and had been there seven years when I got there.

'Yami put the three of us in a room. He said, "You three are going to work together. We've been running a health service for two years. The good thing is that the numbers coming to the clinic have increased. People are more comfortable coming in."'

But the people were not getting any healthier, especially with regard to trachoma. The leading infectious cause of blindness globally, trachoma occurs in communities with inadequate access to sanitation and water. Though the disease had been eliminated in much of the developed world and white Australia, it was still prevalent in the community. 'And Yami said, "Uwankara Palyanyku Kanyintjaku. A Plan".' In Pinjara, the words meant a Strategy for Well-being. 'No one out of the three of us could say those words. So it was shortened to UPK.

'It was a very short meeting. Yami was direct and to the point. He said, "This is the problem. We need to stop people getting sick. In the next room, there are 18 Aboriginal people who are going to be your bosses and your workers. You can start whenever you want. I suggest – now."

'He obviously had a sense of humour, because he said, "I don't have a clue what to do. We've got no money. You've got six months to plan. Come back to me then."'

Such an offer might not be everyone's idea of a good job. Paul was two years into his architecture practice. There were no travel expenses or any salary offered. 'We had every good reason to say no. I couldn't live there. And Paul the doctor thought the same. Steffi the anthropologist at least lived in Alice.

'I remember saying to Sandra, "I've got this job that looks very interesting." She said, "That's great. Who's funding it?"

'I said, "No one."

'She said, "Fantastic. Great job. A winner."

'And it was.'

Over the next months, Paul Torzillo, the 'medical team', worked on figuring out the health targets. Having worked for the Royal Flying Doctor Service, and later as a chest specialist at the Royal Prince Alfred Hospital in Sydney, he is called 'the best in Australia' by Paul Pholeros.

But that wasn't his evaluation when Torzillo arrived at the architect's office with his findings scrawled on one piece of paper. Paul just stared at him. 'He said, "These are the nine targets in order of priority." I looked, and he had nine lines on a bit of paper. Literally nine lines.

'I said, "Mate, you've been working on this for three months, and this is all you've done?"'

The nine targets were seemingly simple. They were: washing people, particularly children; washing clothes and bedding; removing waste safely; improving nutrition; reducing the impact of crowding; reducing the impact of animals, insects and vermin; reducing the impact of dust; temperature control; and reducing trauma.

'I was really shitty,' Paul remembers. 'I said, "That's pretty bloody slack." The first priority was washing your kids once a day. I said, "You don't need me for washing kids. This has nothing to do with architecture. Get the parents to do it!"

'Anyway, Torzillo said, "You're not impressed. Then come by my office." When I did, he said, "You want to see why they're the nine? Start reading." There was a pile literally table-high full of paper. And the biggest chunk of research he'd done was on priority one.

'What I started to realise was that the goal appeared simple, but he'd done an amazing amount of work.'

But Paul still didn't have any idea what he could do in his role as an architect. Even Stephan the anthropologist, who spoke the languages and knew the clans, seemed to have a more defined role. 'But Yami had this notion that housing was important to health. And I was the bloke that was doing buildings. I admit it: I was a green suburban architect. I didn't know how to listen to what was being said. I mean, the washing thing. "Get the parents to wash the kids!" Yeah, great!

'It takes someone who really is smart to see that you've got to ease people into things. Yami could have given me a lecture. He didn't. He could have said, wake up to yourself. He didn't. He said, "That's fine." And Yami put his arm around my shoulder. He said, "Brother, you're probably right. Parents should wash their kids. But how about thinking about it like this for a minute? Why don't you take a look at some of those houses? Just to check out if they can have a wash, you know?"'

When Paul took a look, it changed the course of his life.

'I walk into the first house. First up is just the straight sheer physical horror of seeing 20 people who have to live in one tiny shed, and it hasn't got any facilities inside it at all. Because it's been built upside down and back to front.

'I still remember the smell of waste water that seeps through every orifice of the house. There's no shower. Taps aren't there. There's no water pipe to the house. There's no water connected.

'The toilet doesn't have a plank at the bottom of it. It's just sat on a concrete slab. After the first flush, it overflows. It never had a pipe to drain out of the house. It would have overflowed from the first time it was flushed. Because the toilet and the other drains like the kitchen sink had never been attached to a proper drain.

'The washers leak, because the taps are poor quality. And the salt in the water decays them in weeks. Therefore, the taps leak more seriously. You put all those things together, and if there's no faeces, there's foul water that's been sitting around for ages, percolating in the house.'

To top off Paul's astonishment at the dire plumbing, he noticed that the broken windows had solid material screwed over them, causing the rooms to be overwhelmingly hot. So the people who lived in the house would stay outside, sitting under a tree to cool down. Later, he and his team discovered the glass had been broken when the contractors transported the building to the desert.

'I remember looking at myself and thinking I had just made the biggest mistake of all. What an arrogant bastard. I assumed that the people were the problem. That's what you have in your head, whether you want to admit it or not: "Why aren't people washing themselves?" Then you see the reality, and think, I've misjudged this badly. And as we got through more and more of the houses, this stuff carried on and on and on.'

Paul sits for a moment in silence, remembering this first experience, then he continues. 'And that was what Yami knew: the people could not wash their kids. They couldn't. No one could. *We* couldn't wash. *We* used to get the first stages of trachoma after almost every trip, with all the dust. *We* couldn't find a tap to wash our faces when we *knew* we had to do that to avoid trachoma. So we'd almost always go back home with the first-stage symptoms. We'd come back to Sydney, have showers, and be fine. But if you lived out there, you couldn't.'

Paul had been confronted by living conditions the Australian population outside the local community had never seen; other surveys had always been done outside the houses. But it wasn't just the state of the houses that shocked him; it was the impact on the people who were supposed to live in them.

'That's probably the horror of it as much as the poor conditions, knowing the faces. The team we worked with knew all these families. They were their relations, their mates, their cousins. It wasn't as if there was some remote removed abstract group, with the guys in the white coats doing assessments.

'At night, we'd camp with these people. And you realise there are a whole lot of people living in conditions I could never have conceived of. You can read books, or you can hear people. But it's different when you see it.'

His anger at the situation increased when he came head-on to dealing with the government. 'The next world you encounter is the bureaucratic world or the government world or the professional world which tells you, "No, you're mistaken. The problem is the people living in these houses are unable to get it right." And it's bad enough to see the physical stuff on the ground, but then you confront a whole conspiracy of people who either don't accept that it can exist, or if it does exist, it's not the fault of anyone but the people living in the houses. You'd be mad if you didn't have some sort of anger, that clearly this ain't right.'

The team travelled through an area of 105,000 square kilometres southwest of Alice Springs, assessing the living conditions of around 3000 people. Over and over they would see the same appalling conditions. And, as Paul points out, these were not problems he or his team could fix themselves.

'For some it was absolutely bloody impossible. I mean, when there's no pump connected to the toilet. That's way outside of the home handyman job.' Yet time after time, the team would spend a week going through the conditions in different communities, debrief Yami Lester, then attend a meeting with a government official and be told that they were mistaken. If the houses were as bad as Paul said, which in the first place the official didn't believe, it was because the people abused them and were culturally unsuited to Western-style dwellings. That view continued even through 2007, over 20 years later.

'We have the resources of a First World country and the attitude of the Third World. Therefore we end up with a Fourth World solution. We recently had a federal minister suggest to us that it'd be better to build Aboriginals houses without showers, toilets, kitchens, because we had to admit by the work that we've done that they're the areas that have the most problems. So leave them out. Because the Aboriginals were going to wreck it anyway was the bureaucratic line.

'And that's the great excuse. Because everyone gets off the hook.

The builders get off the hook; government gets off the hook. "Look at these houses. People sit outside." When I first looked at the houses, I knew why people didn't use them. They *couldn't* use them.'

On a personal level, Paul continued to learn from the blind leader, particularly about how to deal with life and the endless bureaucrats they confronted.

'Yami is an extraordinary man who has a foot in both worlds. He has a traditional Aboriginal foot in that world, and he has a very clear foot in the bureaucratic and white man's world in white politics.

'Before meetings with bureaucrats, he would say, "Don't use all your bullets. Keep a few bullets for the kangaroo." And he'd relate that to a hunting story. He'd say, "Young blokes fire at anything that looks like a kangaroo. Then finally when the kangaroo sticks his head up, you've got no bullets left. And you hit yourself for using all your bullets up on rabbits." Yami would save his fire for the things that actually mattered. He taught me a lot.'

As the team went about their surveys, Paul always wanted to get to work right away. But Stephan advised him how to deal with the situation culturally, as an 'unknown white bloke' – that he needed to sit down and talk with the people for a while, to explain what they were doing and get them on-side. Then, as Sandra had done when she had been sent in to do her report, they could fix things at the same time. 'You never ever go to any problem and look at it and walk away only with a report,' Paul affirms. 'So when we turned up, we always had a toolbox, tap washers, taps, spanners, not a plumber in those days. We did something in every house.

'So when the report came out, it wasn't a statement of what the problem was. It was a statement of the problems plus the solutions and our ability to get to that solution.'

Over the first 18 months, Paul and the team worked closely with Yami Lester as they prepared their seminal UPK report of 1987. The report listed Dr Torzillo's nine targets plus all the team's findings, and it clearly established the links between Aboriginal health and access to clean water and sanitation. The statistics clearly showed the improvement that resulted from environmental changes – which had been Yami Lester's instinct all along.

'Skin infections dropped. Eye infections dropped. The short-term markers of environmental conditions. If you change the environment, health changes,' says Paul.

The team continued to work together, and in 1994 published *Housing for Health: Towards a better living environment for Aboriginal Australia*, a study of 12 UPK houses over the course of a year. This time the publication was launched in Parliament by the health minister.

By now other Aboriginal communities wanted to work with the architect, the doctor and the anthropologist as well. 'Things grew. We started in the centre of Australia. And a mob in Queensland said, well, if you're doing it for them, why aren't you doing it for us? Then New South Wales. Then next the Northern Territory, then Western Australia.'

At the time of writing, the organisation, now known as Healthabitat, has 15 managers around the country and 30 active projects. Most of their staff are local indigenous people who live in the communities they serve.

In order to maintain their independence from all funding bodies, the three directors do not take a salary. But contrary to any notion that it was three white men to the rescue, Paul points out that the whole programme started with the Aboriginal people. 'Yami had great insight about the aim. The initiative didn't come from government, professionals, doctors, institute architects, the university, or the state government. But it was people themselves saying, "How do we solve this problem? We have to intervene." This was an Aboriginal man who intervened. And got a few white fellas to help.'

In the first years, the group did not receive or spend one government dollar. It was the local population working alongside Paul, screwdrivers in hand, or calling in plumbers and electricians. And once the team fixed the houses they remained in better shape, challenging the myth that the Aboriginal people would, as the government claimed, just 'trash them'. 'If you put better things in, if you make sure taps are of good quality, there is a change. We've got hard numbers that show you can knock off 90-plus per cent of the regression by simply doing good work. And while you're doing that, you've got a black pair of hands beside you. And that pair of hands is still around when you've left. Our teams are made of people who are going to stay around. They live there.'

What Paul found was that rather than being the problem, it was the people in the community with the biggest vested interest who were best at fixing the problems. It was the mother, father and the children in each of the houses. If they saw they could get a working shower or toilet, they would lend a hand. 'They wanted to learn how to do it. And then they got screwdrivers and spanners.'

The reason the community had not done so before was that the skills that were needed were outside the range of a home handyman. So Paul's team trained up the local community to become plumbers. For Paul, this wasn't about empowerment, but practicality. 'We don't do that for some romance, that it's nice to have an Aboriginal face doing it. We do it because it would chew up almost our entire fixed budget if we had these other clowns going around doing that.

'This is where people are getting the wrong end of the stick. *Isn't that wonderful, you're creating employment?* No. My job is to fix the houses. If someone can show me a better way that doesn't involve Aboriginal people, I'll look at it. But no one has. And I can't see how they could. They live on the job.'

However much he insists it was only a practical response to the problem, watching the Aboriginal workers develop is part of the reward. 'You realise this is good. We can do this. We can make a difference. And what keeps you going is those people.

'That was a key part of what kept me going, plus working with the two other blokes, Paul – the doctor – and Steffi. You don't get that experience too often in your life, to work with people who are extraordinary on a daily basis. And you're working on things that are big and not easy to solve.'

After the UPK report, Stephan had the idea of making a music album to carry the message across to kids. The community got local rock bands together and recorded a CD, which sold incredibly well. It is still on sale some 20 years later. It features the up-tempo country-style 'Showerblock Song', the rocking 'Septic Tank' ('Septic tanks for you and me / So we don't have to catch disease') and the catchy, upbeat guitar-filled 'Germs Blues' ('There's rubbish on the ground / so why not pick it up / there's germs, there's germs all around'). Paul is as proud of that CD as he is of his houses. 'It got a complex message out to kids, who were our target. And it's been written up as one of the best public health initiatives that's ever been done in Australia with Aboriginal people.'

Paul Pholeros's CV outside this work is impressive, from the luxury housing in Sydney to the sustainable resorts in China. He has also designed and, with Sandra, built a stunningly simple home on Sydney's North Shore. But he spends 30 per cent of his time working for no salary, even now, designing, building and/or fixing bathrooms. To him, it's the greatest challenge in his career.

'What's interesting is getting on with it. Maybe we fail. Maybe nothing happens. At least you give it a go. I've got a very unsophisticated philosophy about that: just give it a go! What annoys me is that professional architects get up and say what a brilliant job they do about the complexity of architecture. But meanwhile there are still people living in conditions that are not right. No one should sit around when that sort of stuff exists in your own country. And when you've sorted that out, go to another country and lend them a hand.

'At a simple level, it's inequitable. It's dividing the world in two unnecessarily. The mansions can be reduced, and the shacks improved. We don't have to have 75 per cent of the world living in abject squalor and 25 per cent living in a way that no one can even understand how rich it is. Ultimately, it's not even of benefit to the wealthy. You can't have a group of people in abject poverty. At some point, that will turn.'

Why did Paul feel compelled to do the work he's doing? Because, as Yami Lester suggested, he did take a look. And once he had, he couldn't turn back. What he says sounds similar to a very old and recognisable idea: do unto others as you would have them do unto you.

'I always relate it to the question, what would it have been like if this was where I grew up as a kid? Our target group was zero to five. At that age, none of us make any decisions about our own lives. And you see the kids are off to hospital for their eighth or tenth visit in the first year of life. Then you ask your mum, "How many times did I go to hospital in my first year of life?" And you find out of course you didn't. And you think, is that equitable? Is it luck of place of birth? Why should that be?'

To Paul, as with Wil and Flor or Siri, the thing is to allow oneself to see and to be touched by what one sees. 'It's not a money thing. It's just people are disinterested. They don't see. If you're in a position where you're immersed in it, it's more than seeing. That's where you need people to help you become immersed in it. Yami Lester made sure I was immersed in it. A far less understanding guy might have severed the link early on by saying, "Look, you're a middle-class bloody hopeless white fella. Get out of here." He could have cut my tenure very short. But he didn't.'

Yami deepened the journey that had begun on a bus trip around Australia. 'You look to start with, like the bus trip – that's all you do. You look. Meet a few kids in classrooms. You meet their parents and have a bit of a yarn. And they're different. But in the end, not that different. Then the next bit is you intervene. All of a sudden, you know their names. And them doesn't become *them* anymore. They have kids, and those kids have kids. I've seen grandkids born to the people I worked with when they were young. So they're no longer *them*, but people with names. And once you know people, it's bloody hard to walk away.'

Paul's altruism, a word he would hate me to use, isn't driven by religious faith. It comes from what he's learned from the Aboriginal community, his experiences, and his own sense of connection, which he relates to his own profession.

'As an architect, you have to worry about what happens on every piece of the site you build on. It can't just relate to the house. It relates to the wind that you don't own, but will return and will have vigour and cooling properties and destructive properties. If you ignore that because it's not the bit you own, then you do it at your peril. We do it with natural forces, so why wouldn't that exact same thing extend to people? It's not a religious thing. It's functional. It's an equation. It's Einsteinian; we're all part of the same matter.'

Paul's luck was getting to know people, and that came from his openness to chance, and having a wife whose hormones wanted him out in central Australia too, which brought him to a blind man who made him see.

'I can't change the world,' Paul says. 'But you can try and work on it where you can.' And, he points out, 'It's bloody good fun.'

From Winnie the Pooh to advocacy

Frika Iskandar

Many people can say that they were born in the same year as John Lennon, or in the year that Neil Armstrong stepped onto the moon. But I was born in 1981, the year AIDS was discovered.

Frika Iskandar was born into a Chinese family in Indonesia. Now in her mid-twenties, she speaks with an eloquence that belies her age. She has been a representative of the Asia Pacific Network of People Living with HIV/AIDS (APN+), with an office in central Bangkok. Theirs is a diminutive building, standing opposite a luxury tower which limousines enter and exit. Frika too is diminutive in stature, with cropped black hair and sharp, piercing eyes, but there is nothing diminutive about her spirit or aspirations.

Her own eyes – and her parents' – were opened, she acknowledges, to a problem that she never thought would impact on her, in the year 1999. Suddenly confronting a harsh reality, Frika Iskandar began to understand the significance of her birth year – the year in which AIDS was discovered.

One day, she woke up in an expensive private hospital in Jakarta with her parents and a doctor by her side. She had been put into hospital to recover from her addiction to heroin, which she had begun injecting with needles. While she was sleeping, the nurses had taken blood for a series of tests. One was for HIV.

In the morning, Frika and her parents listened in shock as the doctor calmly told them she had tested positive for HIV and hepatitis C. At that time in Indonesia, having HIV was considered by many to

Frika Iskandar (Photo: Mikael Enlund)

be akin to a death sentence. But, Frika says, the doctor told them the news 'like I was having a fever or something, saying it like it's not going to change my life at the time, that you have HIV and Hep C. There was no permission [to tell her parents] and no counselling for me.'

Frika came from a well-to-do family; her parents were born into the Chinese community in Borneo but later moved to Jakarta. Like her grandparents, they were businesspeople, and they ended up with a variety of interests, including restaurants.

Predominantly Buddhist, Confucianist or Christian, the Chinese are an ethnic and religious minority in Indonesia, a country of 17,000 islands, 6000 of which are inhabited. In fact, the dominant religion is Islam. Indonesia has the largest Muslim population of any country, of various ethnicities. The Chinese have tended to do well in business, and since the country's independence they have been perceived to be aligned either with the former Dutch colonists or the communists. Whenever there is political unrest or violence, the Chinese have been prime targets.

In 1965–66, during the transition from President Sukarno to

President Suharto, scholars generally agree that 500,000 people were killed in Indonesia. Many of these were Chinese. Suharto also legislated in 1967 a 'Basic Policy for the Chinese Problem', language eerily similar to that used about Jews at the time of the Nazi Holocaust. Chinese newspaper offices were shut down. Chinese religious expression was forbidden outside the home. Chinese-language schools were closed. Though Frika's father managed to keep his Chinese name, her mother's family was forced to adopt an Indonesian name.

Frika's upbringing, however, was relatively normal. She attended a private primary school in Jakarta, as did her two younger sisters, and she remembers as a child being very fond of Winnie the Pooh cartoons on TV.

It was customary for Indonesian families who could afford it to send their children abroad to get a better education. Frika, the eldest daughter, was sent to Singapore for her secondary schooling. For the first two years she lived with a Singaporean family who acted as her guardians. Then, through an arrangement made by an agent of the school, she lived alone in an apartment, in a complex with other student apartments, overseen by another guardian. Her younger sister was later sent to Singapore and lived there as well.

Frika's first experience with heroin came during a two-day trip to Jakarta for the opening of a mall owned by her father. At the reception she met the daughter of a friend of her father's, they started chatting, struck up a friendship, and went out afterwards. That night, the girl told Frika she was using heroin, and offered her some. Curious, Frika agreed to try it, and they cooked it together. 'It felt terrible, bitter, not nice at all. I vomited.'

Back in Singapore, Frika went through the typical teenage feelings of loneliness and insecurity. And she was a long way from home. 'I didn't have enough self-confidence as a teenager. I wanted to fit into this group that I thought was cool. And I felt I was fat, short and ugly. But I wanted to feel like I was cool.'

The girl she had met at her father's opening also happened to be studying in Singapore, and it was here that she and Frika met again. 'She said to try heroin again, until you feel high.' This time, the feeling she got was 'high' – 'I felt I was in my own world.'

This was a surprise to Frika. Her parents had taught her that drugs were evil and that you shouldn't take them. 'But what they didn't tell me was that drugs are nice. They actually make you feel high and feel good.' Trying to fit in, Frika got to know some of the girl's friends and began to use heroin more, at this point only cooking it. 'I wasn't even smoking cigarettes at the time. Some people start from smoking first, cigarettes, then pot, alcohol. Not me. I got right into heroin.'

Like many a cigarette user too, she made the classic assumption: 'I thought I'll do this maybe one time. But I tried a couple of times, and I got hooked. In the first honeymoon period, it felt good. It made me feel high and forget the world for some time. I felt much more confident when I used drugs. And quickly, I went to the latter stage of heroin where you get really addicted.'

She finally felt that she belonged. But the drug overtook any feelings of friendship for the kids at school. If anything, it was the drug that became the friend. 'After we got really addicted, we got greedy. Selfish. We backstabbed each other, to know who was using more or who should get more of the drugs.'

Then in 1998, back in Indonesia during the last major transition of power, the Chinese were again targeted. Many women were raped, and Chinese businesses were burned and looted. Though no one in Frika's family was personally injured, her father lost much of his business. Her parents could no longer afford to pay for both girls to stay in Singapore, so they brought Frika's sister home. Frika was alone in the city again.

The cost of supporting her drug habit also increased as her tolerance for it grew. She couldn't write home to her parents and ask for money to pay for her growing habit, so she had to commit petty crimes. To save money, she started using shared needles, even though she says she had learned at school about the dangers of HIV. 'I had this information when I was in high school in Singapore. So compared to Indonesia, where we didn't usually get HIV education in high school, I did get that. But because of my using problem, I didn't care. This was the "addict" character. I didn't care as long as I could use. I would just see how I could get fixed today.'

She also knew about the dangers of using heroin in a place such as Singapore. This is a country with a zero-tolerance policy, notorious for executing people found carrying drugs. Yet she remained vulnerable to this life-and-death danger as well.

Meanwhile, Frika's parents back in Jakarta had spoken to the parents of one of her school friends. They knew their child was using heroin, and Frika's parents suspected she was as well. At this time Frika was 18 years old and had been using seriously since she was 16. When she came back to Jakarta on a holiday break, her parents took her to the hospital for a urine test. That was how they discovered their daughter was a heroin addict. They put her into a detox programme in a private hospital, and it was there, while Frika was unconscious, that the blood test that changed her life was done.

Although the doctor's disclosure to her parents was a violation of her rights, Frika generously suggests that he may not have been aware of such rights as they related to medical practice. Full of fear for their daughter, Frika's parents asked the doctor what they should do. 'And the doctor said that, because I had younger sisters at home, "You should just separate Frika from the sisters first." Then I was still sharing a room with my sisters. So when I got back from the hospital, my parents followed the doctor's orders. The doctor said, "You have younger daughters, so you have to separate her!"'

So while Frika was trying to recover from her heroin addiction, and having to face the fact that she had HIV, she also had to face discrimination from her own family on doctor's orders. 'Sometimes they act like God, the doctors. He had to come up with something, even though he didn't know the answer. That's what made me angry. I wanted to kill him,' she remembers. 'But now I forgot already what his name is.' And she smiles.

Following the doctor's orders, her parents first separated off Frika's living space, and she moved to a different room from her sisters. But the hardest separation, she recalls, was at mealtimes. Her parents tried to come up with a way to give her separate utensils without her younger sisters knowing what was happening. They remembered the cartoon that had been her childhood favourite. 'They did it in a nice way. They said, "You like Winnie the Pooh, right? Let's buy utensils that are Winnie the Pooh characters." Those would be mine. But there, when we ate together, we put all the food in the middle and then we would serve ourselves the food with spoons. I forgot sometimes, using their serving spoon instead of mine. Then they would toss the spoon away. And that hurt.'

At the time, Frika says, her relationship with her parents wasn't open enough for her to tell them how she felt. She isn't sure if it was just that she was shy, too quiet, or if the culture was one in which she was expected to keep her feelings to herself. Perhaps it was a combination of all of these things, but what her parents didn't realise was just how much the separation was hurting their daughter.

'It hurt so bad I didn't know what to do at home, so I went back into using. Because the loneliness was crazy.'

The loneliness was exacerbated by the fact that no one outside the family was to know about her HIV status; the stigma was still too great, and the family kept the matter private. As she recounts this period in her life, Frika begins to cry. The loneliness of using Winnie the Pooh utensils at 18, getting over her heroin addiction, and facing HIV alone all seemed too much. Winnie the Pooh was just a bear who very much liked his honey – and to *be* liked.

Frika pauses as she recalls the effects of that isolation. She thought that maybe if she wasn't the only one with HIV, she wouldn't feel so alone. 'There was this anger in me where I felt I wanted to give the virus to a lot of people. I felt, why should it be only me? If I were together with all the others, then we'd all feel the discrimination together, not only me. Because I was so lonely at the time. I was disappointed in people, how they treated me. And at myself. Why me? How had I got myself involved into this kind of thing?'

Now using heroin again, Frika went into groups in Jakarta that she knew and, knowing that that was how she had acquired HIV, she shared needles with them nonetheless. Jakarta is not an easy city in which to find needles, but more importantly, she wanted to avoid those feelings of isolation. Even at moments when she wasn't intending to willingly infect others, she continued to share with them, fearing that if she didn't the other users also 'would discriminate against me. And that they would leave me alone.'

Eventually, she realised she could not continue. Even with other users, she felt isolated. She wanted and needed to come out of the loneliness. So she stopped seeing the people with whom she had been sharing needles. A few months later, with the help of her parents, she found a new rehab programme. This rehabilitation centre opened the same year she had first found out about her HIV status. The centre was called in Bahasa, the national Indonesian language, 'Yayasan Harapn Permata Hati Kita' ('Our Children's Hope'). For short, it is called Yakita, or 'Yes, Us'.

The organisation was founded by David Gordon, a former heroin addict himself, and his Indonesian wife, Joyce, a psychologist. It may have been a bonus for Frika to find an Other like herself – David, a Jewish man working in Muslim Indonesia – but it was in this centre that Frika finally found the acceptance she had been seeking.

'I treated David like my mentor. It's because of him, because of him and Joyce, that I can be who I am now. They gave me the start. They showed me the door. I had to walk through it, yes. But they showed it to me. And how to open that door.'

As a former addict, David understood that it was not just the physical addiction to heroin that Frika and others who were trying to come off the drug would miss, but everything else that went along with it. 'There are the four stages, right? The physical, mental, emotional and the spiritual. I had gone through the physical stage where my body didn't need the heroin anymore. But mentally I missed it. I missed the art of using, the art of going to get the drugs, the feeling of burning it. But physically I didn't need it.'

David and Joyce helped Frika focus also on her mental and emotional health, and got her into a support group for HIV-positive people within the programme. Though most people only stayed for one six-month course, Frika stayed for two, building confidence.

It wasn't only Frika who benefited from the programme, but her parents as well. 'Sometimes they had sessions just for the parents. And they learned about HIV and how to deal with it, and that's where my mother and father started to change. In a way, for example in the culture in Asia, in my relationship with my parents, we were not that open in talking about how I felt. And that's where my relationship with my dad and my mum was not that open. But since I got into Yakita and then they went through the sessions, we could talk more.' Her parents, who had of course followed the doctor and their own community in terms of stigmatising HIV, learned to be more supportive of their daughter. And they became more emotionally open themselves.

'That helped me. We could talk more. My dad was the kind of person who didn't want to show emotions. He grew up in a background that said if you are a man, you shouldn't cry. If you cry, you are not a man. And in one of the sessions in Yakita just for the parents, he broke down. He let down all his defences, and he actually cried. After that he was much more open and I could talk with him more.

'I think it would have been different if my parents had put me in the rehab centre and just let me change by myself, without getting involved. But the good thing is when I was in the rehab, they came every week to see me and do sessions. And they would sit there and listen and learn. I think that's also what made them change.'

With the support of the programme and her parents, Frika began to reach out beyond herself into the wider community, to speak to young people in schools. 'As someone who had been a drug user, I knew I'd been selfish. In those days, I would wake up in the morning, and think, what should I do just to get myself high? Or, where are my drugs? Everything had been about me. But now I started feeling, what can I do to help others? This was the turning point for me. It was when I turned from my addiction, and I started knowing who I was as an addict, as an ex drug user. After that I began being positive, learning how to deal with it, and speaking in small groups in seminars in schools.'

The more she spoke out to young people about HIV, the better she felt. This is not to say she felt wonderful every morning, or never got into any tussles with David Gordon. In fact, she was unhappy with him for arguing against her relationship with her boyfriend, who later became her husband. But as far as David was concerned, the man was also in the programme, and a relationship between the two was against the rules.

But stronger than the anger was the feeling she got from working with David and the wider community when she visited schools. 'I felt like I could share the story of my life, so that other people wouldn't follow it. I could try to change someone's life before they got into drugs. And if people already were hooked, I could let them know what they could do to get help. It was a feeling that I actually could do something. Before, what I'd felt was that I *was* junk; that's why they call it a junkie. But now I felt useful.'

But then there were decisions to be made about life after rehab. Now that she was 'clean and sober', and still young, she could return to a normal life. So she decided to open her own clothing shop. With the business acumen typical of her family, she was so successful she opened another two shops in her first year. But whenever she wasn't working at her stores, she volunteered at an NGO. And, as she worked endlessly, the virus got stronger and her immune system began to suffer. She had a choice: to follow her dream of doing social work, or just run her businesses.

But there was another factor too. As the first-born in the family, she felt her parents still wanted her to follow on and take a role in the family businesses. So that is what she did, giving up her clothing shops. 'I became a stockbroker. My sisters were still studying so my parents' hopes were in me. They had a stock exchange company, and I was there to manage it and be the broker.

'At the same time, I was volunteering for non-profit organisations. We'd finish the stocks around 2 pm, and then I left the office because I didn't want to be there. I think my heart was already called; I wanted to do something with HIV. After four months, I realised I couldn't do this.

'But my mom saw my passion for doing the NGO work. And with time, I talked to them about what I learned in the NGO and the issues. And that made a change.'

Frika and her parents began to do social work together. They founded PITA, a support group for parents of HIV-positive young people in Indonesia. 'They created it as a peer foundation where parents could talk to other parents. It started from five families and their feelings of having children who are HIV-positive. And because they got involved with PITA, the parents' group that they actually started, they felt it themselves. They got their own feedback. When they did something about the issue, they felt good.'

Eventually, Frika left the family business to devote her life purely to social work, especially with APN+. She has become an outspoken activist for young people in Asia with HIV, a role model for young women even as she has gone through her own personal difficulties, including the end of her marriage. 'It wasn't just about HIV, it's more than that. It was about life. You can't really close your eyes, and you can't be denying and unaware, ignore what's in life. It can happen to you. For example, like my divorce, it's really unpredictable. I never knew it was going to happen to me. But it happened.

'So it's like in life, now I feel like I can't be poor. But who knows? Maybe in the future poverty will come into my life because something will happen; an accident or ... I don't know. Everything is unpredictable. So we have to be aware. But my turning point, what really made me realise, was when I got HIV.'

Having gone through the experience of addiction and being HIV-positive, and having seen the problem at first-hand, Frika proudly represented young people from Asia at the opening plenary session of the International AIDS Conference in Toronto in 2006. She appeared alongside speakers such as Dr Peter Piot, the head of UNAIDS, the joint United Nations programme on HIV/AIDS, and later shared the stage with guests like Bill Clinton and Bill Gates.

But Frika did not follow the accepted, 'politically correct' line about getting rid of the stigma she and millions of others experienced; she saw it another way. Frika spoke about people like herself empowering themselves rather than waiting for others to give permission for empowerment. 'I say let's not talk about reducing stigma. Because when you talk about reducing stigma, it's been there, generation after generation. Let's not give people false hope. It's better to give people skills for how to live with it and fight back. This is a more positive way rather than a false hope of reducing stigma.'

Frika also appeared in several films at the 2008 International AIDS Conference in Mexico, still fighting for her own and the wider community. She encourages her own community to take the initiative, just as she has changed from a person risking her own and others' lives to dedicating her life to others. Yet she also makes a call to those outside the HIV-positive world. 'On the one hand, there are times that people living with HIV need to have their own meetings or support groups with people living with HIV themselves. But it's not that we're saying that we're separating people living with HIV. Because if we do that, we're making people living with HIV exclusive and marginalising ourselves.'

Having survived that discrimination herself and taken a public stance, Frika feels the most important thing is to be empowered – or even encouraged just to live. 'I came to this point, and other people can too. With HIV, I could survive the discrimination. Dentists were discriminating against me, for example. When I would say I'm HIV-positive, they wouldn't take me. I didn't have to tell them. But I wanted to make sure that they wouldn't use the tools of the dentist again on the other patients. Now if they won't take me, I'm empowered enough to look for other dentists. It's those kind of skills that we need to give people. To survive!'

As part of her outreach work, Frika now wants people to know about her addiction. 'I want to show people addicts can actually change,' she says vehemently. 'You would not have wanted to see me while I was using. I was mad. I was just crazy. But I can come to this point and I feel other people can too. I think that's why the addiction part of my story is important. If I can change, other people should have the chance.

'David at the centre always asked me this question: Are you a taker or are you a giver? I had been taking a lot. I had been self-centred and selfish, taking everything from people as long as it met my needs. Then I got to the point where I wanted to be a giver. And that's the nature of life. Are you a giver or are you a taker? And I want to be a giver.'

Though she is not making the kind of money she made when she was running her businesses, Frika is clear about the value of the choice she has made. 'Myself, I have two personalities. One personality is the addict personality and the old self, before rehab. When I used drugs, I fed the addict personality and became the junkie Frika. But now I don't feed it with drugs, but with social work. I'm much more content with that.

'I think there's a reason why I got HIV. Is it to show people that even though you are Chinese in Indonesia, middle class, you can get HIV? Even though you are not a sex worker or a client of a sex worker? I'm not saying that getting HIV was a gift. But knowing about my HIV status, that's a gift. Knowing it early, and it being not too late to realise what I can do for the future, that's a gift.'

And it's not only Frika who has changed through seeing the epidemic personally and on a wider level, but also her parents. 'They know how important it is for me to work in this field so that I feel I'm useful, that I can be useful in this life. And they understand that, that it is important for me to do this.

'I'm really glad that my parents stayed there with me in the journey, stayed there in the process, and grew together with me. That's what I'm really grateful for.'

Because she has had the support of her parents, as well as her sisters, and David and Joyce, Frika is very open about her status. She is also public because she wants others to see those with the virus and those without. Now she is leaving the organisation for which she has worked, to reach out on her own in the wider community. 'It's a good feeling when you can actually give something. You can give and share what you have with others. It may not be the same when it comes back to you – but what you give will always come back to you.'

Banking on lives

Chung To

Unlike Wil and Flor, Paul and Sandra, or Frika, Chung To made what might seem a crazy choice: he sought out situations that would give him nightmares for years to come. These were not fantasies such as you might see in the movies, but very real horrors impacting on individuals in China. It was a sight that has had an impact on Chung To for life, though he would never say for the worse, no matter how many times he has woken in the middle of the night.

A man in his forties, Chung To is clear and plain-speaking, despite his gentle eyes and demeanour. He gave up a career as a Harvard-educated investment banker to raise money and create a supportive world for young people who came from a place to which he himself had no familial connection. A single man, he is now more connected than he could have imagined – to about five thousand children, who were rapidly orphaned by AIDS following a tainted-blood scandal caused by Chinese officials.

Chung To began life in Hong Kong. His father worked for the

Chung To

government; his family was well-educated and well-to-do. But at a young age, he learned his first lesson about giving to charity. 'I remember my grandmother; we used to go to our favourite restaurant for dim sum lunch as a family gathering. At that time, Hong Kong was a poor place. There were a lot of beggars outside the restaurant. My grandmother would give me a coin and ask me to give it to a beggar. She said, "When you are in a position to help others, you should help others."

'At that time, I didn't understand. But later on I realised why she didn't put the coin into the beggar's box herself, but asked me. She wanted to empower me to be in the position to give, and nurture that mentality in me. So whenever I would give a coin to the beggar, I would know that when I can afford to, I should help others.'

His grandmother had other altruistic tendencies too. His grandparents had fled mainland China when the communists took over, and during the many years she lived in Hong Kong she would help fellow refugees. What she taught Chung To was in line with her own practices as well as her beliefs.

Chung To's lifelong concern regarding the AIDS epidemic arose following the family's move to San Francisco, where his father had got a job in private enterprise. 'I arrived in San Francisco in 1982 at the beginning of the AIDS epidemic. A lot of people were dying, and others were panicking; they didn't know what it was. It was on the front page of the news every day. It was called the "Gay Disease", the "Gay Cancer". As a new immigrant and teenager, it made a big impact on me.'

He also got to see the effects first-hand. 'When I was going to high school in San Francisco, my teacher died of AIDS. So that made it very personal to me. But it also desensitised it for me at a very early age. Because I knew it was not something you would get easily. I saw the teacher every day in very close contact. And we didn't get it. So that also put a human face on AIDS for me.'

After graduating from high school, Chung To went to Columbia University. But even as he focused on his own education, the AIDS epidemic either followed him or he followed it. 'I went to New York for college. That was the mid to late eighties, when many people said the entire Broadway generation was lost. Every day in the obituaries, you'd read about somebody in music or the arts. And as a college student, you did a lot of thinking about it.

'That was during the time of Reagan. And I saw with AIDS how the media, by making it a gay disease, not only further stigmatised gay people but also made straight people more vulnerable. Because they thought, "I'm not gay, I won't get AIDS."'

It was also a time in the US when some popular religious fundamentalists made statements such as Jerry Falwell's famed: 'AIDS is the wrath of a just God against homosexuals.' On the other side were groups like Act Up, who were working to combat such claims and the federal government's refusal to address the issue. 'It was a time when there were a lot of militant protests demanding research and treatment. As a young college student, that was quite an experience living in New York.

'I had friends who died of AIDS, while it was still very stigmatised in the States. We had kids being kicked out of school, people being disowned and kicked out from their family. And church.'

Though he was always aware of the growing crisis around the epidemic, for which there was no effective treatment at the time, Chung

To's focus was on his studies and career. He always contributed to AIDS charities and stayed involved, but work came first. After graduating from Harvard with a master's degree in political science, he worked for Lehman Brothers on Wall Street for two years. Then he joined UBS, working in corporate finance and becoming involved in mergers and acquisitions and the issuing of shares.

In 1995, UBS offered to relocate him to Hong Kong as they expanded into Asia. The chance to work in his birthplace before the handover in 1997 was something Chung To didn't want to miss. He moved to Hong Kong and worked with the bank there for a few years, then with other corporations in finance-related positions.

In 1998, while still retaining his job, he began the Chi Heng Foundation, an organisation dedicated to raising AIDS awareness in China. 'We founded Chi Heng in '98. From '98 to 2001, we did education and prevention for young people, sex workers and gay men.' Then, through friends and contacts in mainland China, Chung To began to hear disturbing rumours. The stories were vague, but the rumours were about tainted blood infecting villagers on a massive scale.

Later, he read a story in a newspaper by a woman he admired, a journalist who was using her work to fight the AIDS epidemic in China. It's rare for a news story to change the direction of anyone's life. But in 2001, that was exactly what happened to Chung To. Her story made him want to see for himself what was going on.

'I read a story from Elizabeth Rosenthal,' he recalls. 'She was the bureau co-chief for the *New York Times* in Beijing at the time. She was also a person who really inspired me. She was a medical doctor herself, then became a journalist. And was very passionate about writing about AIDS in China.

'She heard about the AIDS epidemic in central China, where a lot of people sold blood during the early nineties. Due to unsanitary practices, many of them had got HIV. By 2001, many of them were dying at a very rapid rate. So she wrote about it. She also wrote about an old lady, a 76-year-old retired medical doctor who had been visiting the villages and doing work for the patients. So I was very curious.'

Through his contacts in China, Chung To got the number of the elderly doctor. He rang her immediately. Though she was grateful for his interest, she was fearful of the government.

'I said, "I would like to come." And she said, "No, no, you don't understand. They're very sensitive here."

'Because she was doing AIDS work. At that time, AIDS was considered a state secret in China. Because the blood scandal was partly a government responsibility. These people did not get HIV from IV injection or sex. They were mobilised to sell blood by the government in the early nineties, as a way to make money. This was partly because of the shortage of blood. Because as the coastal areas got richer, people were less willing to give blood voluntarily. So in order to balance the blood bank, they had to go inland.

'But another important reason was a big demand for plasma-related blood products, which could be exported and sold for money. It's a very lucrative business. It's a very lucrative business. A lot of people need plasma-related products, for example if you're a haemophiliac.'

Chung To had several telephone conversations with the elderly doctor, who insisted it was unsafe for him to go there. Yet the more he heard about the conditions of the villagers in Henan province, the more he was determined to go. He bought a plane ticket and went to meet the doctor.

He arrived at her home early in the morning. 'That day was quite scary. I was literally in her apartment for 20 seconds before she said we needed to go somewhere else to talk. She was being monitored and under surveillance all the time. She later told me that the day before four government people, the police, went to her apartment and warned her not to speak to people from the outside. So they must have heard our telephone conversation and knew I was arriving.

'But I arrived at something like six in the morning. So they were not there yet. But after we spent the day together, she said, "You must go now. You dare not stay overnight."'

Angered by the situation, and determined to find out more about it, Chung To decided to visit the affected villages himself over the next months. What he saw shocked him. 'I thought it must be similar to what must have been happening in the worst impacted areas in Africa, if not worse. In some villages that I visited, there was a 40 to 50 per cent rate of infection among the adult population. So half the village either had died of AIDS or was dying.

'I am not trained as a doctor, so I was not used to seeing a lot of people dying. And usually people died at home without any medical care or treatment. That was a time before anti-retroviral treatment was available in China. So there were a lot of side effects, opportunistic infections, and skin disease. It was very hard to see how they suffered. I mean, think if you were the child of the patient, seeing your parents dying in such a horrible way. It's not like a tsunami or earthquake where people die so quickly. It was a very slow and torturous passing away.

'And they were concentrated in the middle generations, because the grandparents wouldn't sell blood, and the children wouldn't sell blood. So it made a stronger impact on the community because the bread-earners got sick more.

'The other thing which had a greater impact was that they sold blood in a relatively short period of time, got sick in a relatively short period of time and died within a short period of time. In Africa, it was more staggered that people got ill. But here, because it was not staggered, the safety net provided by the government, and the villages, did not work.'

A village might be composed of three or four families. When a few of them were sick, they could take care of them. But when half of them were sick, the whole traditional family network disappeared.

On another level, though, what Chung To saw in China *was* eerily like Africa, where I had seen grandmothers taking care of their own children's children, sometimes six to ten at a time. 'Just like in Africa, the grandparents had to witness the passing away of their own children one after another. I know many families where the middle generation was completely wiped out. So the grandparents had to become parents again. They had to work in the fields and make an income to support their grandchildren.

'And for the middle generation, they got HIV, suffered physically, and didn't die in peace. They thought they were leaving behind their underage children without people to take care of them, and hadn't done their job as a parent.'

As for the children, they became orphans. Many were deprived of basic education and care. And all three generations suffered from the stigma of the disease. At first, no one knew how people contracted it, so it was just a dark and mysterious thing. Later, word got around that it seemed to be spread by sex and drug use, so those who had it became stigmatised and vilified.

It was the sight of two boys living in unbearable conditions that shocked Chung To into taking more action. 'I saw two brothers who lived in an eight-foot by eight-foot tiny hut. The original home had collapsed due to rainstorms. They had lost both parents to AIDS and were jammed into what was originally the kitchen of the house. So three metres. No heat, no electricity, no water.

'It was so cold the first time I visited. And imagine the boys, one 15, one 12, living in such a place. When it got dark, it got completely dark. At the same time, I saw a Kuan Yin statue, the goddess of mercy, or the equivalent of Mother Mary in Catholicism, in the middle of the hut, very shiny and a big contrast to the messy hut. I asked, "What is this?" The older one said, "Oh I picked it up from the neighbours'. And I pray to it every night." I asked, "Why is that?" And he answered, "Because I want to have a better life."

'All my life I had been doing finance-related things. But in that part of China, I saw such suffering that I thought I had to do something. A lot of people think, you're so great to sacrifice your job or put aside your career. But I'd been working for ten years. Giving back a few years to society wasn't that difficult a decision to make.'

The reason he had to do it right away, why he couldn't wait, was the children. They wouldn't wait to grow up. Chung To felt that if he didn't help them, and now, they would grow up uneducated, and miss any opportunity for a future. They were absolutely vulnerable.

He went to the villages over and over, and made many visits to the children's homes. He saw them at 12 or 13, dropped out of school because they had no money. 'So I thought the best thing was to get them back to school. If I didn't do that then, we would miss the chance; even two years later would be too late. So I had to make a decision. It was either do it now or never.'

But it wasn't just sympathy Chung To felt for the children. 'I admired the children a lot. They not only had to bear the physical burden of taking care of the parents, taking care of the siblings, making dinner, doing the housework and going to school, but also the emotional burden of seeing the parents passing away in such a horrible way.'

Why couldn't he have just raised money on the side, as opposed to literally giving up his career? Chung To's answer to that question is, 'At that time, it wasn't the money that was the main problem. It was the resources. I couldn't find anybody willing to do what I wanted to do in such a way. I looked for people. They were so scared of AIDS that they wouldn't work in AIDS-infected villages. And there was a lot of political sensitivity: I could not bring a lot of people there at that time.'

Chung To was capable, willing to travel to remote areas because of his belief, and willing to work for free. So he had to be the one to set it up.

He also had previous experience to offer. He had worked with groups that were building schools in remote areas in China, and poverty-relief programmes in mountainous areas. He had been involved in fighting the epidemic in Hong Kong, and had been well aware of its effect from the time his teacher had died. 'So it was a good combination of my past experience. I knew I should start something, which could be scaleable. Because I wasn't interested in helping just one village. I wanted to start something which could help a lot more people. But we had to start small and gain experience.'

But Chung To decided his model would not involve building orphanages for all the thousands of needy children in China. That would disrupt the young people's lives, take them out of society, and most importantly, it wasn't possible to take on to a large scale. Instead, he would build on the existing infrastructure. Let the children live with grandparents and other relatives in the same village, and get them back into the local school system with other non-impacted children.

In China, for the first nine years of a child's education, primary and junior high schools charged no tuition fees. However, there were book, uniform and other fees, for which each school charged differently. So Chung To began with providing these smaller amounts of money, sponsoring the existing education system rather than starting schools from scratch, as for example the religious missions had done in the 19th century.

'This enabled us to grow very quickly from the first semester, where we helped 127 students in one village. As of now, we are helping over 5000 kids. If we were still building orphanages and schools, we would not be able to expand and help as many children.

'The beauty is we don't have a physical location or the burden of running schools. We leave it up to the local education department to do that, but we enhance the quality of the education of the whole school, like building a reading room.'

Such contributions mean the schools co-operate with Chung To's foundation, because it is working directly with them. 'We send the teachers to extra training. We buy extracurricular books. So we enhance the quality, but we don't touch the curriculum. We respect the local position. We don't want to interfere and change people's minds. But we will help the school in any way we can, to enhance the quality of the teacher, the quality of the school facilities and so on. That way we can grow quicker. After 11 consecutive semesters of growth, this model has proven to be a sustainable model which can be scaled up quite rapidly.'

The other needs Chung To saw were what he calls psychosocial: to enable the children to have the courage to express themselves, with emotional support. That was the labour-intensive part, and it took time to find staff. It also involved creating even more programmes, getting children to draw, bringing them to summer camps, or simply being and speaking with them. 'Just like with your own child, you don't want to just pay for the school and the education. You have to talk with the child, to spend time with them. You have to show them that there's someone in the world that loves them and cares about them.

'I always see them and think about how to help them as *my* children. If these were my children, what would I do for them? So I write letters to them. I send small stationery and gifts to them. I see them and play with them. And encourage them not just to study hard but also how to be a good person, sending them books not just about knowledge but about good ethics. To be honest, to be a person with integrity.'

Chung To has built his Chi Heng Foundation to the point where he is not needed full-time for the moment. 'The past six years I have done this work full-time. But I have used up a lot of my savings. A few months ago, some former colleagues asked me to work again, so I've been working for a few months back in the banking industry while I continue to be involved in Chi Heng as the chairman.'

Because all his co-workers know of his dedication to these children and this cause, to which he promises to dedicate the rest of his life, they are supportive. His boss, who adopted an orphan of his own accord, also ensured the investment bank donated money to the foundation.

But over the years, Chung To basically depleted his own funds for children from a part of China, as his mother pointed out, with which he had no familial or historical connection. What does he get out of it then?

'Seeing the children growing up and knowing that their life has improved because of what we do is one of my greatest rewards. It's like seeing your own child grow up. There's a lot of joy, because we have three hundred kids in universities. Others have graduated and got good jobs.

'It's made me a much stronger person too. Not long after I started this, the virus SARS broke out in Hong Kong. There were a lot of people committing suicide, jumping off of rooftops killing themselves because their investments went bad as a result. But after seeing the children, I was so impressed that they had to deal with much bigger issues, seeing their parents dying and with a much worse future. Still, they were not complaining.

'We have children who draw art therapy, saying that tomorrow life would be better. We had those two brothers, who despite losing both parents to AIDS and their house collapsing, two brothers living in a small hut without anything, still had not given up their hope in life. So compared with them, we have a lot more. We should work with what we have and make the world better. If they can do it, why can't we?'

Regarding his own willingness to engage with the suffering he witnessed, Chung To brings up an analogy. It is the story of the Buddha, who began life as a young prince with all the riches one could imagine. The only thing his father didn't want him to see was the suffering in the world. But there came a day when the young prince insisted on going outside the palace gates. There he observed what was happening – the beggars, the poverty, and the struggle of humanity. It was the day that began his difficult path – the path that ultimately led to Nirvana.

'Of course, there's the dark side of it,' Chung To says. 'I felt very scared seeing people dying. So I try to suppress them, but in the middle of the night I will have nightmares. I will wake up and start crying, not with a pain but just starting to cry. Sometimes you blame yourself because there are people whom you couldn't save, like a lot of the adults that died of AIDS.

'But I gained a lot more than losing, always. Seeing it and doing something about it, and being proud of the fact that I have done something about it.'

For Chung To, AIDS remains the key focal point for addressing issues globally, even issues of poverty or discrimination. After all, he points out, one can still be refused entry to many countries in the world if one is known to have the HIV virus, including the United States and Iran.

'I always tell people AIDS is a big issue, although many people don't see it. I always talk to students in university with this notion: ten years from now, would you rather gather again in this room and say, "Gee, I wish I had done something about it, had I known." That was what happened in Africa 20 years ago. A lot of people say, I didn't know it was going to be like this.

'We did know. We know what is going to happen in Asia. If we don't do something about it, we could say the same thing ten years from now: "Oh I wish I knew and had done something." Or would you rather congratulate each other ten years from now that you did something and saved some people's lives?'

Chung To can sleep better, it seems to me, certainly on the last point. And the two brothers who had been praying to the statue of Kuan Yin would agree. As I hope would the goddess herself, who is the embodiment of compassion.

Chapter 4

Listen up

> We have two ears and one mouth so that we can listen twice as much as we speak.
>
> Epictetus

Like Chung To, Siri had nightmares about what she had seen. And like him too, she quickly realised, 'You can't help and cry at the same time. Because when you're crying, you can't hear.'

Whether it comes from embossed four-colour dossiers issued by the World Bank or a drunk at the bar, we can always get advice. We can get it for free, or for the price of a drink, or we can pay through the nose for it. Advice on anything is available – whether it's the best car deal, who we should date, or even the latest advances in penis enlargement or breast reduction – and such advice is freely offered by people we don't even know! There is also plenty of advice on privatisation vs nationalisation, the implementation of democracy, global markets, epidemiology, peace commissions, etc. Yet chaos, famines and wars still ensue, even as governments, the UN, think-tanks and NGOs spend ever more money on advisors.

What they don't spend money on is listeners.

Listening isn't easy. When we do listen, often what we hear defies our expectations. Yet as John Steinbeck wrote, 'Nobody wants advice, only corroboration.' The fact is, most of us just want to be heard. As any therapist will tell you, we each know the solutions to our problems, even if they are surprising even to ourselves. It's a matter of getting to those answers – that is, listening to ourselves.

What the people in this book all discovered was that by listening to the community or the individuals they worked with, they indeed found needs and desires other than those they had anticipated. That held as true for the rebel from Darfur as the man devoting his life to working with street children in Cambodia. When each really listened, leaving their own preconceptions behind, they were surprised by what they heard. But then their own efforts became more successful; they were actually giving people what they wanted. And the people's own solutions worked.

My own cultural mores and preconceptions were severely challenged when I listened to a woman who represented a community of people condemned by just about every society worldwide. Yet her thoughts echoed what an African-American minister had said to me: 'We'd be surprised at how strong people are with the right kinds of support. They actually make a lot of the good decisions on their own.'

The woman I was challenged by couldn't agree more. Her name is Rachel Wotton. Her views, and those of the thousands of workers she represents, are rarely listened to. Governments legislate against people like her and her clients supposedly 'for her own good'. Charities try to 'rescue' people like her and abolish their way of life, claiming that the vast majority of them are victims.

Rachel is a sex worker. She claims, as do many of her peers and peer organisations around the world, that they choose to do sex work. That they want people to realise that 'sex work is work'. Most importantly, that theirs is a voice that also needs to be heard. Because, if it is not, their rights are in real danger, including often their right to survive.

A different calling

Rachel Wotton

On behalf of Scarlet Alliance – the Australian Sex Workers' Association – and many sex worker groups from around the world, I am extremely proud to address this conference. This is the first time a sex worker has been granted the opportunity to make a keynote speech ... Sex workers have been objectified and medicalised for far too long. But we are not just objects to be 'managed' and controlled. With adequate support, sex workers can lead the way. And so, whether it is in the boardroom, on the street, in the brothel or the parliament, there should be 'nothing about us, without us'.

From Rachel Wotton's keynote speech to the International Harm Reduction Conference, Poland, 2007

Rachel is a somewhat petite strawberry blonde. Her face has wide cheeks and a defined jaw, and wears a winsome smile when she chooses. On her website, under a pseudonym, she advertises her services as 'a genuine independent escort'. In some of her photographic poses, she can look extremely kinky. In others, as she says, she appears like the wholesome girl next door.

Whether or not girls next door are all wholesome, Rachel feels good about what she does. 'I look nothing like what people assume a sex worker is. I do look like the girl next door. Clients and people outside the industry say, "I'd never think that you were a sex worker." But I say, "We come in all shapes and sizes." And by me choosing to be open and public and a proud sex worker, people can start to shift their paradigm of what the sex industry is and who's involved in the sex industry.'

Rachel, who is in her early thirties, was the international spokesperson for Scarlet Alliance, the Australian Sex Workers' Association. In addition to having written many papers on her industry, and working on a master's degree, she was the first sex worker to be a keynote speaker at the annual International Harm Reduction Conference, hosted in Warsaw, Poland, in 2007. She is also a founding member of a non-profit organisation devoted to fighting for the sexual rights of people with disabilities, Touching Base Inc. While it may run contrary to many people's expectations, Rachel is satisfied with her chosen work. 'At the end of the day,' she says, 'my industry's all about pleasure. My whole job is to make someone feel good about themselves and to feel happy.'

Rachel's story goes against the myth of the 'troubled-childhood, drug-addicted, victimised prostitute'. A child of English parents who had migrated to Australia, she was born in Sydney's south, with her brother following three years later. Hers was a normal suburban upbringing, and she claims to have always been an A student. Like many children, she grew up with parents who eventually did not stay together. They separated when she was 11 years old, and then divorced. Her father remarried soon after – 'I had the usual evil stepmother,' Rachel says with a laugh – and she ended up with three stepsisters, a stepbrother and a half-brother.

Despite the normality of her suburban life, even as a teenager Rachel was attracted to sex work. 'People go into it for all sorts of different reasons. I was always attracted to it. I always remember cutting out and reading articles in magazines like *Cleo*, or I'd look at the newspaper articles.

'I didn't know how to get into it actually. And when I was being forced to move up to Queensland with my father at 16, I was trying to find a way I wouldn't have to go.' She thought prostitution could be a way to stay in Sydney, although she didn't believe she could do street work, which she had read about. She didn't know then about safe houses, and didn't feel comfortable with the idea of getting into someone's car. She also didn't believe she had the good looks to be a really 'glamorous' call girl, the sort she had read about in the wanted ads. 'I was still a virgin then, mind you. I thought they would just laugh at me. If I think about it now, I would have made a fortune.'

So she moved to Queensland. She finished secondary school, then left home to attend Queensland University, moving in with her boyfriend of the time. For her second year, she transferred south, to the University of Wollongong in New South Wales. Here she studied toward a Bachelor of Arts in Psychology. As she describes this period, she makes her life sound prosaically normal, even as she says matter-of-factly, 'Then I took a year off in '94 as I started to get into the sex industry. I moved up to Sydney. And in '95 I did third year at Sydney University.'

The way she started in her line of work, while at university at Wollongong, was through becoming friends with her boyfriend's ex-girlfriend. One day when the boyfriend was out of the house, 'his ex-girlfriend confided in me that she'd started working in a brothel. And

Rachel Wotton

I asked her all about it. I said, "Could I do this?" And she said, "You'd be fine."'

Before Rachel did any work at the brothel, she first started working on 'a swinging cruise'. 'I worked on the swinging boat a few days before my first shift at the brothel. And while that was technically the first time, it was really easy.' As many readers will know, a swinging club is where people can 'swing' – i.e. have sex with other people consensually. But letting the cat out of the bag a bit, Rachel says some swinging clubs pay girls to get the party started and to make sure people have a good time.

The first time she did this it felt very simple, she says; it was a fast way to make good money. 'Back then, I was working in a bottle shop for ten dollars an hour. I remember being on the back on the jet cat from Manly back to Sydney, and the first time I earned $300. And I remember thinking, "Oh my God, I've got $300 for five hours of my time." I'd always been really independent, and this was a way for me to secure my independence and do the things I wanted to do.'

Her introduction to work in the brothel was slightly different. The ex-girlfriend had called her up and asked if she wanted to do a shift the following week. Rachel was 20 years old, and it was Valentine's Day 1994.

While one might think this would have been a traumatic experience for her, she recalls it as a humorous incident. 'The first time in the brothel it was funny because I got there and the receptionist thought that my friend had filled me in. And my friend had thought the receptionist would fill me in on all the details. Then my first client arrived shortly after. He booked me for an hour.

'So I just went in winging it, pretending I'd been working somewhere else for a year. And my first client – he had the second-largest cock I think I've seen in my life. And I remember thinking if I can do this, I can do anything.' She laughs easily at the memory.

Rachel's experiences with sex work from then on, she claims, were almost uniformly positive. 'Once I got into the sex industry the most amazing thing for me, straight from the word go, was how normal everyone was, and all the differences between people. I thought you had to be this high-class glamorous model to do it. And that was a very quick learning curve in the sex industry. When I do presentations now, I often say to people, "Pick an age, an occupation, a hair colour, an eye colour, a body size, a skin colour, religion and an ethnicity and you've got someone working in the sex industry."

'The diversity of the clients is as far as your mind can see in the general population. If people think religious people don't come to the sex industry, they've got another think coming.' She laughs. 'Because there've been many stories in my career talking to other sex workers – and my own experiences – where people who are in front of the congregation come to see sex workers, and that's female, male and transgender workers.'

On top of the diversity of the people she met, she felt she was doing what she was meant to do – a business where she gets to give pleasure. 'Some people call it a calling. Some people may grow up, and they always wanted to be an astronaut. Or they always wanted to be a fireman or a graphic designer or architect. I was always attracted to this. I've never had a problem with anything I do. People say, "How could you be doing this?" But I don't feel bad about it. I don't think that

I'm unworthy. I always like learning about people. I get to see a variety of people through my work, and I get to maintain my independence.'

Contrary to my own expectation that she might feel powerless, always at a client's beck and call, she says the opposite: that she grew to feel more empowered and independent. And it made her feel better about herself, even physically.

'I developed a much better and healthier body image. I've never liked my bottom. And for 15 years, all these guys have been paying me and saying, "You have such a great ass." Even now I look around and say, "Are they talking to me?" My ability to be more empowered and stronger has increased tenfold. I always say that the sex industry has probably saved my life because of my ability to negotiate safe sex and know about sexually transmitted infections.'

However, even if she was proud of her work, she was well aware of the stigma attached to it by the wider community. She did tell her brother and his friends after a year or so, but for many years she kept her profession secret from her mother.

And having finished university, the more she worked and began to listen to other sex workers she got to know, the more she started to realise it wasn't so easy for many of her peers. 'When I first started, brothels were still illegal, because the decriminalisation of running and operating a brothel only occurred in '95 in New South Wales. And I had no idea about laws or anything like that. But I guess I had an innate thing about rights, and the old question, why? Why was the wider community, or the police, so horrible to many of us? I started to realise that there was a lot of inequality.'

She heard about the International Conference on Prostitution, ICOP, which was to be held in 1997, only a few years after she'd begun working. She was fascinated by the idea of a conference where she could meet others who were working as she did: people from all over the world. 'I was able to get to my first International Conference on Prostitution in Los Angeles by saving up my money and funding myself to go to it. When I got there, I was the "baby whore", I used to say,' she laughs. 'I was one of the youngest there.

'I'd never been with so many different sex workers and people presenting on different things. I was lucky, because there was an outreach worker from the New South Wales sex workers' organisation, SWOP (Sex Workers Outreach Project), who took me under her wing. It was a real eye-opener. I met so many amazing sex workers at that conference, many of whom I'm still in contact with today.'

After hearing about the difficulties many of her fellow workers presented from their experiences and their communities, Rachel was moved. Listening to the others, she was able to see just how hard the profession was for some of her colleagues internationally and even in Australia. She also began to realise the extent to which what she did was condemned worldwide, and as she heard, the situation was getting worse. On her return to Australia, Rachel decided to volunteer with SWOP.

'There was this horrible thing around the world, this backlash against sex workers. I mean in some ancient cultures sex workers were highly revered. Somewhere along the way, and this I believe has to do with religion, sex workers have been dropped to the bottom. And everyone is suffering so much discrimination and stigma that they become these anonymous faces. Both the clients and the sex workers are demonised. The clients are portrayed as "dirty old men who are violating women". The sex workers are portrayed as "drug-affected, unworthy people". They're viewed as being not a good mother, a good friend or a suitable partner. And this is so wrong.'

Rachel's sex work now also became a way to fund the volunteer work she was doing, which related to sex workers' rights. She took additional courses, then, two years after she started volunteering for SWOP, she landed her first paid job with the organisation. That in turn led to wanting to tell her mother what she did, with pride.

'My first "real" full-time job was at SWOP. I was only volunteering before then. My first role was as the Sex Work and Massage – SWAM – Project Officer, where I wrote a resource that was funded by the Attorney-General's crime prevention unit in New South Wales. The launch of the report was to be in 2001. I wanted to tell my mother about this launch and have her there. But I wasn't sure how or where to do it.

'I thought long and hard about it. I didn't want her to be at my place, because if she were upset or angry, then she'd have to drive home like that. And I didn't want that. And I didn't want to tell her at her place. So I told her in a shopping centre. I went shopping with her on the halfway mark between my place and hers. And I told her in the food court.'

Amidst the hustle and bustle of people eating kebabs, meat pies, Chinese food and ice cream, Rachel revealed not just her profession to her mother, but her calling to help others. 'I didn't just say, "Well, I'm now a sex worker," but I told her that I was also employed at SWOP. I had different articles I'd written for the sex worker magazine. And I could show her what I was working on in this position.

'And she was more than a bit surprised.'

Her mother, though obviously not delighted, was supportive of her. Rachel also realised that it wasn't easy for the parents of sex workers. 'It's really isolating. It's not so isolating for me because I have a huge group of friends and supporters and colleagues and peers and I'm very out in the sex worker community, but people around you are really isolated. Like parents and partners of sex workers.'

But even if she felt she could be open herself, the marginalisation of sex workers continued to drive Rachel to do more than her own work, saving up so that she could afford flights and attend conferences overseas. 'I always wanted to help people, to support and empower people. And by being an outreach worker and being part of this, I was able to help impart the knowledge I've learned and learn more things to empower people to be able to assist themselves.'

She also did local outreach. 'When I was doing outreach on the streets, the street-based sex workers were some of the most amazing strong and empowered women I've ever met. But there was one time when we were out there, and I got a phone call saying someone's being strangled. And we got there and found the guy in the car, and the woman is hysterical and upset. And the police say, "He says he paid for the service, so it's his word against yours." And I was thinking, for a sex worker to be crying, especially on the street, means that there really is a problem. Yet the police don't take her statement and won't even charge him.'

Rachel points out that this is just one example of how marginalising sex workers puts their lives at risk. To her, society's view on sex is itself a double standard. 'Sex sells everything these days but when you're actually selling a sexual service it's looked down upon. You can sell a car with a near-naked woman. But if you're a near-naked woman getting paid for your time, that's looked down upon. People just treat sex workers like we don't have a brain. That's wrong. And they also treat clients as predators. What we say is that clients are your sons and cousins and uncles and friends and colleagues at work.

'People need to start recognising that it's an occupation. It's an industrial issue. I could never be a garbage collector. I could never get up at three in the morning, never do such a rigorous job and deal with people's garbage all the time. But I'm glad there are people who choose to do that job. I don't care why they're doing it. What I do care about is that their occupational health and safety rights, their industrial rights and their human rights are being respected.'

Whereas for a sex worker, as she points out, their profession affects even simple things such as getting a credit card, renting a flat, or even getting a home loan. If a sex worker were sexually assaulted, there would be a strong chance that their job would be brought up in court even if it had nothing to do with the case.

In the same way that HIV-positive people are discriminated against worldwide, so it is with sex workers. 'The United States can ban me from going there just because I am a sex worker in Australia, even though I may be just going to visit friends in San Diego for a week. Yet people should be able to freely move around.'

In the developing world, besides the beatings from the police and the other dangers that occur as sex work is criminalised, the issue of HIV casts an even wider shadow. In the US, the Bush Administration passed bills aimed at fighting the AIDS epidemic, with billions of dollars earmarked for prevention worldwide, but with the proviso that no money could go to any organisation that was working with sex workers, unless they were facilitating 'exit programmes', i.e. helping them leave the profession. The United States Global AIDS Act, passed in 2003, barred the use of federal funds to 'promote, support, or advocate the legalisation or practice of prostitution'. 'And the bravest thing that ever happened,' she says, 'is that Brazil just contradicted the US government and said they support the sex industry.' (The Obama administration is reviewing this policy at the time of writing.)

As part of its campaign against HIV/AIDS, Brazil's government did actively listen to this marginalised group, especially to Davida, an organisation originally set up by sex workers. Davida helped raise its own money by establishing a clothing label. 'They got sex workers to model their own range of clothing. And after the Brazilian government rejected $40 million from the US, it was another way to raise money to be able to assist the sex industry. But for a lot of organisations, it's been horrific.'

This was especially true in nations where poverty was rife. The right of sex workers to use a condom to protect themselves was at risk, since to exercise that right, one would need access to condoms, and they would have to be affordable. Yet the 'gag ruling' has been accused of preventing the distribution of condoms to sex workers in places hard-hit by the epidemic, such as in Africa or Asia. A well-established Thai organisation, the Population and Community Development Association (PDA), had previously worked with the US government agency USAID. But as it insisted on distributing condoms among sex workers as well as the general population, it lost its US funding. In another case, a United Nations official condemned the US and the Ugandan government for warehousing condoms in the badly affected African country, when there was a known shortage.

Rachel grows livid when talking about this issue. 'People say, "Why can't they just say no? Or why can't they just use a condom?" Either there are no condoms, or they're so expensive in those countries that it's more than the cost of the service. And governments just put their heads in the sand. They say, "Well, this shouldn't be happening." And blame it on the sex workers or on the clients who are paying for the services. How is that attitude helping anyone?'

She contends that many governments, while claiming to try to reduce the epidemic, also claim that the problem is with the people they are trying to help: the sex workers. This echoes Paul Pholeros's findings, with the Australian government claiming to want to help the Aboriginal communities while describing the Aboriginal people as the problem.

'It's not good enough for governments to say, "Sex workers have such a high rate of HIV; what are we going to do?" and then not look at the legal environment. If you give people rights and an environment in which they can go to the police to report crimes, where they have access to affordable safer sex equipment, where they are treated with dignity and respect, then you can really start a constructive way forward.

'What the governments are saying in these countries is that sex workers shouldn't exist. So therefore they're outside the law. Decriminalisation is the way forward to protect people's health and safety and human rights. It's already been shown that it doesn't work for governments to act like ostriches and put their heads in the sand. And one of the things we often say is, "If we don't speak up, then what's going to happen?"

'The reality is that humans like to have sex. They like to have company. And they like to engage in different things. If people want to have mutually negotiable arrangements, then people should be able to do that in a safe environment.

'Hopefully if we advocates do enough work, write enough things and present at enough conferences, than it's a bit like that drop in the water. It's just one drop, but it can reverberate. And reverberate with the right people. So you just have to keep going.'

Today, Rachel's community can finally be listened to, and heard. After eight years of presenting at conferences as a representative for Scarlet Alliance and SWOP, she is now finishing her master's degree in Sexual Health at Sydney University. In addition, she is spending more time in the next phase of her work with Touching Base, the organisation she co-founded, which has been active since October 2000. Says Rachel: 'People with a disability have an intrinsic right to sexual expression.' Touching Base assists people with disabilities and sex workers to connect with each other, focusing on access, discrimination, human rights and legal issues and the attitudinal barriers that both marginalised communities face. So her base of advocacy keeps widening.

What Rachel herself gets out of her volunteer work, she says, is simply 'making a difference'. 'We find it hard to do when you're up against adversity all the time, but it is good to reflect, take stock and take a moment to appreciate that the hours of endless sleepless nights writing or reviewing documents do actually make a difference and can benefit sex workers in a positive way.'

And more importantly, as a representative she can give people hope. 'I can be open and honest about the work I do without the constant fear of arrest, harassment and persecution. I am very lucky to live in Sydney and be able to be who I am without those fears. And we always hope that our small wins here can help change things for the better overseas.'

As a representative of sex workers worldwide, Rachel's wish is that they can 'achieve their right to live in society without being marginalised, to end discrimination and stigma, and for our human, industrial and labour rights to be recognised. For sex work to be recognised as work.' Her belief is that the solution to the problems of marginalisation and human rights lies in the community itself.

If people will listen.

Marketing lessons from L'Oréal – to Phnom Penh

Sébastien Marot

Listening involves more than just hearing another's viewpoint and assuming you understand what they mean. Sébastien Marot discovered that listening means listening and listening and listening again, until you finally understand what the person or community is really saying.

In Phnom Penh, a friend and I went for a meal at the 'authentic Khmer' restaurant my hotel recommended. The capital of Cambodia is a dusty low-rise town, still recovering 30 years after the genocide of millions by the notorious Pol Pot and his Khmer Rouge. Even today, compared with other Southeast Asian cities like Bangkok, with its high-rises and malls, or Ho Chi Minh City in Vietnam, Phnom Penh feels poverty-stricken and stuck in time. Alongside the cars of the wealthy, the poor pedal rickshaws, and beggars compete for tourists' attention on cluttered streets.

The restaurant turned out to be expensive but tasteless, with sullen service. Outside were many young street children begging for money, some with parents perhaps nearby, waiting for them to return with their spoils.

We walked back a different way, towards the still-decaying temple, Wat Phnom, for which the city is named. En route we passed a simply but colourfully painted restaurant called Friends. We decided to stop for a coffee and dessert to overcome the sour taste left by our earlier experience, and I was enchanted by the enthusiastic young staff. They raved about the appetisers, so we tried these – they were tasty and inventive. On the menu there was a description of the restaurant and its purpose: it is part of a street children's vocation programme, with the profits going back into the operation. The lively waiters and kitchen staff are former street children and drug addicts. The organisation is called Friends International, or Mitt Samlanh ('Good Friends').

The operation is the brainchild of Sébastien Marot, a lean man in his forties with dark hair, an open smile and inquisitive eyes, who I met the next day. Fourteen years earlier, he had listened to a group of street children similar to the staff in the restaurant. What they said was that they wanted an education. So, with his life savings, Sébastien started a school. But within a month, 16 of the 17 kids had dropped out and gone back to the streets. 'That's when you realise that you're doing everything wrong,' Sébastien says. 'That what you think is great is not necessarily what they think is great. And therefore, it's not them, but you who's wrong.

'But instead of quitting, I started doing something different.'

And by listening again and again, he found what works.

Originally, Sébastien comes from the capital of the country that was the former coloniser of Cambodia. That is, Paris. His father was French and his mother German. His father, a psychologist, was a corporate human resources consultant. His mother, a scholar professionally, took care of the children. Growing up, Sébastien excelled at secondary school, and his scores propelled him to l'Institut d'Etudes Politiques de Paris, where he studied, of course, political science. As he says, 'With that, pretty much one could do anything.'

Except get out of military service which, at that time, young French men had to do. But Sébastien – and eventually the street children of Cambodia – was lucky. 'Because of my background, I was sent to the

French consulate in Osaka, where I fell in love with Asia and especially Japan.' He was posted there for 18 months. After his tour of duty, he worked with the Asahi Broadcasting Corporation, a television station, for another five months. Then, after two years in Japan, instead of going home, he decided to see more of the continent and spent the next year backpacking. He travelled to China, Hong Kong, Taiwan, Thailand, Malaysia, Singapore and Indonesia, eventually landing up in Australia.

Anyone who has travelled in Asia has heard the plaintive cries of street people, and especially children, as Sébastien did time and time again. But at this point in his travels he had no intention of starting programmes for them. Like many other thoughtful and compassionate tourists, he would give the children food rather than money. This way one was giving the child something directly, rather than supporting their parents who might be keeping them on the street or out of school.

After his travels, Sébastien returned to Paris, but he kept his Asia connection going by helping the Asahi Corporation set up a Paris operation. When that was done, he needed work. With no background in the field, but the reputation of l'Institut working in his favour, he landed a job in marketing with L'Oréal, the cosmetics company. 'I had no experience in marketing, but somehow my school is special. So when they saw this on your CV, they would usually like you. So they didn't mind taking me on. My specific brief was a focus on shampoo for babies,' Sébastien laughs. 'Which I guess was my link to children!'

He worked on a wide spectrum of activities, including the making of commercials, branding and market research. The focus of the latter was on learning to listen to the customers – in this case, the shampoo-needy children and/or their adoring parents.

For Sébastien, three years at L'Oréal were enough. And he yearned to be back in Japan. 'I learned a lot but hated every single minute of it, and I decided it was time to move on. I didn't like the philosophy of the company. There was no coaching, no support, no teaching you how to do things. It was just swim with the sharks. Eat or get eaten. And the best will survive.

'I wanted to go back to Japan. Luckily, I got released from L'Oréal with a nice severance package at the end, and with the money to get

Sébastien Marot

established in Japan. Because I had the money, I decided I'd stop somewhere in Asia I hadn't been. Just for a few weeks. I had a choice between Vietnam, Laos and Cambodia. I chose Cambodia.'

He arrived in 1994, on April Fool's Day. 'That should have told me something,' he says. 'I always look at this date and have a good laugh.'

But the situation in Cambodia in 1994 was anything but funny. It was only 15-odd years since Pol Pot had ravaged the country, and two years after the country's first elections, supervised by UNTAC, the UN peacekeeping operation. Western aid had come flooding into the country with various strings attached, and the Khmer Rouge – with Pol Pot still at its head – was still given credence as an active political party.

Nationwide, the country was still being de-mined. Both the poverty and the riches made from foreign aid were endemic. There was a much looser sex trade here than in Thailand, which had begun cracking down on bars and suppliers of children forced into prostitution. So sexual predators were now exploring this country. In addition, people operating in the local economy could not compete with the high salaries and ever-increasing prices paid by the international aid workers.

'Cambodia in '94 was hell in many ways,' Sébastien remembers. 'It was after the war, the Vietnamese occupation, and the end of the time where a huge international army destroyed everything by trying to rebuild it, in the sense that all the prices went crazy. Some people got extremely rich in a very short time as reconstruction started. There was no electricity, no water, and guns everywhere, shooting all the time. Even Phnom Penh still had mines. I remember they de-mined the corner of my street.' He adds with a hint of irony, 'An intense place.'

Everywhere Sébastien looked, there were children living on the street. And as far as he could see, there was really nowhere for them to turn.

What changed things for Sébastien was a simple sight: the juxtaposition of street children and a certain car. 'I was coming out from this restaurant at night. At nine-thirty then, it was really late and dangerous. And I saw about twenty kids asleep on cardboard on the road.

'I'd seen street kids before. I saw them in Indonesia, horrid, disabled, crawling in the train or pretending to need to crawl and asking for money. In China, I saw kids inflicting wounds to their hands as a show to get money. I had been shocked and horrified, but I was not pushed to do something.

'But this time, I saw a big black Mercedes drive by. It was this very defining moment, there at the central market at night, with this big black car, and those kids sleeping. And that just horrified me – the kids, the Mercedes, the rich people making a lot of money – you knew that money was not legit, but made from abusing and walking all over people.

'Then I started to learn more about the history, and how a lot of people had got involved in helping the country to get back on its feet. But seeing the kids there, I realised it was obviously going to fail big-time. Millions of dollars came into the country for rebuilding, yet they were forgetting all the kids. It made no sense.'

So he started consciously trying to help that first group of street children, which consisted mainly of boys. 'I started doing what everyone does stupidly, which is bringing food and bread and water to the kids. And of course the boys were grateful.' But he noticed that often they weren't as hungry as at other times. 'Suddenly I realised that two other people were doing the same, and so the kids had eight meals a day. It seemed fantastic to the kids; but then I recognised it was negative and harmful because we were actually keeping them on the streets. I was doing everything that should not be done here.'

In Cambodia, far from his European background, a world away from his middle-class upbringing, Sébastien witnessed a few organisations occasionally taking his 'feeding programme' to the nth degree, yet nothing they did created any change. 'Organisations would come with a big truck and everything,' he says. 'Then the kids would get the shower, the doctor, the big meal, new clothes, and go back on the streets. And that was "charity". They would give and move on, without making the situation better.' The children would remain on the street, having had a check-up, and now with a full stomach, and slightly better dressed.

Or compassionate tourists, like Sébastien, would give food to the cute, dirty, helpless little girl or boy on the street. But the more he began to talk to people, the more he started to realise what that meant. 'Because the child doesn't move away from the street, they would end up as an unskilled, unproductive adult. They know a bit of the languages, because they've begged from Japanese, French and German tourists. Because they're 13 or 15, and no longer so cute, they have no other option. They end up in prostitution. Or they have a kid on the street, then two or three kids. Suddenly, exponentially, you have generations of street people.'

Sébastien and the two other adults who were feeding the street children met. They decided to do something about the situation. But as the others worked full-time, and he had his money from L'Oréal, it was decided that Sébastien would be the one who would specifically focus on the project. 'After we met and decided giving food was the wrong thing to do, the group said, "Sébastien, you need to be in charge of this." I didn't sleep for 48 hours thinking about everything, about the possible consequences for me and my life, and Japan, or not. But I had money saved. I was the one. So I said, "Let's try the adventure. Let's do it."

'But I felt lots of things. Angry, upset, and crazy ... I was 29. Young for a guy, I guess. Women are more mature. They wouldn't have done this.

'But I never thought I would stay long. I was going to stay three months, teach the guys how to do it and go off to Japan.'

Sébastien's first plan of action was to find out what the local children themselves wanted. He knew that he needed to start by listening, as a company might do market research, feeling the pulse of its audience through surveys. But unlike Paris, his target audience here were wearing rags and living on the street. The other difference was that he was a westerner. So that he wouldn't impose his own views from outside the culture, he hired a local man to work with him. Then they met with the group of 17 boys.

'We met them on the street with the Khmer guy. "What do you want?" I say. They say, "We want education. We want a place to stay."'

Education. So be it. Using his savings, he did what they asked, while his future life in Japan continued to wait. Fulfilling the boys' request, he and his now small staff opened a dorm – a place to stay – and a school for their education. He hired a teacher, and the boys began to attend school immediately.

Almost as immediately, they began to leave and go back to the streets. 'Of the boys that were there, 16 of them left and just one stayed.' That was within one month.

Sébastien's face betrays the shock he felt then. Here he was working hard to give these children an opportunity, giving them what they had asked for. But once they got it, they didn't seem to want it at all, let alone appreciate it. 'That's when you have to decide that maybe everything you're doing is wrong,' he says now. First, he had the normal reaction of being angry, then disappointed. 'I'm giving everything to them, I thought; they should be happy and stay.'

He thought again, and decided to listen again as well. 'Therefore assume that you're wrong. And try other things.'

So he began to study children other than this first group of boys. He took younger children in. Asking and listening over and over to how these children wanted to be taught, he worked with the teacher to create a programme that was more fun. The idea was to make school a place where they would want to stay, somewhere more enjoyable than the streets.

This time, the marketer achieved instant success with his target audience. 'Within a month, we suddenly had 50 kids. Literally, it went from one to 50. So that showed me I was in the right direction again, with education for younger children. That younger children liked school.'

But Sébastien still wanted to know what the original boys, the teens, wanted, these more hardened ones who had supposedly wanted education. 'For that older first group, I went back to them and said, "If you don't really want school, what do you want?"'

Asked and listened to again, they clarified what they meant by education. 'They said they wanted jobs. They wanted money. They wanted to learn, yes, but only within another context.

'That's when we started vocational training. But I said, "You need to learn also because you cannot be stupid and not know how to read and write. Because otherwise you won't keep a job."'

So that they could get and keep a job, one of Sébastien's innovations was to take vocational training to a new level. The children would actually work in the jobs for which they were learning skills. One example was creating the restaurant. The staff work in every capacity, from being a waiter to washing dishes to learning to be a chef. Over time, they discover what they're best at.

Another idea was a beauty salon, where girls could learn to do manicures, pedicures or hair-cutting, easily transferable and desired skills in the city. 'In Cambodia, there's a big business for weddings. Or you go to the market and you have your tools and baskets and go from stall to stall to the women selling. And the former students can make reasonable money. That's why we still try to keep them as long as possible. We try to get them to stay longer, so they will have more skills and more skills and more skills. The longer they stay, the higher their salaries get. And the girls often start their own businesses.'

By having the programme train the young people in real work, the children not only have skills but also experience to offer employers afterwards. But unlike Sébastien, who came to his first job with a pedigree from a respected higher institution, these were troubled street youth. They would bolt at the earliest sign of difficulties in their first jobs. So, taking on board the lack of support he had felt at L'Oréal, Sébastien took the opportunity to rectify every practice he had experienced and detested himself. He fashioned his programme to coach and encourage the street children.

'The thing is vocational training looks great, but it's only a little piece of what a child needs, a really small piece. You need affection. You need shelter. You need sports; you need general education. Vocational training is great as part of that, but you need all of the rest.

'One of the differences between Friends and other organisations was that we were forced by history to build this huge service that is really holistic. Whenever we looked around, trying to find someone or something to refer to in Cambodia, it did not exist. We had to build it ourselves. It's difficult to build, and not every organisation has that chance, but now we have nearly everything here. Like us, other services may have the restaurant, but they don't have the rest around it. It just doesn't work as well for the really hard-core kids where you can really go from drugs, or everything really, to normal life.'

One of the most important things, he points out, is for the children to have a sense of a future. Just like the country rebuilding itself from the ashes of history, the young people need to have an idea of how to rebuild their destiny. 'What you really need is something St Exupéry, the French writer, said: "If you want to have people build boats, don't give them just the tools and the wood and tell them about how to build a boat. Tell them about the beauty of the neverending sea and the infinity of the seas." So it's really giving them a vision about their own lives. That's what's important. Once they have that, they will train and they will move on. They have to dream personal dreams of a future.'

Sébastien agrees wholeheartedly with Siri's comments about her own first wish for shoes. 'Small dreams like the shoes are essential. Street kids do not have much, but what they have, you have to pull it out and make them think it's possible. That's true for any child, but street kids especially.'

His own dream is to keep growing Friends internationally, as people get weary of hearing about the crisis of street children. That is another reason he started the businesses. 'There is donor fatigue. That's why you have to be autonomous. That's why you have to have businesses.

'Then you become not a charity but a business, a social business. We are in between, because we have donors, but really that's the philosophy of the base we're trying to build up. That through this kind of business mind, we are able to make change. If you are a charity in the sense that you ask for money from donors, and then you give out money, you maintain a logic where you go beg from someone, then expect people to beg of you. It's a begging system. It's not healthy.'

Of the original 17 children that Sébastien first worked with, all came back, stayed and finished the programme. As have thousands of other children in the 14 years since. Now the Cambodian government has asked Friends to branch out further into the country, and the Thai and Laotian governments are asking them to model their programme in their countries. Sébastien has begun another programme, called Childsafe, which extends to Europe as well. The idea is to get businesses and communities to take responsibility for the safety of their children.

Sébastien has received the Order of Australia, and a major award and grant for social entrepreneurship from the Skoll Foundation in the US. So from his first 'getting it wrong', after listening again and again, Sébastien feels he is now getting something right. And as he meets individuals from other countries, ranging from Thailand to Kenya, he discovers their findings are the same as his: that by learning to listen to what the children really want, worldwide, one realises that they all seem to desire the same thing: a future. And with the right encouragement, they'll get it.

The rebel who put his ear to the ground

Idris Azraq

We rebels were more romantic, and we were not practical. Because we were away from the suffering of the people, and we were looking for something idealistic. Before, we thought that, as intellectuals, we knew what was happening.

Though Sébastien Marot claims he got it wrong at first, I met someone who claimed to have got it even more wrong. That he hadn't really heard the desires and needs of the people for whose lives he and his colleagues were literally fighting. That man is Idris Ibrihim Azraq, chairman of the Democratic Justice and Equality Movement, one of the major rebel movements in Darfur, Sudan, where the government is committing what has been called the first genocide of the 21st century.

Sudan is the largest country in Africa. The region of Darfur lies to the west, bordering Chad and the Central African Republic. About the size of Texas, it has a population of six million people, primarily Muslim but of African ethnicity. After the ongoing civil war with the predominantly Christian and animist south was seemingly settled at the start of this century, the Islamic and Arabic government of Sudan, based in Khartoum, escalated a harsh campaign in Darfur against the Africans, supplying and encouraging Arabic tribal groups in their pursuit of 'Arabicisation'.

This led, from 2003, to a more organised rebellion on the part of the Africans. In the following five years, approximately 2.5 million people were uprooted, according to the UN. The international consensus is that at least 200,000 people were killed during this period. In an expected contradiction, the Sudanese government claims it is only 9000.

Although Idris Azraq is the leader of one of the Darfur rebel groups, he lives a hand-to-mouth existence in the Netherlands, fully aware of what the consequences would be if the government in Khartoum knew his exact whereabouts. He dresses as elegantly as his budget allows, in a jacket, slacks and white shirt. Like him, his clothes have seen better days. He has a disarming and toothy smile, but his looks are not movie-star material. What he does have is idealism, conviction and passion.

As he talks about the situation in Darfur, Idris equates negotiations between the international community and the government in Khartoum to Chamberlain's talks with Hitler. He says leaders can give people a vision either to raise themselves up or to act 'like beasts': 'Even an advanced country like Germany, under Hitler, acted like beasts.' He also reminds me that after the Holocaust the words 'Never again' were used. But, he claims, 'never again' is happening right now.

Idris Ibrihim Azraq

Idris had spent years with his cadre, living in exile, leading the fight for his people and convinced about what had to be done, when he had his own shock. When he decided to really listen to the people on the ground, his own ideas were severely challenged. But strangely enough, he says, that gave him even more courage and a stronger conviction to fight for their rights.

Though most teenagers rebel at some point, becoming a true rebel is not a normal career choice. Few high school career advisors suggest taking up the profession of rebel leader. There is no career path, no benefit entitlements, and the hours are long. The pay, according to Idris, is not good, and completely uncertain. As is the outcome of one's whole mission. But Idris was seemingly raised to fight against injustice: shaped by his father, by his high school and university days, and even by his years as a refugee.

Idris comes originally from Jabal Midob, the Mountain of the Midob, in northern Darfur. He grew up in a village near the town of Amalha, which means salt water. 'The Midob people are Nubian people,' he says with pride. 'They came to the region a thousand years ago.' He describes the landscape with affection too, as a treasured mix of mountains and plains. 'Our land is semi-desert and very big. We are nomads, and semi-sedentary. We rear all kinds of animals from cows to sheep, goats and donkeys.

'My father too kept all these animals, except camels. And he was rich according to our context. The house I grew up in is called a Midob house, built with wood and thatch. But it was big, maybe 30 square metres. It was divided into a place where you can meet people and a place of sleeping, and had two fireplaces. One fireplace for the meal or for visitors, and a fireplace for cooking. But we lived like other people.

'Here in the Netherlands, people are more individualistic. They are connected with each other, but in terms of the nuclear family. But in Darfur, in Africa, it was more extended. People lived collectively. If you did not have money, you could still eat.'

After years in the Netherlands, and now accustomed to eating herring, cheese and bread, Idris still recalls his childhood meals with affection. 'What we used to eat was asida, a porridge made with millet. That is my favourite.' People familiar with eastern or southern Africa would recognise asida as similar to ugali or pap, which are now made from cornmeal.

'Near Amalha, we had our own village, which consisted of my family and my relatives, uncles and aunts and so on. People loved each other, and everyone embraced you. When we had a holiday, they would bring you new clothes. We lived a really nice life.'

What Idris calls a nice life might be called poverty by Western standards. But, as he says, it depends on the context. The situation has also grown worse with the war, as he points out – 'the way people have to work now is almost Neolithic, and it is especially difficult for women, who spend a third of their lives searching for water.'

Growing up, Idris learned a lot about leadership from his father. 'My father worked as a sheikh, a leader. And he solved family disputes between the people.' Though his father was not educated in a Western sense, he did have the capacity to listen. His father also became involved in politics as a youth. 'When he was young, he joined the Umma Party. The Umma Party developed from a religious group, a Sufi movement, and fought fiercely in the 19th century against Egyptian and Turkish domination of Sudan, as well as the English.' Idris laughs. 'But the English were more clever, and domesticated their leaders.'

Before marrying Idris's mother, his father went to the capital on behalf of the party. When he returned, he became influential in the community. Though he was Muslim, he was also proudly African, and had very strong ideas about how to keep his culture's traditions alive in Islam.

'For example, we had these rain rituals done by women. Which were pure African. Those who believed in the Koran thought that it was very bad. But my father began to do these rituals – *with* the Koran. He may not have been learned, but I learned many things from him.'

Idris began his formal education by attending both a normal primary school and a traditional Koranic school, which he went to in the afternoons. However, he realised that what he was learning was actually memorisation, rather than how to study. On top of that, 'You had no time to play,' he says with a laugh, and there were beatings. So his father agreed to send him to boarding school.

Unlike many in Darfur, especially those with the status of a leader, his father was monogamous during the period he was married to Idris's mother. But life changed for Idris after his mother died during the birth of his younger sister, who would also later die in childbirth. His father took on more wives. At the time of his mother's death Idris had five siblings, but over time, as his father took three new wives, this number reached over twenty. Though most of them went to some form of school, it was Idris who continued to receive the best education. The younger ones would not get the same opportunities as the Islamic government in Khartoum began, as he says, 'to prevent people from regions like Darfur to go on to further education'.

Intermediate school gave Idris his first taste of different cultures, a yen for diversity he has kept throughout his life. 'I went to intermediate school in a place called Maliet. It was an astonishing time for me, because for the first time I discovered other groups. One of them African, the Berti, and one Arab, Zyadin. They were different from us, in their traditions and their way of life. For example, the Berti were agriculturalists. And the Arabic tribe, Zyadin, were pure nomadic.

'Those were the happiest days of my life. I found new people and new friends. Because they were different, we learned from them. And they discovered many things from us.'

For his secondary schooling, Idris returned closer to home. And now, having encountered other cultures and their views, he began for the first time to become involved in politics, rallying people against the government. 'Ever since I was in secondary school at the end of the 1970s, I believed in political activity. I would give speeches that we must do so and so. And we students had clashes with the government of Nimeiri, when he applied sharia law. In our community too, some people began to exploit those laws to become harsher.'

Colonel Gaafar Nimeiri had seized power in May 1969, espousing socialism for the country rather than Islam. He concluded peace agreements with the rebels from southern Sudan in 1972 and instituted free education. However, after oil was discovered in the south, in 1979, Nimeiri pushed an Islamic agenda, making Arabic the official language of the south rather than English. The war against the south began again, resulting in over a million deaths. The Islamic agenda also began to be pushed in Darfur, with the African community.

'At that time, my father was with me. He too was against the law of Nimeiri. He said, "This is not sharia. Because they beat women." There were also people who were poor and drank. Because of that, they were punished. We knew that is not the true Islam.'

Following his father's lead, Idris took matters into his own hands. In a way, he began his career of rebellion here. 'When I was in secondary school, the leader of our region collected about 400 sheep from the people to give to the vice-president on his visit. When he came, the leader said to the vice-president, "We are going to give you 400 sheep as a gift." And the vice-president said, "Good. But I will leave these 400 sheep, so that you can build schools."

'But after that, the sheep vanished. Nobody knew where. And people began to talk secretly.

'I was young and enthusiastic in those days. So I spoke in public, in a mosque after Friday prayers.' Idris raises his voice, as if he were addressing the congregation of that mosque today. 'I said, "Where are these sheep? They are deceiving people, and this is corruption! And we must so and so ..."' He laughs, remembering the high school boy preaching justice.

'The leader of the region became furious. They brought the police and took me to prison. But only for a day, as my uncles got me out because they had influence. But that gave me publicity.'

His father stood with him. 'He said publicly, "What my son said is right."

'People divided into two groups. The majority were with me, and a very few who were benefiting from the situation sided with that leader. I brought the issue to the court. And the court began to make an investigation. But the elders came and said to me, "Settle this. People are going to be divided, and it will make a problem." So I said, "If it makes a problem, then I will let it go."'

After leaving school, Idris went to the University of Khartoum to get a degree in education, with a focus on English. But as he had studied French in secondary school, he was forced to study that instead. 'Yet since I graduated in 1985, I have never worked with French or spoken it.'

He retained his enthusiasm for politics, exploring different groups to match his own growing ideals. 'I tried social justice and the Marxists. Then I joined the Muslim Brotherhood, because my father was a Muslim. When we were in university, they were always saying we should have a multi-party democracy. That it would be like the University of Khartoum, where you could hear all voices, and what they want.

'And I was happy at university, because there we found not only social diversity but also political diversity. Yes, at the time of Nimeiri, there was only one party group. But inside the university, Nimeiri couldn't control us. So there were different political ideas and different organisations. And people could discuss things freely.'

After graduating, Idris returned to Darfur and began life as a teacher of history – and, ironically, English – in a secondary school. He left the Muslim Brotherhood, feeling it had become fanatical, especially after the coup of 1989. 'They imposed martial law, and they brought people to prisons. And they imposed two agendas, an Islamic agenda and also an Arabic agenda. I am Muslim, but I was not convinced by that version of Islam. Secondly, I am not Arabic, and I wouldn't adopt Arabic nationalism.

'So others and myself from Darfur began to oppose the government of Sudan.'

In the meantime, the government's war against the south continued, and the population there was devastated. Idris paid no heed to the fact that the southern Sudanese were primarily Christians or animists. At his school, he urged his Muslim students to understand the plight of their African brethren, even if they were of a different faith. 'Some of my students wanted to go there and fight for the government. "You must not go there," I said. "What is going on in southern Sudan is not a jihad. For the government to go there and kill people is a crime. That is their land. And even if they are not Muslim, they are human beings. You cannot go and kill people to force them to adopt any kind of belief."'

Increasingly outraged by the killings in the south and what he began to see in his own Darfur, he began to rebel more actively against the government. It was no longer enough to make speeches at the local mosque, hoping his uncles would get him out of trouble, or to consult the elders in hope of appeasement. This time, he intended to take up arms.

'There was a man called Daoud A'Habolla. He was an Islamist, but he also had the idea that we should oppose the government of Sudan. The government had begun to organise Arabic tribes in Darfur in order to Arabise all our people too. And he took up arms.

'I had secret contacts with him. He was supposed to arrive in Darfur. When Daoud was to come to Jabal Midob, I was waiting. I was going to join him and his forces.'

But before he reached Idris's district, Arabic tribes in southern Darfur caught wind of Daoud's arrival and notified the government. Daoud was captured and promptly executed by the government. The armed attempt at rebellion had failed. And Idris was named by an informant and taken in by the police.

'The government brought me to a prison. They asked me, "Do you have a relationship with Daoud?" I denied that I had any relation to him. And they insisted, "Write that you are not going to practise any political activity."

'So I wrote that I would not. I lied.'

Idris was released, but knowing he was still in danger, he got some money together and managed to reach the port of Sudan. He had been told about a boat going overseas, though all he knew about it was that it was going to Europe. The rumour was that it was going to England.

This was appealing, because of his knowledge of English, and he had heard that opposition leaders had begun to organise there. He thought perhaps he could join them.

He found the boat, and embarked. However, the boat – and Idris – landed in Rotterdam, in the Netherlands. His only choice was to ask for asylum there. And, he acknowledges, he was fortunate to get it. But now he had to learn yet another language: Dutch.

While waiting for his status to be clarified, the son of the sheikh survived by doing whatever odd jobs he could, such as picking tomatoes. Later, after he had been granted official status as a bona fide refugee, he was accepted into a master's programme of arts and culture. This was a joint programme between the Netherlands, the UK and Spain. Idris studied cultural anthropology.

Though he looked for political movements to join, he found none that shared his idealism. So he began what one might call 'normal life'. He finished his master's. He got an apartment and his Dutch passport. He started his own import-export company and was doing rather well. Until again he started to hear reports of what the government in Khartoum was doing.

'In 2001, when information became available, I realised how people of African origin now had to be either assimilated into Arabic culture or become second-class citizens. They were being killed systematically, as the government was arming some groups. In collaboration with Arab tribes they began to burn villages in western Darfur. They burned about seven hundred villages, but luckily not of my tribe. My tribe was made of fierce fighters, so nobody could take their rights.

'But I am not a tribalist. For me, we are all human beings, and in one country. All our people must live together, either Arabic or African.

'We had to do something.'

As Idris started to explore what he could do, he began to find a few like-minded Sudanese who also believed that something had to be done. Most importantly, he met another man, Khalil Ibrahim, who seemed to have similar ideals. Idris's gut reaction was to be suspicious of Khalil, as he had worked as a state minister of education in Darfur. However, Khalil claimed to have had problems with the government, and thus had had to flee to the Netherlands. These were desperate times, and rather than listening to their initial intuition, Idris and the others decided to trust him. 'After a while, we included him, because he had fresh ideas. And we formed the Sudan Justice and Equality Movement – JEM.'

Idris maintained his business for the next two years, and a semblance of normal life. However, all that changed in 2003 when the civil war exploded. 'My import-export business was going good. But in 2003, when the government destroyed even more villages and millions of people were forced to move outside and so on, I had to dedicate all my life to this cause. Because what was the meaning if I have money? It was nothing for me if my people are suffering.

'I could try to become a brilliant academic or successful businessman or so and so, but I felt it would achieve nothing. But if I could be a successful politician and put together a good framework in Sudan, I felt I could put everything on the right track. And so I began to live hand to mouth.'

Khalil Ibrahim was voted chairman of the movement, and Idris its spokesperson. They put out information which they claimed proved that since independence the government had been controlled by northern peoples. Meanwhile the insurrection movement gathered an alleged 15,000 armed fighters on the ground. Other rebel groups formed to fight the government, some achieving more notoriety at the time, but then they splintered into ever more factions.

As we talk and drink fresh mint tea in a café in Amsterdam, Idris acknowledges that the rebels did fight violence with violence. 'Violence became the nature of the governing state of Sudan. They never accepted dialogue. They killed about two and a half million people in southern Sudan. And now in Darfur, how many have died?

'In natural law, if you find a small ant, and you try to crush it, it will try to defend itself. It is an instinct to defend yourself. So we were not using violence for violence, but to protect our people. We would kill government soldiers who came to attack us, and we even gave orders to our people not to attack cities or outside Darfur. We won't take innocent people. But if we find those who are perpetrators, we will do it.'

Idris is proud of the fact that the rebel movements were getting the message of what was happening in Darfur out into the world, in contrast to what had happened in southern Sudan, 'where over one million people were killed by the government. Yet then, the international public was not enamoured of the issue.

'We were able to attract the attention of the global community. Everybody now knows about it. More people died in southern Sudan than in Darfur, but we were successful either by media or demonstrations, and concentrating our efforts, to tell people that there was something bad going on there. There were many bad things going on in the Congo too, but we were able to uncover the ugly face of our government.'

But divisions began to occur within JEM too. Though Khalil and Idris were both opposed to the government, they differed in their ideologies. 'When we started, we said we could each work from our tribe, but we must work for the whole Sudan and for the national purpose. That we must adopt something far from religious influence, a secular democracy. But after a while, we found that Khalil Ibrahim still had connections with a religious movement. From his Zargawa tribe, he began to tribalise our movement.'

Idris claimed Khalil had installed relatives in key positions within the movement, creating an imbalance of power. Within the movement, it was obvious that it was time for a change. Some in the movement followed Khalil, who kept up the fight, and moved back to Sudan and Chad.

But in January 2007 a group of those opposed to Khalil met in Addis Ababa, Ethiopia, and selected Idris as their chairperson. He says it was because of his ideals. 'My strength is not my tribe, the Midob. My tribe in comparison to other tribes is small, only about 100,000 people. My strength was my national agenda. In the movement, they elected me because I was against Arabisation and wanted a secular state, and also a united Sudan but a federation. That our history and our destiny was one.'

Although he continued to lead his movement he had ever more limited success. Getting the ear of governments as a rebel leader, unless one has won a military advantage, is not easy. Idris realised that the movement was not moving forward in the way it needed to, regardless of his commitment and idealism, and the atrocities that continued to be perpetrated. He knew he was getting nowhere trying to negotiate his idea of a united secular Sudan, even with secular

Western governments. He felt the voices of non-profit organisations from outside the region were listened to more than those who actually represented the people, such as his group.

Yet the question that began to plague him even more was this: did he indeed represent the people, or his own group's point of view? Why wasn't there a groundswell to make a federated Sudan, for instance? He needed to try to figure out what was going wrong.

In 2007 he returned to Darfur secretly. 'To some extent, we had been more romantic, and not practical. We were away from the suffering of the people, and looking for something idealistic. We as intellectuals thought we knew what was happening.

'So we organised people from the village levels all the way to the province level. We met with our people on the ground. And they said to us, "You want to solve the problem of Sudan and to restructure all the country. But this is a very long struggle. And we cannot wait for that. If all the regions were uprising at the same time, then it would be a good idea. But if other regions are not paying attention and we are the only ones paying the price, why don't you ask for something like what happened in southern Sudan? Self-determination. Then after we become established, we can look to other regions."

'We made a survey among everyone: refugees, students, Darfurians who were married or unmarried, even those in the Darfurian forces. They all said that the best way is for Darfurians to have their own state. That we must not enter any negotiation with the government of Sudan unless the issue of self-determination is included.'

Idris and a colleague then took a month in England to study what the people had been saying. After all the years of pursuing their own ideology they now decided, based on what they heard from the people, to change the goal of the entire movement – to press for an independent Darfur.

'Now, for me,' Idris says, 'a leader's role is to dedicate his time to study the options for the people. And let the people choose what options are better. Because they also have their minds and their experiences, so they can choose.

'Many leaders think a leader is somebody who can think better or has more vision than other people. But if you as a leader think that you can choose what must be, that is when a dictatorship can begin.

And that is the problem of so-called revolutionary leaders. They think that they have a kind of eternal wisdom.' He laughs. 'But nobody can monopolise wisdom, eh? So for me the only way is the participation of the people.'

Idris studied what the southern movement had done to keep its identity, inspired by the example of the famed leader John Garang. Even though the people of the south were mainly Christians and animists, and Darfur was Muslim, Idris saw a model that could work to achieve what his people wanted.

Towards the end of 2007, the movement he admired so much invited him to southern Sudan. They offered him safe harbour from the Sudanese government, and arranged meetings with other Darfurian rebels as well, so that Idris could voice what he had heard from the people. 'We gave our proposal for unification to the other rebel movements. Because most rebel groups are tribal, the only condition was they must believe in accommodating the diversity of all the social groups.

'Theoretically, all agreed. But in practice, they didn't agree. And further, we were losing time. So I left some of my group there to negotiate with them. But I came back here. Because on the ground, we are in need of help. And the international community are not enthusiastic about efforts to separate the region or make it independent. Even though we have seen what happened in Kosovo, where they were supportive,' he says ruefully. 'But in Africa, they want to maintain colonial borders.'

Meanwhile, the split in JEM has had serious consequences. In 2008, Khalil's faction fought alongside the president of neighbouring Chad against that country's rebels. The government of Chad had supported JEM in the past, but Idris would not commit his people to fight against the Chad rebels, who were also indigenous – this would violate his and the movement's principles.

Then Khalil's troops, feeling confident after some of their military successes, tried to invade Khartoum. They got all the way to the suburbs of the city but were eventually defeated by government troops, and many of the rebels were captured and later executed. Sadly for Khalil, because he kept his movement tribal, many of these people were his relatives.

Militarily, Idris's group is trying to keep its diversity alive. They are trying to bring in at least 50 fighters from each tribe within Darfur. And with 80 tribes in the region, that adds up to a decent number of fighters. Though Idris admires the purely non-violent methods advocated by Gandhi, he points out that his own people are not only fighting for their rights, but are facing genocide. 'Without a military side,' he says, 'our political ideas would be just romantic poetry.'

Idris remains committed to the cause of his people, even at the cost of the 'good life'. 'If I was born in the Netherlands and all people were living up to some kind of standard of life, I could enjoy this kind of life. But I came here as a refugee.

'I live in the Netherlands. But psychologically, I'm still in Darfur. My mentality, my memories and emotions are still there. Even if you give me a palace and money and say, just don't do anything in Darfur, I would not enjoy that life. Because I am not only myself; I am nurtured. I cannot eat and enjoy if parts of my family are still hungry. It is better for me to share rather than to take alone. For me, life has no meaning, unless I give also some kind of meaning to other people.'

Though the zeal of his mission is still in his eyes, Idris is more at peace these days. He still wants to help his people, but in the way they want to be helped. He knows change depends not only on the West listening, but on his own people helping themselves. 'We must not depend on help that comes from outside. Until now, all of us only cry to the international community for help. Yet our groups have not even produced one unified proposal to how we can solve the problem.

'Our people must take the initiative themselves. We must strive to protect ourselves, not only hope for international groups to come and help. Some have a good intention. But sometimes they perpetuate this conflict resolution, and it becomes a factory, an industry.

'The development of water wells or producing our food, we must take initiative to do all these things. Not only wait for the non-government organisations to bring food from outside. Because that is also the problem of the NGOs. They don't always give help to emancipate you. But it makes you more dependent. They bring food, and you stay in a camp.

'But if they would give us machines to produce things or bicycles to use for transportation, it would be like the Chinese proverb: instead of giving fish, teach one to fish.'

Whether the NGOs are doing the harm he suggests is open to question, but Idris says he will continue his work, no matter what. 'In Sudan, our people are living a way of life now that goes back to the Stone Age. They draw water from wells, still using donkeys. We have seen the world, how humanity has progressed. My own sister died in childbirth. We have to work to change the life of our people.'

Having been educated, and seen and heard other ways of life, that is what he wants people in his home to know: that there are other ways of being, which can only come through listening and exposing oneself to other cultures and ideas.

He admits that all help, over time, makes a difference, whether it is work like his or school children in other countries who take the time to learn about a place like Darfur and send small donations and letters to the children there. Those children will remember that someone from outside cared, and eventually become curious about them as well.

'Education lets you compare your life with another life. This is the only technique with which you can liberate yourself,' says the rebel, after years of armed struggle. 'You cannot discover yourself and know where you are unless you compare yourself with others. If I had not come here in Europe, I would not have discovered that we were backward, not only in material things but also in many cultural aspects.

'But everybody can learn from one another. From the very primitive, the most advanced can learn. The Europeans may be advanced technologically and with governance and so on. But the West can learn how people like ours can be connected with each other. That even when they have very little, they can share. You find meaning in your relations with other people and connectedness with other people.'

Will the people of Darfur get an independent state? Only time will tell. But at the very least, one of their leaders is listening to the desires of the people he is trying to help, as well as his own heart. And as we part after one of many meetings we have now had over years, Idris leaves me with words that sound optimistic and, knowing him, are fervently believed: 'We embrace diversity. And from the heart of darkness, we can light a candle and let people come. If you are a real revolutionary, the welfare of people is your goal.'

Chapter 5

Use what you know

Whatever you can do, or dream you can, begin it.
Boldness has genius, power, and magic in it.

Johann Wolfgang von Goethe

Idris Azraq says that once the community is heard, everyone has something they can offer, whether they are within that community or outside it, whether they are a child raising funds at their school in London or a doctor in Médecins Sans Frontières. What we offer may not be billions of dollars, as someone like Bill Gates or Warren Buffett may offer. It may be the skills of a nurse or a truck driver, an event planner, a football fan or a journalist, a Buddhist monk turned teacher or a Catholic priest who provides comfort to the dying through simple companionship. Each uses what they know, with a creative twist. And each touches numerous lives, while gaining more fulfilment from this work than anything else they can imagine.

From nursing and trucking to activism

Naomi Mayers and Sol Bellear

Like Idris's people in Darfur, many Aboriginal people in Australia have

Naomi Mayers

been asking for self-determination for a long time, and at the very least to control their own lives and services. Naomi Mayers and Sol Bellear, both in their sixties now, both with sparklingly intelligent eyes, are today the major forces behind the Aboriginal Medical Service (AMS), the first indigenous community-controlled medical centre in Australia.

Naomi, a nurse, and Sol, who was formerly an interstate truck driver, both grew up with discrimination in Australia. They knew first-hand that things had to change for their population. So they took the skills they knew – for Naomi, practical medicine, and for Sol union organisation – and used them to learn to fight for their community's rights. They have become two of the most effective activists and advocates in their community. AMS has received recognition internationally, including from the World Health Organization, Naomi has been awarded the Order of Australia, and Sol has served with numerous organisations including the Aboriginal and Torres Strait Islander Commission.

Naomi's family was originally based on Cummeragunja Aboriginal Station in New South Wales, on the north side of the Murray River bordering Victoria. She was born in 1941, only two years after the Cummeragunja Walk-Off, the first mass Aboriginal strike in Australia. The walk-off was in protest against the harsh conditions the residents were forced to live under at the station, under the firm control of the New South Wales government's Aborigines Protection Board. The residents crossed the border into Victoria. Though it was illegal and they faced serious consequences, others in the community provided support and provisions. The rebellion was widely covered in the media, and the protestors' actions led to changes in the law.

Her people's fighting spirit lives on in Naomi who, though regarding herself as one of the 'lucky ones', has had her own tough times. Her early years were spent happily, she recalls, with her whole family, but later her parents separated. Naomi and her sister spent many years away from them, first in an orphanage in Bendigo and then in Melbourne.

However, she knew even then that many children her age had been taken away from their families altogether. 'The government in the thirties and before thought that Aboriginal people would die out. That's why they took kids away – the stolen generation. They took kids that had a bit of white blood in them, gave the Aboriginal people the dole and thought they'd go away. "Smooth the dying pillow", they called it.' This was a policy based on social Darwinism and the early mainstream 'science' of eugenics, a theory bent on improving the hereditary qualities of a race or breed. Similar theories about the inferiority of racial groups were also used in the first part of the 20th century by the US government to keep the African-American population subservient, and by the Nazis to justify extermination of the Jews. Thankfully, eugenics was widely discredited after the Second World War.

However, its theories were also used in Australia and its impact on the life of the indigenous population was severe and traumatic. Even prominent white advocates for Aboriginals, such as anthropologists, claimed the Aboriginals were not equal to whites. The idea that the full-blooded Aboriginal population would just die out was used as justification to keep them on mission stations, use them as servants, and treat them as second-class citizens in general. In contrast, Naomi decided to devote her life to ensuring Aboriginals stayed very much alive. She started as a nurse at the age of 18, going first to the Home

Hill Hospital up in Queensland, then to a Jewish hospital in Sydney, and then back to Melbourne.

Sol Bellear grew up in a family that stayed together, which he credits with giving him and his siblings the strength to persevere. His mother was clear that each of her nine children should get a good education. Affirming her dream is Sol's brother Bob Bellear who, having served in the navy and become the first Aboriginal petty officer, later became the first indigenous judge in the country.

Still, Sol also faced the realities of racism growing up in the late 1950s and 1960s. 'It's the same all over the world in depressed communities, the hopelessness, the frustration. It was more than one teacher that told me that, when you look around the world, blacks are only good sportsmen or singers. I couldn't sing, so I had to play sport.' He laughs at the memory. 'But that's the sort of thing that's put in your head. And you do start believing it.

'I was always told at school that for Aboriginal people, there's just no jobs. And in '65, there weren't. Your average school had what they call a career advisor. In your last couple of years of school, they'd look at your marks and advise you as to what you could be and what you should be. They said I was going to be no more than a technician working for Telstra [the telecommunications company]. But I was interested in current affairs. I was always interested in politics.'

Eventually, being told what he couldn't do inspired him *to do*. Sol found his own activist inspiration outside Australia. In the late sixties and seventies, he turned to African-Americans in the US. It was only a few years earlier, in 1964, that the Civil Rights Act had been passed, giving African-Americans full rights as citizens.

'I had started out going to University, at Sydney Uni, but six months into that, I had an opportunity to go to the Congress for African Peoples in Atlanta, Georgia in 1970. There, I met civil rights leaders from the US as well as leaders from Africa. Every black nation on earth was invited there,' he says. 'You didn't have to be of African descent.

'I got involved in all the politics and met a lot of people. At that stage, Australia was unknown to them. People said, "Gee, we've got black brothers and sisters in Australia?"' The African-American community took an interest in Sol, wanting to learn about his background and struggle, and in turn he was fascinated by their

Sol Bellear

work. His original six-week tour of the US was nowhere near enough time. 'I had gone over for six weeks, but I ended up staying 18 months. But I saw what was going on over there. And we used it here in an Aboriginal context.'

Sol's visa expired well before he came home, and he says the Australians were out looking for him, as well as US officials. An underground network hid him while he got to meet leaders such as Angela Davis and Jesse Jackson, as well as Elijah Muhammed who founded the Black Muslim movement. He also studied the ideas of the slain civil rights leaders Malcolm X and Martin Luther King.

Back in Australia, Sol got work as an interstate truck driver. Through driving, he got involved in the unions. 'We were the younger ones coming through and started taking over. The older leadership, the Aboriginal leadership here, wasn't that strong, but it was very conservative, very church-controlled.

'But younger people just got sick and tired. Cops were bashing us, and land rights demonstrations and all that started because of our support with the union movement, particularly the builders, labourers, wharfies and that. You'd start off with about ten or twenty blacks that were in the marches. But then that grew. And the next year there'd be more and more.'

Sol lived in Sydney's Redfern area, along with other young Aboriginal leaders who were coming up. Even after 1967, when the law changed their rights on paper, the indigenous person's life here was that of a second-class citizen. 'There was only one pub here that allowed Aboriginal people to drink until probably 1971, the Empress Hotel. And the cops used to come there. That's where they'd train up their detectives and riot squads. They'd come in, lock the doors and just bash the hell out of blacks. Then they'd throw them in the vans and cart them off.'

This was where Sol and his crew first became more active. As they could not get adequate legal representation in court, and certainly nothing initiated or funded by the government, they decided to found their own organisation, the Aboriginal Legal Service (ALS). They brought sympathetic law students, magistrates and barristers to the pub to sit down and have a beer – to see what was going on for themselves. This might be one time when anyone would have to agree that alcohol consumption led to the well-being of the community!

'At closing, in those days 10 o'clock at night, the people we'd brought down could not believe what the cops were doing. And out of that grew the ALS, where these solicitors would volunteer their time to appear in court. Because of that, the whole police system changed. Before, if I was arrested and brought before a court, there were no arguments. "Bang, you're getting two months." But when we started even pleading not guilty to being drunk, cops had to start being a lot smarter. Because the blacks were getting legal representation.'

Naomi's expertise came in handy in the next institution the Aboriginal community decided to set up. In a situation similar to their legal difficulties, there was a desperate need for medical services. 'The hospital here, Rachel Forster, just up the road, wouldn't see blacks. They could be dying on your doorstep but if there were whites sick, they wouldn't see you,' Sol says.

An Aboriginal activist named Shirley Smith, along with Sol and other members of the community, and the now famous white doctor named Fred Hollows, decided to set up the Aboriginal Medical Service. The concept was that the community would control its own services, meaning the people would be better served, as they could trust their own people. The organisation was the first of its kind in Australia.

'The legal service was set up first, in 1970,' Naomi recalls. 'And the medical service was in 1971. I was in Melbourne then. But they said, come up and help us, 'cause I'd done nursing down there. So when I come back up here to Sydney in October 1971, I was on the board and then I went for the co-ordinator's position. That's when I started working at the AMS, in 1972.'

Young medical doctors, including Paul Torzillo, who works with architect Paul Pholeros, volunteered their time. Locals created an improvised ambulance service. 'The community would go pick up patients in their cars,' Naomi remembers. 'The doctors used to work after hours when they closed their practice or jobs. They used to start at about 3.30 and work until ten o'clock at night.'

Even though the AMS was providing a government-mandated service, there was no government funding for the first 12 months. That pattern continued even when the community set up similar services nationwide for other Aboriginals. 'The second one that we helped set up with donations was in Broome, Western Australia. Then the German organisation, Bread for the World, picked it up. Until the Australian government were so embarrassed that an overseas agency was paying for the service, that the government had to fund it. A lot of things happened like that, where they were forced to fund them.' There are now approximately 130 such services throughout Australia, including the site where Yami Lester was the community leader.

The concept of the local community controlling its own resources is critical, Sol claims. 'The state government unsuccessfully tried to mirror this when we started to get a lot of patients turning up. But their thing was community-*based*, not community-controlled. It was still a state government instrument.' Considering the treatment of indigenous people over the last two hundred years, trust in the government is not high in the community.

Trust would become an especially important issue in dealing with such taboo subjects as HIV/AIDS, primarily a sexually transmitted disease. While the government and many in the media have portrayed the Aboriginal community as unable to take care of itself, Sol points out, 'When HIV first started breaking out in Australia, we were the first to see that we had to put some preventative things in or we were going to be wiped out completely.'

In fact, the AMS was lauded by the World Health Organization for its work on HIV/AIDS prevention in the eighties. As Naomi and Sol say, because locals led the initiative, the community responded. Sometimes the leading was gentle and, as Naomi points out, it sometimes had to be done in a no-nonsense fashion, something a nurse used to dealing with stubborn patients would know about. 'When we put up notices about condoms in the waiting room, a couple times the staff took them down,' she says. 'The older ones didn't understand and were ashamed. So eventually I had to say, "If you take these notices down about using condoms and AIDS, I'll sack you."' She bursts into a loud laugh.

'At the time, condoms were not accepted either in the non-Aboriginal community or the Aboriginal community. So essentially Aboriginal women decided this was what had to happen. Within 12 months, condoms were being used in the Aboriginal community.'

The AMS staff put together an educational video, which won international recognition, but they also realised, as many international organisations did later in Africa and Asia, that to fight HIV young women needed more self-esteem. They needed to be able to protect themselves if young men refused to be responsible. 'So we started having self-esteem classes for young people,' Sol says. 'Teaching the posture, the way you walk and this, that and the other, even teaching young girls to put make-up on. And the outcome was we got invited to take ten or twelve models to Paris, France. Aboriginal people designed all the clothes. All the models were Aboriginal. All the music was Aboriginal. Paris didn't know what the hell hit them. And they loved it.'

'That's the sort of thing that came out of the local community,' Naomi points out. 'All those models, now they've all got good jobs and self-esteem. And the others see it and say, "That's our lot who went from Redfern to Paris." Let us run our own show the way we want to, and there is an outcome. Force something on us, and there's no outcome.'

Because he has reached his sixties, Sol is sadly a rarity, just by being an older Aboriginal man. 'We've got the youngest group of any population in Australia,' he says, shaking his head. 'You get to 45 and 50 and we die off.'

But still, Sol and Naomi's notion is to use their skills, together with the wider Australian community, to find a way forward and create a population with longevity. Though medical skills are important, as they have seen, the health of the community also involves the repair of self-esteem. As Sol and Naomi see it, this is where the general population in Australia, and in other nations dealing with marginalised peoples, can contribute, even with such simple things as an apology or recognition of past errors.

'We need the country to admit about the massacres of Aboriginals and the stolen generations and all that. It's not about who's responsible and litigation. But by admitting that, this is the beginning of the healing for the community's emotional scars.'

On 13 February 2008, the Prime Minister of Australia, Kevin Rudd, did apologise to the Aboriginal population on behalf of the government and the Australian people, in a ceremony in Parliament. Many people in Redfern and from the AMS watched the ceremony live on-screen. In his speech, the Prime Minister said, 'To the mothers and the fathers, the brothers and the sisters, for the breaking up of families and communities, we say sorry.

'And for the indignity and degradation thus inflicted on a proud people and a proud culture, we say sorry ... We today take this first step by acknowledging the past and laying claim to a future that embraces all Australians.'

'It's the first step towards healing the emotional grief of the Aboriginal people that were victims of that callous action,' Sol says. 'One thing all communities know how to do is apologise; it's something we're taught as children.'

And it was one of those things, Sol and Naomi note, that didn't cost a cent. It was a case of the Prime Minister, and his party, using their own skills to add to the process that people like Naomi and Sol have been working on for years. As Sol says, it was a start. 'One simple word is the beginning of that healing.'

Beluga for the homeless

Ronni Kahn

Ronni Kahn, an energetic woman in her mid-fifties, paces her office as she argues on her mobile with a client. She's wearing a smart red dress to match her auburn hair, definitive earrings, and – importantly – stylish high-heeled shoes. The office – a studio space on the ground floor of a two-storey terrace house in Sydney – is crammed with tables of flowers, coat racks strewn with dress costumes and feather boas, and various party items.'What I do is put on special events,' she says. She's an event planner, from corporate parties to weddings and everything in between.

She's arguing about a fundraising affair in support of a Jewish organisation's project to help people suffering from drug addiction or depression. 'When they came to me,' she says later, 'they'd already chosen the theme. Now what do you think a religious group would choose as a theme? Rio! Bums and sex! But I have to bring them a Brazilian model wearing the huge regalia, with no g-string and in a full dress. And the dress I've got is at least off the shoulder. But,' she says laughing, 'they tell me – shoulders no good!'

Ronni, though, is not too worried about losing this battle. She's someone who has survived change after change in her life. And now, besides arguing for such things as an off-the-shoulder dress, she primarily fights on behalf of the poor through her foundation Oz Harvest, getting them delicious gourmet food from the elegantly catered plates of the wealthy.

Ronni grew up in a suburb of Johannesburg. When she was six, her father, an architect, had a major car accident that led to two years of recovery in hospital. By the time he came home his practice was out of business. 'After that, he never really made it financially, so my mother always worked. By the standards of my peers, we were pretty poor. Birthday presents were knickers and socks, while my girlfriends were getting ponies. Still, we were certainly privileged, because I was white growing up in white South Africa. And they were wonderful positive parents.'

Ronni Kahn

A big influence in Ronni's childhood were the family's next-door neighbours, Selma and Jules Browde. Although both were known as anti-apartheid activists, it was Selma whose work on behalf of the black population in the townships of Soweto would change the course of Ronni's life, 35 years later.

'To describe how close the relationship was between our families, they tore down the fence between our houses so we could use their pool. And when Selma went to medical school my mother fed her three kids, who would come to us every day.' In a sense, Ronni's first experience of catering to others came with her mother's returning Selma's kindness.

The family's other friends were also anti-apartheid activists, including Arthur Goldreich and his sister. Goldreich had hidden Nelson Mandela and 18 other African National Congress members at his home in Rivonia, where they were famously and sadly arrested. Arthur escaped and later made it to Israel.

But Ronni's parents were nervous about getting involved in anti-apartheid activities. They focused instead on instilling alternative Jewish values into Ronni, rather than those of the Afrikaans government. 'I belonged to a Jewish youth movement from the age of ten. In South Africa, it was one way of exploring ideas that were not open to you at school, such as democracy and socialism. These were things that were fantastic to explore when the rest of white South Africa wasn't talking about such things like the equality of human beings.'

After graduating from secondary school, Ronni couldn't continue to live according to the status quo. 'Staying in South Africa felt very difficult if you weren't going to be involved. And to live a life that you weren't exploiting people all the time, it seemed a better option to leave. My parents, who weren't Zionists, still felt the importance of the state of Israel. So early on, I knew if I didn't stay in South Africa, Israel would be the place to go.'

Her parents couldn't afford the fees for Ronni to attend university in Israel, but fortunately she qualified for a scholarship. She moved there in February 1970, three years after the Six-Day War. Still, the country felt like a haven after South Africa.

At university, Ronni met the man who would soon become her husband. After graduating in English and art, she made another big move: she followed her husband and his friends, who were committed socialists, to live on a kibbutz. (The term originates from the Hebrew word for 'gathering'.) The kibbutz they moved to was called Yizreel; it was a collective farm where no one held private property. 'It was literally a commune of 300 families, based on early communist principles.' Here, she and her husband had their first child, a boy.

While there, Ronni and her husband were sent to Australia for two years, as emissaries for the same Jewish youth movement she had been involved with as a young girl. In the intervening years, her brother-in-law had married an Australian and her sister-in-law had moved there as well. Ronni's second son was born in Australia during those two years. Still, she felt she belonged in Israel. And when the time was up, the family moved back to the kibbutz.

But over the next few years, Ronni realised that this way of life did not live up to her expectations. 'Initially the idea was that living on a kibbutz would fulfil some ideals: that people are equal and should be treated equally, each according to his ability and each according to his needs. But it was disillusioning,' she says. 'When the kibbutz movement started, women were equal. For example, when women had babies, they first put them into children's houses so they didn't interfere in their lives. But then women became firstly carers of children, while men had greater options. I thought that wasn't fair.

'Also, other people in the committees were making decisions about my life. I had to abide by decisions that I often didn't agree with. Some things I could live with, and some things I couldn't, all of which made me decide that I had to do something that *I* could control.'

So Ronni and her husband started life all over again. They had little money in hand, as it was up to the kibbutz to determine how much money was apportioned to those who left – in her family's case, after they had lived and worked there for ten years, the sum the committee came up with was a mere US$4000.

Despite her dissatisfaction with life on the kibbutz, Ronni still wanted to give the dream country of her youth a chance. The family moved to Haifa, where her sister had a florist shop, and Ronni began to work there. Occasionally, customers wanted flowers for parties, and that was how Ronni began to learn her special-events craft. In addition to supplying fragrant bouquets, she began to organise the catering for various affairs, mainly weddings to begin with, but eventually working up to orchestral concerts.

After eight years, she decided yet again that it was time for a change: to leave Israel, in order to keep her sons from having to serve in the army later. 'I had brought up two Israelis. The cut-off date for the army for leaving Israel was age 14. If we stayed until after they were 14, if they ever set foot back in Israel, they were liable for the army. And they could still be called up from another country.

'I had lived through a couple of wars in Israel, the '73 war, then the Lebanon war. And I hadn't seen that as a solution to anything. And there was disillusionment that there would ever be peace with our neighbours, including the Palestinians. So the question was: did I believe enough in Israel to give my children up for this belief?'

Her answer was no. But she would not move back to South Africa, which was still under apartheid at that time. Another of her sisters lived in the US, but she and her husband were familiar with Australia, and that was where they chose to start life over.

'We came here with nothing, no job, and a 13-year-old and a nine-year-old. So we put our heads down and butts up to make a life that was worth living. And I determined that the only thing that I wasn't going to do was the event business!'

Ronni laughs – because that was exactly what she did, setting up her own company. 'It took about ten years for me to establish my business. And my husband did his MBA part-time, as he also worked. We struggled through to reach a point where financially things were just starting to turn a corner. We had just finished building a house. To all intents and purposes, we had "made it", having been together almost 30 years.'

It was then that Ronni decided she needed another change, this time in her relationship. She had witnessed her parents scrimp and save for an ideal retired life, with her mother dying shortly afterwards. 'My parents' story showed me that there was no such thing as preparing and waiting for when you have your dream life. That it had to be right now. I realised that I was in a marriage that was good but wasn't good enough. And I felt that my life was too short to make compromises.

'It was a brave, foolhardy move, but I left.'

On her own, Ronni continued her event-planning business. Shifting course, she began a relationship with a man whose focus, she claims, was only on living the high life. For a while that suited her – fine dining and travel on a whim. But she couldn't help but see that her current life and her adopted country had their own sets of problems. 'I realised in many ways it was similar to South Africa – not without the black and white problem, but without it being in everyone's awareness.'

She also began to notice at her events just how much quality food was being thrown away at evening's end. So she looked for an agency where she could donate it once in a while. 'I either was lucky or unlucky to have found a place to take food – the Matthew Talbot Hostel for Men. I'd driven late at night down where the house was, and you just had to do that once to see the poverty here. It is one street behind the Porsche dealers, the Ferrari dealers, the Maserati dealers. But there were probably between 300 and 500 men who ate there.'

What she saw left her troubled. Her life of glitz and glam at the parties, her friends by the beach and her new relationship were at odds with the desperate poverty she glimpsed at the hostel and a few other shelters to which she began to donate the leftover food.

It was around this time that she took a trip. 'I was going to a wedding in Israel. And I had the choice of flying via Europe or South Africa. South Africa was more expensive, but the family of Jules and Selma Browde was very special to me. I hadn't seen them since I'd been out of the country for 35 years. What made me know I had to go that route, I don't know. But I knew I was looking for something.'

She spent her time in South Africa solely with the Browdes. One morning Selma, now in her late seventies, said, 'Come with me to Soweto.'

'We stopped first to visit a black woman there who ran a little kiosk. I had not been back to South Africa since before Mandela came out of prison. So my image of South Africa was completely the apartheid South Africa. Just seeing these two people interact was pretty mind-blowing.

'As we're driving, I said how the place had improved. And Selma turned around and mentioned how she had helped bring electricity into Soweto. Then I went with her to her new project, clinics educating women in each neighbourhood about AIDS, so they could do grass-roots education. Here was somebody about to be 80 who had affected so many lives and was still an extraordinary example of what one could do. And I thought, "I wake up every morning and run to Bondi Beach and then go to work. And what else do I do?"

'That was my epiphany. Just two days in South Africa totally galvanised me, knowing I would come back to Australia and my life would never be the same. That's when I decided to look at my skills and see what I could do. What am I good at? What do I know?'

She returned to Australia. There were two major problems as far as she could see. One was the discrimination against the indigenous population. 'But when I looked at my skills, I asked, could I really help them, and in what way?'

But she realised she had a skill and an asset she could use for the other problem. 'What's common to every single event I do is food. Corporate clients, individuals, social, all different kinds of clients. It could be a product launch, a gala dinner, a bar mitzvah, a wedding, or a 21st or 50th birthday. The common thing was that food unites people, and people get together around food. And while there was food left over at every single one of my events, I knew that there were people who were hungry.'

As she thought about how to get her food from events to people in need, she decided to stay with her sister in Los Angeles, to give herself some time to focus. In preparation for her trip, skimming through a US events industry manual, she came across a company called 'Angel Harvest'. It was a food rescue programme that connected with event companies like hers, but in America.

She immediately called, but only got an answering machine. So she phoned her sister and asked her to find out who had set up the agency, telling her she didn't care where they were in America, she would go and find them.

When her sister met her at the airport, she told Ronni she was in luck. She had got through to the founder, Helen ver Duin Palit, and she lived in Los Angeles! Ronni called Helen and said she was going to set up a food rescue programme in Australia, and needed her expert advice. Helen agreed to meet.

Ronni smiles at the memory of her next big dilemma: what to wear for the meeting! Shoes, so important to Siri's childhood dream, were a crucial component. 'I get dressed for the appointment. I put on a divine outfit. And then put on brown stilettos this high' – she gestures with her hands – 'where the sole was hot pink. My sister said, "Ronni, in the not-for-profit world, Helen will come wearing a kaftan with beads coming down to her toes."

'She arrived not in a kaftan, but she did have beads down to her knees. I said, "Can I get you some tea?" She nodded. And when I turned around to get the tea, she said, "Those shoes are awesome." And that broke the ice.'

So wearing stilettos with hot-pink soles, Ronni learned everything she could from Helen ver Duin Palit. Angel Harvest had become a nationwide US programme, bringing together event-planners and people feeding the homeless. But Ronni could be both. As an event-planner herself, she had direct access to food.

'When I came back to Australia and told people that this was what I was going to do, they must have seen the fire, and they said, "What can we do to help?" But it still took about a year and a half from the day that I decided I was going to do it before Oz Harvest could be born officially.'

She continued her research in Sydney, getting to know the agencies who were helping the needy and volunteering herself to see who really could use the food. 'If I was going to do it on a commercial basis, I had to do my homework before I could sell the concept.'

She began volunteering with a programme called Just Enough Faith, run by a former restaurateur named Jeff Gambin. His own epiphany had come while he was sitting on a bench outside his restaurant, when a homeless man offered him a blanket thinking he was cold. That was the moment that prompted him to start his feeding programme. When Gambin later literally won the lottery, he decided to devote himself to the programme full-time. 'Jeff was the first person I went to and said, "Listen, if I do this, will it be helpful?" And he said, definitively, yes. His programme fed about 300 to 500 people a night.

'The important thing is that out of his van he provides about five choices of meals a night. Because, he said, for these people this is likely to be the only choice they have in their lives. They go to the bureaucratic offices, and they can't choose what home they're going to be in, or anything else.

'I saw the guys and women and families that would come and eat there. They looked just like my family. And that made me more determined. For whatever misfortune, whatever happened in their lives, they had gone to the other side of the fence. And it could have been me. And still could.'

One of the things in Ronni's favour was that, because of her work, she did know people with money. 'I knew if I had to rely on government funding, I'd never get it up. The bureaucracy would take years. So I went to an investment bank and asked if they'd give me the money. And they took a chance and gave me $50,000.

'Three years later, we now have four refrigerated vans on the road, four full-time drivers, a full-time logistics and co-ordination manager and a part-time business strategic development person. And how we fund it is by talking to people. For example, the Paul Newman Foundation last year decided to give ten charities $100,000. And Oz Harvest was one of them. So that allowed us to buy two more vans.'

be smug and think that only other people have misfortune. It could happen to us.

'Certainly I was brought up to do unto others as you would like them to do unto you. And that was the value of my family; we have to look after other people as well as ourselves. Though it's not a religious thing, but a human value thing. My parents didn't ever say to me do it for Jews. They said do it for anybody.

'What I get out of doing this is a deep sense of fulfilment. I have achieved something bigger than just my life. And that feels amazing. That each of us in our own little lives can do something that makes a difference. My heart now feels full. So I feel a millionfold lucky, knowing I've done this and that there's still more to do.'

Today, her grown-up sons have their own band. They play music dedicated to peace, perhaps validating her decision to keep them from the army. She is happily married again, to a barrister, and maintains a close friendship with her ex-husband, also in a new relationship. But she puts her well-being down to Oz Harvest. It was her particular way of finding how she could use her skills. 'This was my way because this is what I knew. But every one of us has a way.'

Her mobile phone rings. The first call is from the casting agent of the models for the Jewish organisation's party, to see how the Rio off-the-shoulder-dress discussion is going. The following call is from a shelter, asking about the next delivery of food.

Then she leaves for a flight to Canberra. She is off to open the newest office of Oz Harvest, at the centre of government in Australia. 'We're opening there this week. With those board meetings and government parties, and all that food, there are about fifteen shelters that we're starting off delivering to in Canberra.'

As a result, someone who is homeless, jobless and broke will literally be eating the same food as the prime minister had that evening, whether it's beluga and smoked salmon or a traditional meat pie.

Inventing the game

Mel Young

South Africa, 2010. In the stadiums, hundreds of thousands of fans from around the globe cheer football stars like David Beckham. Hundreds of millions more watch the games on TV and root for their teams as they fight it out for the FIFA World Cup.

But if you'd been in South Africa in 2006 or Melbourne in 2008, you'd have also seen thousands of diehard fans in the stands yelling for teams from around the world. In the city centres, players in uniform battled for the ball. After each game, children mobbed their heroes and begged for autographs; TV crews and newspaper reporters hustled the players for interviews.

Just months earlier, some of these players would have been ignored if they'd asked for change on the streets. Because back home, these men and women had no homes.

But this event was theirs – the annual Homeless World Cup.

In the stands watching was a lean, dapper man with shaggy silver hair, a sharp nose, and eyes that don't miss a beat. This devoted football fan is Mel Young from Edinburgh. His journey, to create an event that has changed thousands of lives, was as unpredictable as any game. 'My path was sure not a traditional route to the top of the bank,' he says. 'But the culmination of all my learnings are coming together in this.'

A daunting castle towers above Edinburgh. Nearby, within the city walls, winds the Royal Mile with its ancient buildings of grey stone. Below is the 'New Town', now over 200 years old, built on what was once bog and marsh. But everywhere you go are comforting pubs where when the weather's crap, as people say, a dram of whisky or a pint can warm one's chilled bones.

Through meeting Mel, I was privileged to see some other sides of the city, including a housing estate and even the homeless within the regal city walls. On an evening after I had tried haggis over mashed turnips and carrots, a few older guys hailed me over. Instead of crossing the street as I might usually, I went over. While I petted his black dog, one man talked about having worked on an oil rig off the coast of Norway. His life sounded as nomadic as mine. One of his friends offered me some liquor. When I had to leave, they kindly insisted I come back and visit Scotland again.

During the day, a young man in a black jacket tried to sell me a magazine. Noticing his accent, I asked where he was from. Paris. Unable to get work, he had come here. Would I like to buy a copy of *The Big Issue*?

Yes. Because only hours before, I'd been speaking to its local founder.

Mel Young was born here, but his own family bounced around, from one military base to another. Although trained as an accountant, his father enlisted underage near the end of World War II, wanting to fight for his country. Afterwards he stayed in the army, preferring a soldier's life to balancing books. 'I was moved around a lot, because an army life is nomadic,' Mel says. 'The military command would say, in three months' time this whole bit of the army is moving. Then even in that place, they were doing exercises somewhere else. So the family would move to Germany, they would go to France to play with their guns, and you'd get left behind.'

Mel remembers a particular move to Berlin when he was five years old, which had all the suspense of a Cold War Le Carré tale. At the time, the city was divided into Russian, French, American and British zones, surrounded by East Germany. 'I don't know if it was my mother's anxiety that I picked up, but we were passing through the Iron Curtain. And the train was stopped. There were military guys on the platform with guns, checking the passports. They wouldn't let my father on the train, because there was some ripped corner of his identity card. And he was on the platform yelling, "Just go. Go and I'll get there somehow."'

So Mel, his brother and his mother had to proceed on their own. On the train, a soldier came to the two boys. He told them not to worry but just to sleep as they went through East Germany. 'He said, "When you wake up, you'll be in Berlin. But no matter what, don't open the blinds. If the train stops, it's because there's a problem. But it won't stop, you see? And we'll see you in Berlin in the morning."

'I woke up in the night, and the train was stopped. But the man said if it stopped, there was a big problem. I thought, I'll just have a

Mel Young

look out there. So I opened the blind. On the whole platform of a small station were these East German soldiers with their rifles pointed at the window.'

'I thought, oh no, I've started World War III, all because the guy said don't look out the window.' Mel laughs as he recalls his childish belief that his actions could change the world. It's a belief carried at heart by everyone in this book, including Mel, but in a rather more benign way.

Luckily, World War III was averted, and their father rejoined them. Mel refuses to complain about his childhood, but recognises that the mobile army life was hard on his mother. She had trained as a nurse. 'She would try to get some jobs wherever she was; it wasn't easy for her. Because you're not in control of your life.'

Still, he claims to have learned to care for other people from his mother, in spite of her difficulties. 'I learned a lot from my mother about values. I think it comes from this Scottish stuff about community: that we're all in it together. If you look at Scottish history, we created Adam Smith who created capitalism. But then we have strong links with the communists in the early days of the Soviet revolution, and a strong church background through Protestant times. These things mix. So people in Scotland who are very successful financially connect with you as ordinary people. They don't have any airs or graces. And that was very much where my mother was from. That you have to respect the other people around you.'

In a sense, Mel grew up in a movable city. The people stayed the same, it was only the landscape that changed. 'On these army bases, the whole British community would move. So we weren't really in Germany, and I can't speak German. So you'd get a whole community of people, cinemas and all that in a British zone.' Even in the schools, teachers were brought from the UK on a rotating basis. Sadly, this caused a child's education to be endlessly shifting.

What remained consistent was Mel's boyhood love of football. He followed Edinburgh's Hibernian Football Club, no matter where he was. He loved watching the game. But unlike many children who dream of being a star themselves, he invented his own club – and more – in his mind. As he says, he was an imaginative child. And entrepreneurial. 'I used to even make up my own leagues. I'd create my own football tournaments as a child.' It was a dream that would come true but in a way he couldn't then have imagined.

Unlike many on the base, Mel was exposed to people from outside the military as well. 'Families became very close naturally. I was lucky because through my father's friends who weren't in the military, I was always speaking to other people. For me, that wasn't a big deal.

'Much more of a big deal later,' he says, laughing, 'were rulings in court telling people to cut their hair. Or the Rolling Stones getting arrested.'

Mel was attending secondary school in the late sixties, and even on a military base, he says, 'I was against the military, in a real rebel phase. We were all long hair. I was 17.'

Luckily, he was off to university in Edinburgh, the first of the family to get a higher education. Enrolled at Heriot-Watt University, he chose economics. 'I didn't know what to do. But I didn't enjoy it.'

It was now 1971. Protests against the Vietnam War were going strong, and disagreements grew between generations. 'I think my parents were despairing of me. But a lot of parents were despairing of their offspring at that point. As younger people they'd been through the Second World War, and the austerity after that. What was our generation doing? Playing loud music and talking about a communist takeover.'

During his university years, his father and he stayed out of contact. Yet even as he and his friends and opposed authority and the military, Mel still saw the side of the people serving their country. 'Some friends would say the military is evil. And I would argue, the government directing it may be evil in that sense but not the people. I mean, what do you do as a country? Not have any soldiers?'

Mel threw himself not into economics but into university life. Like his father, who had left accounting to serve his country in the army, Mel searched for another way. 'I didn't realise at the time that what I am is entrepreneurial. So already now I wasn't following a career path. I learned a lot about politics. I became vice-president of the students' association. Drinking, women, talking about politics, and lots of music – Pink Floyd, the Rolling Stones, Van Morrison.

'I was also influenced by a lot of good folk music. At a bar called Sandy Bell's, there were a lot of folk musicians. They just arrived with their fiddle or guitar and sat down and started playing. And a great poet, Hamish Henderson, was always there. So on one hand was this fabulous music, and on the other hand we were talking about how we fight fascists.'

Thirty-odd years later, the night I visit the bar, sadly, there's no music. But there are plenty of chatting locals in the plain smoked-wood bar. I get a shot of Macallan's single malt for two pounds and feel like I'm back in college myself.

At the end of university, Mel decided not to graduate, one of the regrets of his life. But what he did glean was an interest in journalism, writing for the student paper. 'To begin with, I wrote about music. Apparently Richard Branson began writing this way too. Because if you'd review a record, you'd get to keep it. "Who wants the latest Led Zeppelin to review?" "I'll do that!"

'Then I started writing about politics in the paper, and then editing it. We'd sit up all night. So that's where I got the bug, not just about writing but putting it all together as well.'

After university, he freelanced as a writer for local papers, got together with mates to support the Hibernian Football Club, and still listened to music, as punk took over. But economics and journalism merged with his entrepreneurial bent. He and some friends started a magazine called *Citylinx*, a kind of *Time Out* for Edinburgh. It was a mix of entertainment, listings and politics, published cheaply out of a basement office. 'I must have been 23. We just started it, and drew just enough money to pay the rent and have a beer.

'It was ridiculous the way we used to run it, by giant committees. So we'd have an editorial meeting of an evening, and 20 people would be around deciding what was going on page two. And it didn't matter if we'd never seen you before, you'd have your say. It was fabulous.' Mel laughs, remembering the raucous meetings.

The method made for the success of *Citylinx*, but after three years its dissolution as well. 'Get this! Sales were going up. Advertising was going up. But the committee split. At the end of the meetings, one half went to one pub, and the other half to another.' He laughs again. 'So we had this in-fighting about politics, one more left than the other. We were just mirroring how rock bands can't get on. We were young, and everything really mattered. So we just stopped.'

Mel was unemployed for some months after that. But while at *Citylinx*, he had met a young woman who had moved into his shared flat, a social worker. They began dating. While he was unemployed, they married. Perhaps because she had a similar bent to Mel, she didn't blink when a friend came across a job for him with little pay, in Wester Hailes.

Even today, the housing estate of Wester Hailes feels bleak. Far on the outskirts of Edinburgh, it's built over an old quarry cum landfill. Highly incongruous high-rises look out over the promise of rolling blue-green hills. These kinds of estates were built in the UK in the sixties for the poor, similar to those in other cities in Europe or the US.

What happened in Wester Hailes was similar to what Paul Pholeros discovered in the housing that had been built for Aboriginals in Australia. 'Millions had been spent on it, but contractors had used second-rate building materials. They skimmed off the top. So the houses were not very good. There were no stores, no cinema. No bus service. Completely isolated. People had very little money. And their kids wandered around. And the government went, "Uh-oh, we've got some problems."

'So there was an initiative to create a sense of identity. Part of that was a small newspaper called the *Wester Hailes Sentinel*. They wanted somebody to edit it and help develop it.'

His friend had thought if anybody in the city should apply for the job, it was Mel. Obviously, so did the people in Wester Hailes. Unlike many who just talk about social justice at university, Mel began to live it. 'I don't have to tell you all the typical things on an estate: youth, mass unemployment, heroin, and AIDS starting to kick in. There was a family where you had five kids all dying of AIDS.'

At the time, Edinburgh had a reputation as the AIDS capital of Europe, with the affected population primarily injecting drug-users. And Wester Hailes was particularly hard hit.

Co-ordinating all the projects on the estate, and a man who would be influential in Mel's life, was a community worker named Laurence Demarco. His view was that local people should have control. 'At the time that was quite radical, because the power came much more from government. So he used to have this fight with the authorities.' Many years later, Mel and Laurence together set up a social entrepreneurs' network called Senscot, which is still in operation today.

As the eighties progressed, so did the *Wester Hailes Sentinel*. It carried local news items, sports news, even recipes. Over time, Mel began to grasp his real mission: to help the community gain control of the newspaper itself. 'Whenever I go into things, I never think I know anything. But I've learned to listen to what the people there are saying. There were fabulous people there who led that community and changed things. I went in knowing how to put this paper together. But it was their paper. I wanted to leave, so that I was handing over to an editor coming behind me who was local. Which I was able to do.'

While at Wester Hailes, he became friends with a social worker named Tricia Hughes. She was in charge of creating youth and single-parenting groups. After five years Mel left the paper, but the two still talked about the seemingly intractable and growing problem in Edinburgh and Glasgow: the homeless.

Mel's entrepreneurial instinct kicked back in. He wanted not just to talk, but also to do something. 'We're always very good at talking; we're quite good, Scots, at moaning. We sit in a bar and say, "The weather's dreadful." "Yeah." "The football team is dreadful." "Yeah."

'So Tricia and I said, let's do something positive instead of just talking.'

On a trip to London, Mel saw homeless people selling *The Big Issue*, a recently launched magazine that took a new approach: to give the homeless a job. 'What I liked about that, *The Big Issue* was giving a hand up not a hand-out. The idea was more about creating the framework, so that they could help themselves, to rebuild their community if you like.' So Mel, with his knowledge of publishing, and Tricia, with a background in social work, wrote to Gordon Roddick, the founder of *The Big Issue*. His wife was Anita Roddick, owner of The Body Shop. He suggested they meet John Bird, the editor of the magazine.

'John was a different kettle of fish. He'd been homeless. In his youth, he'd been in trouble with the law. But he had experience with publishing and was passionate.'

Mel suggested to John Bird that he publish *The Big Issue* in Scotland, but the organisation had no extra time or resources. Instead, Bird suggested Mel just sell the London magazine there. What Mel knew though, from his Wester Hailes experience and *Citylinx*, was that the magazine had to be local, or 'Scottished'. So John suggested Mel and Tricia start their own organisation, and their own *Big Issue*. They would be free to use the London magazine's national interviews, but could do their own local stories and listings as well.

So Mel and Tricia decided to do just that. They forged ahead in Edinburgh and Glasgow. They began by scouring the streets, meeting with homeless people to see if they'd be interested in selling the magazine. 'It was a big gamble for us. Homeless people think very short-term. It's all about surviving today to get to tomorrow. And we said, "We're bringing this magazine out. Would you be interested in selling it?" And they'd say, "Yeah. When is that?" We'd say, "In about three weeks' time." "Three weeks?" they'd say. "Don't know where I'll be in three weeks."'

So when Tricia and Mel started publication, they didn't have one committed seller. They'd invested their own money, got some friends to invest as well, and 'supporting subscribers', people investing £100 a year into their organisation. As he says, they were diving in the dark.

What happened defied even their dreams. 'The first issue we printed 25,000, and we sold them out completely. The people just came and started selling. It went around this fast.' Mel snaps his fingers quickly. 'You want to get a message around the city? Tell a homeless person. They'd speak to other people and say, "I sold this magazine and I have ten pounds." And the others would go, "Oh, can you do that?"'

The next issue they printed 30,000. The next, 40,000. 'Within six months, by Christmas time, we sold 140,000 copies across Scotland out of a population of five million. By this point, the printer was saying, "My machines are going to blow a fuse!"'

The success was due partly to the homeless people selling the magazine, but also the population of Edinburgh and Glasgow. 'People went, "Yep, that's us." They bought three or four copies of the same magazine. It was almost a badge of "We're supporting our boys out there," like a war front. It was a great community feel. It was not about saying how many people are homeless. It was about this is a person called John or Fred or Ian, and they're big or small and old or young and male or female and good or bad, but they're just people. They're not statistics.'

How much each vendor made depended on their efforts. The magazine cost 50p and the vendor received 20p. 'Some sold very few copies and some lots, particularly if there was a loan shark chasing them or something like that. Everybody got just above the minimum wage if you wanted an average. And some could use it to move on.

'The money and job were important. But it was about self-respect and self-esteem. Before, people had just ignored the homeless and walked past. But now they were with the people on the street. By just saying hello and how's the weather and all that, it made them feel part of society.'

Mel also made sure the magazine was good. People asked him why he was paying professional journalists to write for a non-profit paper, and he'd reply that they wanted to produce good copy, to get more sales. 'It wasn't a pity purchase. It was about that person telling you that this is a good magazine. And that was about the seller's self-respect and self-esteem.' To prove his point, the magazine and the journalists won numerous Scottish Press awards.

Like Sébastien Marot and the Friends restaurant in Cambodia,

Mel's business model was not to make a profit but to be self-sufficient. 'We were running a social enterprise. You get income, you grow it, and you make it effective. If you make a profit, you put it back into the development. We got salaries. But we weren't making money out of it.'

The Big Issue also transcended political divides. 'At this point, I was getting cynical about party politics. But *The Big Issue* got cross-party support. The left-wing parties supported it, because we were doing something about the poor people. The right wing supported it, because it was about self-help, not about hand-outs or government.

'We came along not as a political intervention, but something that was fresh and new. Of course, the more we got into it, the more challenging it got. Because we got to know the homeless people and their issues. And getting them out of their situation was not simple.

'Some had many problems but were trying to find ways to work through them. And a lot of times it was bureaucratic crap they were going through, stuff that was invented in this society.

'And you had terrible days when someone died. I mean, health is an issue. A lot of them are taking drugs, so you have overdoses. You have mental health issues. They get depressed, and commit suicide.'

According to a study by the organisation Crisis, the average life expectancy of homeless people in the UK is 42 years. The national average is 79 years, a difference of 37 years! In Montreal, Canada, another study showed that the risk of homeless men dying was 12 times that of the general population, and for women in Toronto, ten times higher.

'We had one week where three died, one after the other. So you have some bad days. But other days you have some very uplifting times.'

One such day came out of the biggest challenge Mel had yet faced. Six months in, *The Edinburgh Evening News* claimed to follow one of their vendors – to his home. The headline blared that *Big Issue*'s homeless sellers were not homeless at all. 'For us at the time, this was dreadful. And the sellers go, "This is the end of the world."'

The story put the whole enterprise at risk. Normally, Mel and Tricia asked sellers standard questions to determine if they were indeed homeless, and anyone who'd been on the streets even a few days would know of them. In this case, the seller had only just got himself a place to live, but was an alcoholic and barely surviving. 'He was distraught, because he felt so bad about causing damage to the project. But we said, "Of course you can sell the magazine and be with us."'

Mel finally decided, as in his days at *Citylinx* and the *Wester Hailes Sentinel*, that the only way forward was as a community, even if it was a homeless one.

He called a meeting. 'All the sellers came. And you should have seen a meeting like this. Everybody just talked all the time. So many people were smoking, you couldn't see. Nobody had any sense of time. So people were coming in late. And,' he remembers, laughing now, 'there was someone playing a flute!

'So I stood on a chair. I said, "Right! Three things are going to happen, when you sell the newspaper tomorrow. One, you'll get people who'll be aggressive towards you. Secondly, you'll get the opposite. Somebody'll say, oh you're just wonderful, and can I buy two magazines? Thirdly, most people are going to ask, what was that? And it's up to you to tell them the truth. We can make this work."'

As Mel spoke, the people began listening intently. Finally he looked down. 'I remember this guy in the front row. His eyes were bulging. And he went, "Yeah. YEAH!"'

The meeting finished, Mel spent a restless night. Next morning, at the office, there were more sellers than ever. 'There was a queue all the way upstairs. All of them had come to sell the magazine. They were going to get abuse, but they were not scared of it. And exactly what I said happened. Some assholes spat at them. But the sellers said to most people, "Well, it was just one guy."

'And it was the best sale-day ever.' He smiles, still delighted. 'It wasn't a boring job! We had rollercoaster times.'

As *The Big Issue* in London and Scotland became successful, other street papers began around the world. Mel helped many of these start-ups, for example in Russia and Eastern Europe. As the movement grew quickly, just one year after establishing *The Big Issue* in Scotland he co-founded the International Network of Street Papers.

Today, there are 88 street papers in about 37 countries. Back then the International Network had few resources, but still the heads of the papers managed to meet once a year, meetings that Mel describes as 'absolutely electric'.

At one meeting in Cape Town in 2001, Mel and Harald Schmied, who headed a paper in Graz, Austria, were talking into the night. This was also the year Mel was selected by the US-based Schwab Foundation as one of the world's leading social entrepreneurs. 'We were very tired, and we're drinking beer. And we were saying, "This is a great conference, but there are no homeless people here." And we thought, maybe we could do a conference with them, but then there are problems of languages.

'Then we thought, "Ah, but there is an international language called football."'

Harald was a former semi-pro, and Mel an enthusiastic fan – and a creator of leagues in his childhood imagination. 'I just loved watching the sport, the whole community around it, going to the pub before, then the game, the banter. It was being part of something. So I said, "Some of our sellers in Scotland have a semblance of a football team." And Harald said he had the same in Austria. I said,"Tell you what. We'll be Scotland, and you'll be Austria."'

Both men claimed, because their teams always lost, they had to win. 'So then we had more beer. As you do. And by the end of the night, we'd invented the Homeless World Cup, and wanted every country to join in!'

Many late-night beery talks are just that: talks. When the alcohol evaporates, so does the idea. But when Harald and Mel met the next morning, they determined to carry through with the concept.

Harald worked on organising Graz, while Mel sorted the international arrangements. Street papers in various countries organised people to play football. Then a team was selected to come and represent their country.

Street soccer is a fast game, and the players had to be fit. There would be a maximum of four players per team on the court, three outfield players and one goalkeeper, plus four substitutes. There would be two halves of seven minutes. Pitches would go up in the city centre, and admission would be free.

A year and a half later, in July 2003, teams from 18 countries showed up in Graz for the first Homeless World Cup. Just as he had had no idea if there would be any *Big Issue* sellers, Mel couldn't know whether any spectators would show up. Or whether it was worth raising money to bring homeless people from around the world instead of building houses, for example.

From the first game, all doubts were set aside. 'It was an amazing week. We had three incredible outcomes. One, the homeless players were changing in front of your eyes, standing upright. They were playing football, for their countries. They were singing the national anthems better than the professionals. They were a team. They were proud to be representing their country, when to date they'd had no recognition at all, ever.

'The second thing was the audience. We didn't know how many people would come, five or whatever. But thousands turned up to watch. The stands were full all the time. And people were screaming for the teams. Children were going up, and the players were signing autographs, like international football stars. Normally these people in the stands would cross the road before talking to a homeless person. Now they were applauding them.

'The third change was in the media. By the end, there were banks of television cameras from all over the world, including countries that weren't participating. And 100 per cent positive stories, when normally the media portrays a negative image of homeless people.'

The only discouraging thing for Mel was that Harald Schmied had been right: Austria won. This time.

Even more surprising to Mel than the success of the event were the results of the follow-up research. Eighty per cent of the players had got jobs and found homes. Many had got off drugs and continued to play football, or to coach. 'I'd worked with homeless people since 1993. And you just don't get figures like that. So we checked the figures, and they were the same again.'

The figures were happening worldwide. 'If you are homeless, you live on your own. You're selfish in a sense, because you have to survive – today. But on a team, you have to pass the ball. You have to think where you are when they pass the ball to you. So you become part of something. 'And you meet other people from another country who are maybe worse off than you. Then you start to think, maybe I can get out of this.' Though it had been conceived as a one-off event, now it was agreed, 'Okay, let's do it again.'

With help from all over, Mel's childhood imaginings of his own football league were transformed into an annual event. And with the Cup taking so much of his time, Mel Young and Tricia Hughes gave ownership of the Scottish *Big Issue* to John Bird, leaving a strong management team in place.

In 2004 the World Cup was held in Gothenburg, Sweden, with 26 countries attending. In 2005, the Cup was held in Edinburgh. In 2006, they returned to Cape Town where Mel and Harald had invented the game, and where more African countries could attend. In Copenhagen in 2007, there were teams from 48 countries. In Melbourne in 2008, 56 countries.

Following each event, the players continued to change their view of themselves as the fans saw them in a new light. 'The people are the same. The day before they were lying on the street. Then we put them in a football strip, gave them a ball and built some stands, and you're applauding. But they are the same person.'

Reflecting on his own youth, when he moved from base to base with the same population, Mel says, 'All we have done is changed the landscape. We stopped looking at people who are homeless as problems, but as people that could make a positive contribution. Instead of excluding them from society, they were involved.'

Many of the formerly homeless people not only changed their own lives, but they were also recruiting other players and coaching them, on the field and off.

Today Mel's staff work out of small offices in the area of Port Leigh, Edinburgh, at the top of three rickety flights of stairs. The Cup itself is held only one week out of 52 in the year. The other 51 weeks Mel keeps an eye on projects on the ground in about 70 countries, which as far as he is concerned have as great or a greater chance of enabling people to transform their lives. For example, at a national championships in Nairobi, 3000 homeless players gathered, with audiences of 500,000 over the five weekends of the tournament. During the year, the players get certificates, become captains and start their own street leagues.

'The critical thing for us is that this works. It's about impact. Changing the people who are playing is the main thing; the second part of it is changing the attitudes, and now we get governments saying, what are you doing?

'We're simply building a movement through football. We're using football as a method to create change.'

Though not as well-known perhaps as David Beckham, Mel Young is having a worldwide impact, with the support of FIFA and corporate sponsors.

'It depends on which figures you believe, but one says there are 100 million people homeless. Incomprehensible figures. So you could get paralysed. But I believe you do what you can. And you try to be replicable all over the world. That's what we do.'

Like others tackling the big problems, Mel stays emboldened because he doesn't work on statistics but stays focused on the human story.

'We just work with the people who are right in front of us. Then the more impact you make and the bigger it grows, you start to create change. Our aim now is by 2012 to have a million homeless people involved. We'll get there because of the Asia and Africa numbers getting involved. But if there's a hundred million homeless and we've affected a million, well, that's one per cent. So it's all tiny tiny little steps.

'It's like sharing a dream. Everybody who's seen the World Cup gets it. Some of these players just go off, running street leagues all over the place, in Afghanistan, in Zimbabwe, everywhere.

'Harald and I were right. It is an international language. You can play in every country. And it's very inexpensive. Ball, kick it. Anywhere. You can involve everybody. So it's a beautiful way of tackling some of the issues.'

Mel believes his wish to eradicate homelessness is similar to that of most people he meets. 'I do lots of talks and always ask: "Who thinks poverty's a good idea? Who thinks homelessness is a good idea?" In all the years, not one person has said yes. I've spoken to some of the richest people in the world. Nobody wants it. So why have we got it then? We create problems in the "have world" because of this. So let's just end it. Then we'll all feel much better and live in a better world. It's kind of obvious.'

In terms of using what one knows, it's as if Mel squeezed every bit of knowledge from his experiences, so even those economics classes came in handy. 'I've been on a platform with an entrepreneur and a social entrepreneur. And the DNA is very similar. But the only difference is that entrepreneurs are driven by money, and sometimes power.

'But for me, what I get, for example, is when recently, I got on a bus. And the driver looked at me. And he said, "I was on the football team. Remember, a couple years ago? Now I'm driving the bus." He said, "I'm married. And I'm not homeless anymore."

'And I just felt, that's what I get out of it. And music to my ears, at the last event, Higgin, this homeless guy, said to me, "After this, I'm not homeless. Because I am changed." He's now a taxi driver. But he plays football as well in his spare time.

'It makes me feel really good. That I've contributed something worthwhile. It is about the people, and it's not about statistics. I've given you my 80 per cent figures, which are true, but what's powerful to me is the human story. That's what gets me going.'

Mel's mother died young, and his father had retired from the military to care for her. So she only got to see Mel at Wester Hailes. But his father became a big advocate of *The Big Issue*, insisting all his friends buy the magazine. Meanwhile, Mel stayed married, raising three children who are now in their twenties. As he quips, his generation left home as soon as they could: 'Nowadays, they won't leave the bloody house!'

Over the years, the *Wester Hailes Sentinel* changed its name to the *West Edinburgh Times*. In the library, a kind and concerned librarian with silver hair showed me the last published copy. I mentioned Mel Young, and she smiled. He'd done a lot for the community, she said. But in the past two months the Edinburgh council had decided not to fund community newspapers. Instead, it wanted to promote its own magazine, publicising its own activities.

Mel is resigned about this, saying that maybe everything has its time. But what could be seen as misplaced priorities on the part of councils or governments doesn't change his fundamental faith in people.

'I believe in human beings. I think you're dealt some cards or a path takes you down to some space that's not so good. We've created a world where some people who are rich now are unhappy. I've been in conferences with them talking about it. Then there are some people living in poverty that are happy but challenged because they have nothing to develop with. It's crazy. I inherently believe in human beings. It's just a question of how you change the system to get people together.'

Proving Mel right finally, Scotland won in Copenhagen, which as he points out would never happen in the FIFA World Cup. And years after he didn't graduate, Queen Margaret's University gave him an honorary degree. And his childhood dream of having his own league is an enduring reality.

It doesn't matter what you know – the skill can be anything

The range of skills one can apply to make a difference is almost endless, and it doesn't matter how big or small, complex or simple, they seem.

Brendan Touhey, a young American, was another who used sport to good effect. While playing professional basketball in Belfast, he was moved by the political conflict between the Catholics and the Protestants that was still playing itself out among the Irish kids. The enmity was obvious. What hadn't been obvious until then was that they could do something together without killing each other. Basketball being his skill, Brendan got the children to work out their tensions on the court.

It was in South Africa that I came across his programme Playing for Peace, which had branched out internationally. In Durban, one could now see people of all races in this apartheid- and AIDS-ravaged nation playing together and finding a bit of peace, while learning life skills from their tutors.

Music was the skill used by the noted Argentinian/Israeli conductor Daniel Barenboim and the late Palestinian/American scholar Edward Said. Together, they created an Arab-Israeli orchestra that first assembled in Germany, and has since performed around the world.

In New York City, at the Project Renewal programme, master chefs teach homeless people and former drug addicts to be chefs themselves. In professionally outfitted kitchens in the shelter's basement, a teacher hands fresh sage to the students. They smell the herb. And after years of McDonald's fare, or injecting drugs, it is as if the rich fragrance of the herb itself gives them a high.

One former student is a young African-American named Duane. When I met him, he was assistant pastry chef at One If By Land/Two If By Sea, a prestigious restaurant in New York's West Village. He made a chocolate confection that was exhilarating. Originally from the state of Georgia, he had ended up on the streets of New York, and finally at Project Renewal. Now desserts have become his calling.

One could see the delight in his eyes as he made, smelled and spoke about confections, and the quality of chocolate or meringue. His was a life transformed, by people who were sharing their passion for what they knew and loved: cooking. And now Duane also teaches at Project Renewal on some of his days off; as he says, 'I'm passing on what I can now.'

To eat sweets, of course, it is helpful to have teeth. Just as Sandra Meihubers has trained up dentists in Nepal, so Paul Kotala decided to use dentistry his way. He sold a successful practice to train dentists in Laos, one of the least developed countries in Southeast Asia, which had suffered under years of communist rule and isolation. But rather than feeling he is doing some grand deed, what touches Paul is that his concern for the people in the rural areas is matched by their concern for him. Though he was excellent at fixing their betel-nut-stained teeth, and training up staff, they grew worried about the state of his finances – specifically, whether he could even afford clothes.

To do his work, Paul had outfitted himself with special lightweight grey shirts with pockets that could carry all his dental utensils. Each shirt cost about AU$125. But each was also the exact same design as the others, and the same uniform grey.

'The Laotians said, "Dr Paul is very generous, but he's only got one shirt."' He laughs. "So they decided to raise money to buy me another shirt. Until finally I showed them the other shirts – that they were all the same colour.'

Paul learned his lesson. 'When I travel to new rural villages and stay a few days, I have three different colours.' But, appropriately for a dentist, people still bring him gifts of things that they and he can eat.

In neighbouring Cambodia, there is a young man who decided to use what skills he had learned too, though his education was meant to prepare him for a life of religious devotion. For him, however, meditation alone was not enough, if the people of his community, especially the children, were in need. He chose instead to follow in his persecuted father's footsteps, and teach.

Out of the ashes – a father's son

Brak Sareth

Under the incongruously named banner of Democratik Kampuchea, the Khmer Rouge seized power in 1975. One of their most infamous actions was to take an ordinary high school in Phnom Penh and turn it into a prison. They divided classrooms into cells, where they extracted what information they could from those they tortured. That included members of the intelligentsia, doctors, Buddhist monks and teachers. Strangely, the head of the operation, which was known as Security Office 21, was himself a former mathematics teacher. Even Pol Pot, the head of the Khmer Rouge, had taught history and geography at a private school at one time.

Now this building houses the Tuol Sleng genocide museum. Besides some of the torture cells, there is a gallery of thousands of bleak black and white photographs taken by the prison guards. The victims' faces look out at their tormentors, and now at visitors to the museum. Some of the condemned people seem to be smiling. My guide, a woman with eyes beyond sad, looks at me calmly and says the guards tickled the prisoners to get these ghoulish grins on camera, even as they knew they were going to certain death.

Many of these people were executed just because of their intelligence. They were accused of being against Pol Pot's Year Zero Policy, meant to wipe Khmer culture and history from the face of the earth.

Years later, in defiance of that annihilation, in the small village of Samdech Oy, a young man named Brak Sareth became a Buddhist monk, a testament to keeping Khmer culture alive. Small and wiry, he is now only 30 years old. Wrapped in his orange robes on a crowded street, his frame seems so frail he might float away in the wind. But his keen eyes and smile counter that impression with obvious strength. Brak is determined to follow in his father's footsteps and impart to others the gift he was given: education.

In April 1975, the Khmer Rouge invaded the city of Phnom Penh, toppling the US-supported government of General Lon Nol. The army forced the city's two million residents into the rural areas, including the village of Samdech Oy, 49 kilometres and some hours' march away. Anyone of learning, anywhere in the country was a target. In that village of Samdech Oy, Brak's father was a marked man. A former translator for the French, he was also a teacher who could speak English.

Though Brak was not yet born, his family's story is firmly imprinted in his memory. 'The regime took my family to prison together. Then they called someone to check about my father's profession. But my older brother and sister kept telling them that my father is not a real teacher, only an informal teacher.'

The troops, many of whom would themselves still have been at school elsewhere, separated the family. The mother was put into one camp, where she would help to grow rice for the community, and her children were put into another. 'My father, they brought to prison because they wanted to kill him. Then afterward, they arrested my mother too. They put irons on her hands and legs.' But after three months, she was released. The Khmer Rouge needed people to grow rice.

Brak's father managed to escape the fate dealt to so many of the educated people, and he lived on the run for the next few years. When the Vietnamese defeated and chased out the Khmer Rouge in 1979, the family was finally reunited, unlike millions of others. They were lucky: of Brak's seven older siblings, only one sister had died.

Brak was born in this poor area, in Kampong Seu province. Today it is a one-hour drive to Phnom Penh, because there is now a road. But at the time he was growing up, it was still several hours' drive to the city.

Unlike many of the traumatised adults in the community, Brak's father was determined his son would have an education. Even if there were no schools left. 'We learned under a tree. When it rained, we

Brak Sareth with some of the children he teaches.

would go into the temple.' But many of the generation older than him, including some of his own siblings, remained uneducated.

Brak was later sent on to secondary school, even though his parents were having a difficult time financially. 'School was not free. At that time, the government of Cambodia asked for 40,000 riel per year [the equivalent of about US$10 today, a lot for a rice farmer]. But my parents paid.

'My secondary school was 25 kilometres from my village. Because it was so far away, few students went to high school. If you rode a bicycle, you could arrive there in 30 minutes. But I had no bicycle. So I walked. Every day it took me two hours to get there. Then it was two hours back, arriving at home at seven o'clock.'

It was while he was at secondary school that his desire to become a monk arose. He would listen to the quiet men at the temples, whose practice had survived the Khmer Rouge's fierce attempt to cut their religion from the heart of the nation. As someone who loved studying, Brak was impressed by their life. 'A monk could not go outside to play football or go dancing. They had to stay in the temple to read books and to make their character. But my parents always told me, "We don't have anything to give you except for knowledge. And knowledge is the most important thing." So I asked my parents if I could be a Buddhist monk, and they agreed.'

To be a monk, though, he had to start secondary school again – under Buddhist rules. Normally, one had to redo one's primary studies as well, but luckily Brak's excellent grades made that unnecessary.

After graduating, again with high marks, he gained a scholarship to Panhasastra University in Phnom Penh. Here, he studied philosophy, 'because philosophy can get you more knowledge'. He didn't only study Buddhism, but learnt about as many religions as he could. Like Idris Azraq from Darfur, he wanted to compare other ideas to his own and to give himself as open a way of seeing the world as he could. Also, at that time Muslim and Christian missionaries were coming into Cambodia, and some were starting schools.

But Brak always intended to come back home and teach, like his father. So after university, he returned. 'I went to the countryside to become a volunteer teacher in the community, in my village. I stayed at home three years. I lived in the temple, but in the morning the students came to the temple to study. I taught the Khmer language, mathematics and English. Like my father.' Sadly, his father died soon after his return, in 2001.

Once back home, Brak started to learn other things about the difficulties his community faced, things he had never known even though he had grown up there. Now a monk rather than a student, he began to see that the needs of the children were much greater than he had realised. Even though he offered free education, some children were not able to go to school. Many parents didn't want their children to attend. They said the only thing that would lead to good jobs was having connections. And having themselves grown up uneducated under the Pol Pot regime, they had been indoctrinated to believe that learning was wrong.

As for the formal schools nearby, though they too were supposedly free, they still charged money. 'They'd always say they needed to support the teacher. One day, it was 200 riel [about 5 cents] a week. Another day, 200 riel per day. And the teachers would get the money.'

On top of these problems was the current government's own lack of care for the area, 'because the village voted for the opposing party. So the government didn't care about our area.' Brak also noticed how often the children who did come to him became sick. Just as Siri had in Buriram, he began to investigate why. 'They had no sanitation. They'd drink the water from the pond, which people used for cows, chickens and pigs. The children had bad health. Some would die at seven years old, eight years old, even four years old.'

So, at the age of 25, armed with a university degree and what he had learned about conditions in the rural areas, Brak came back to the city. He wanted to meet his university friends who were now at Wat Ounalom, the temple that is the centre of Cambodian Buddhism. Built in 1443, supposedly to house one hair of the Buddha, it is a narrow but prominent building in the Khmer style, with a red and gold roof – providing a stark contrast to the poverty in Brak's village.

'I told my friends about the children's situation in the countryside. That if we do not care about them, we won't know how will they stand in the future.'

His friends were moved, and together they decided to found the Raise and Support the Poor Organisation (RSPO). They would go to the countryside and explain to parents who wouldn't send their children to school 'that if one has no knowledge or no skill, one cannot find a good job'.

'We said, "People who have a motorbike, a bicycle, or a car, a restaurant, or a big business, they all have knowledge and education." We would say, "You should not abandon your children, just because you were not allowed to study. And my organisation will not take money from you. Remember, it is free."'

The people began to listen, and children began to attend Brak's school. Three years later, 13 people work with him – ten monks and three lay volunteers. At the moment, he and his colleagues still work out of the local temple, teaching Khmer, English and tailoring. The latter skill is especially for the girls who, unable to survive in the countryside, often migrate to the capital and get low-paying work in the factories. But as Brak points out, 'If they know how to make clothes themselves, they can find their own customers and keep their salary for themselves.'

RSPO also has an office in Phnom Penh, where they teach English, Chinese, Japanese and, Brak says softly and confidentially, computer classes. The monks teach Word, Excel and Photoshop. The money for the computers and sewing machines has come from donors from the United States and Japan. Brak's organisation also supports some orphans from the community, sending them to secondary school and covering the costs of their fees, as well as materials and uniforms.

Ever his father's son, Brak can't help but talk about the value of education. 'Education is the most important thing. If you have no education, your idea and thinking is short-term, not long-term.'

As to why a monk should be busy educating children and teaching computer skills as opposed to purely praying for people or focusing on his own enlightenment for the betterment of the world, he says, 'Some people think that the monk can only pray at the temple. But the monk has to help in the society. The monk is an example for other people, so we must take time to share our capacity, our knowledge.

'I am a human being. I must complete the rule of human beings: to help each other. If we think of only ourselves, our society cannot develop. My life is my community's. I must open my eyes to look around me, and see who is suffering, who is happy, who is healthy, who is not healthy. I must look. And I must help as long as possible.'

What he gets out of it, he says, is happiness, the balanced happiness which he believes Buddhism offers. 'I feel so happy. Not long and not short, but the middle happiness. Our life is meant to get happiness, but we want others' lives to get happiness as well. If today we have food, then we want them to have food. If today we have knowledge, we want them to get knowledge.'

Brak remains heartened by what his organisation has accomplished in a short time. He treasures the fact that more and more children show up at the temple for classes. But with the government's refusal to help, there was still no official school for the children to attend in the community. So Brak took his duty further: not just to teach but to build the school itself. 'We are not only there to teach the students, but we also build the structures, the schools.'

On 17 February 2008, he held a ceremony to collect the last of the money needed to complete a school that would serve 13 villages. Filled with confidence, he says with a smile, 'We have 43 per cent of the school built. All we need to finish is the roof, the door and the windows.'

Until then he will continue to teach under cover of the temple or a tree, like his father did before him.

The skill of being

Father Michael Bassano

Father Michael is another kind of monk – a 'monk from Christian' is what Buddhist Brak Sareth would call him. Though the priest's body is thin and frail, his handshake is strong, and the eyes behind his thick black glasses flash with enthusiasm every time he smiles. He is equally comfortable either facing dire poverty or at Dunkin Donuts, opposite the shopping malls of Bangkok's Siam Center and the impenetrable traffic of taxis and three-wheeled tuk-tuks.

Father Michael's journey has taken him from an Italian immigrant family in Binghamton, in upstate New York, to a Buddhist-run hospice for severely ill AIDS patients in Thailand. He has spent these last years dealing with the dying, the stigmatised and the friendless. Still, he smiles often. In the midst of the suffering he has witnessed, he has found a healthy measure of what Brak calls 'middle happiness' for himself and for those facing death.

Yet as he says, all he has to offer is his presence.

Michael Bassano's desire to become a priest began in elementary school. He admired the young parish priests who would come to talk to him and his friends while they played stickball, an old schoolyard game like baseball but with a simple stick and a rubber ball. During one conversation the priests suggested they become altar boys, and so Michael did.

'I wanted to be like those priests, my heroes. But first of all, my hero was Jesus. He loved everyone with no exceptions, whether rich or poor or Jewish or Phoenician, all these peoples. Somehow I knew I wanted to be like that.'

When he first told his parents he wanted to be a priest, they were silent. His father wanted him to be a barber. His mother had come over from Italy with nothing and wanted her son to have a good middle-class life. Michael's aunt later told him that when he had announced his intention of becoming a priest, his mother was so upset she went to the parish priest and begged him to discourage her son. And this is in fact what happened – when Michael went to the local priest, an older man, to tell him his ambition, the priest tried to dissuade him, saying Michael would never make it. But if the boy still had the desire to become a priest later, he said, they could talk about it then.

As his parents didn't have the money to send him to a Catholic school, Michael attended Abraham Lincoln Public School. Which was what his Catholic friends called 'pagan school'. Even now, Michael remembers their taunting rhyme: 'Lincoln, Stinkin'/what are they drinkin'/Beer or wine/oh my God, it's turpentine.'

But public school meant he met kids from outside his own ethnic group, such as African-American and Jewish children. His notion that there might be other views that were different from those of his own faith clarified when he gave a class talk on the life of Jesus. He spoke about how Christ was crucified by Romans at the request of Jewish leaders. 'Afterwards, Carol Rosen, one of my Jewish friends, said, "Michael, do you think *we* put Jesus to death?" And I slowly answered, realising, "No, it wasn't you. That's just what we were taught."

'At the time, she was in a gentle way challenging me. I was only 12, but I thought, maybe she's right. I'd never thought of that. I'm directly accusing this person I care about of being responsible for His death. It made me uncomfortable. So she invited me to her synagogue, and I began to get an awareness of a deeper truth.'

He remembers also being told at Catholic services that it was a sin to go to a Protestant church. Yet even the priests would go every Thanksgiving to those 'outcast' churches and hold an interfaith service where all the parishioners would gather. 'That was a way for me to see what *they* are like. Since I was told *they* are not like *we are.* And I had accepted all that previously.'

When it was time for him to go to high school, Michael, still determined to be a priest despite the discouragement he had received, begged his parents to let him attend the Catholic school. Although still against his becoming a priest, they nevertheless came up with the school fees. After graduating, he attended junior and then full seminary in northern New York.

Father Michael Bassano

At the seminary, he faced his first personal predicament in his life of faith. He had been taught to have no weaknesses, but he had a major one: sometimes he didn't feel the presence of God.

'Like Mother Teresa. It was a real crisis, thinking I wasn't worthy enough to be a priest. Maybe it was my upbringing, my father saying, "You're no good," or the church saying, "God is watching everything you're doing." But I got through the crisis by coming to a different notion of faith. For me, faith became a decision to keep believing that somehow God is present, even if you don't have a sense of it at every moment.'

The other challenge was chastity. In high school, he'd had girlfriends. And he continued to date one young woman even in junior seminary. 'She got very upset when she knew I was getting close to the time to make a decision. She got mad. She said, "Yeah, God gets the best, and the girls get the rest." It was tense for me too. Could I go without being married and having a relationship with a woman?

'I went for counselling for it. "No big deal," the counsellor said. "Just go down to the brothels and do it a few times." But I couldn't do that. Not use a woman.' So he made the decision to be chaste and struggle through. Unlike many of the seminary students, who dropped out because of the rigour of the training, Father Michael stayed with it.

His path was challenged again when, three months before his ordination, his mother died. He missed her tremendously. 'At the wake, people came up to me saying you must be very angry at God. I never felt angry but I certainly was sad. I didn't understand her death but didn't feel anger or bitterness, but totally grief.

'I remember my father saying, "Now, you have to stay home and take care of me." I was the middle son. As a responsible son in an Italian family, you had to take care of your father. So a correct decision would have been to stay home. But after the funeral, all I could sense was that I knew what I had to do. So I waited a week and told my father, "I know you want me to stay here and take care of you. But I have to go back."'

Father Michael returned to the seminary, became ordained and was given his first parish. 'Those first years it was good, doing the rituals. And when my father was ill, I was assigned to an upper West Side, ritzy parish. Then I got caught up in the whole idea of "I'm a priest; aren't I wonderful?" Some people think they're literally God when they become a priest, as if to say, "I'm all-powerful, don't question me."'

But he did remember at times what it was that had brought him to the priesthood in the first place. 'Being a priest was a way of helping people at the most difficult moments, whether it be at a funeral, or at happy moments, like a wedding.'

Three years after his mother died, his father passed away too. Even as he continued over the next few years in the same parish, his father's death served as a reminder of his initial wish to be of help, like his hero Jesus, to all, rich or poor. 'There were families even in the wealthy parish who were really poor. I knew one family who had nothing. There were five children. Even though the mother was living in a house in the upper end of town, she was struggling. I was drawn to them, and learned a lot from them.'

At this point, Father Michael might just have continued a career as a parish priest, going further up the ranks if anything. As he remembers it, 'So here I am. I made the goal. But I always felt a need to be among the poor, to be aware that if there are any poorer people than ourselves around us, we needed to respond to them.'

He began to pay attention to goings on in the Catholic Church that were seemingly far removed from his community. In El Salvador, after Archbishop Oscar Romero spoke out against the right-wing government on behalf of the marginalised and poor in the country, he was assassinated. Later that year, four nuns from Maryknoll, a missionary movement from the US, were raped and killed there because of their commitment to the poor. 'So all of a sudden I started becoming aware that the church was more than my diocese. And it was the time when John the 23rd said a tenth of our priests should go help the poor in South America. Those things made me wonder if I were being called to go beyond my normal life.'

The opportunity to go a bit beyond came in 1982 with an assignment in an inner-city church in Utica, in central New York State. He worked there for five years, contending with the problems of drug and alcohol addiction, violence and poverty. 'There was a lot going on there, with alcoholics coming in, a mental health clinic next door. But it wasn't enough. The only thing I could think of was Oscar Romero and the Maryknoll sisters, missionaries who went beyond their diocese. I had to find out if that's what I was being called to do.'

On New Year's Day 1984, after mass, he went to visit the Maryknoll Catholic missionaries in Ossining, a town an hour north of New York City. He entered the building – a large stone structure, which had at its centre a tower with a roof like that of a Chinese pagoda – introduced himself, and met some of the brothers and sisters. They invited him to stay for lunch. This group had just been in Tanzania, and they told him about their experiences in the most trying of circumstances. Hearing about this excited him about doing mission work overseas. But he still had mixed feelings – wondering first if he was unworthy for the work, and second, could he learn a new language? And the third thing, would he disappoint the diocese? The priest – who was meant to advise others in times of crisis – was afraid.

But he decided to explore the idea further. During his vacation time, he did a two-week course run by the Sisters of St Joseph in Mexico. He worked with refugees from El Salvador, and people in the slums. 'I was very moved by what I saw. I had never seen such poverty. It was then I sensed I had to do an overseas mission.'

Even then, he wouldn't have to commit to missionary work for the duration of his life. The diocese could let him out for five years. Still questioning his abilities, he went to a counsellor to ask his opinion. 'The Catholic counsellor said, "No matter what issues you have, you'll work them out. Let life be therapy for you."'

In 1987, he was finally accepted to work with Maryknoll in Chile, for a try-out period of five years. He remembers telling his parishioners in Utica he was leaving, and their disappointment. One young man accused him of betraying the diocese. 'But I knew that I was onto something, to be part of the larger experience of life. So that I wasn't just an American who thinks it's the only place to be and no one else matters.'

He spent the next five years in the toughest slum in Santiago, learning a different view of the United States, whose government had actively undermined the democratically elected but allegedly communist-leaning Salvador Allende. In 1973, Allende died during a military coup, after which the infamous General Pinochet took power, becoming dictator until 1990. Where Michael worked, 'all the people were considered communist because if you were poor and against the government of Pinochet, you were a communist. So priests were considered that too.'

Not only were Michael's eyes opened to a different view of America, but to a different way of being Catholic. 'We helped Christian-based communities where the people themselves would be the church, not the priests. They shared the homily. And before every liturgy, they would tell what was going on during the week. "The soldiers took Mrs So and So." That became the prayer of the day. It gave you a whole idea that this liturgy is not just – we pray to God, help us, we go home – but that it was part of life.'

Michael and the other priests became involved in the struggle against the government, and he went out onto the streets with the people protesting against the widespread torture and violation of human rights by Pinochet's regime. He was only arrested once, being protected as a citizen of the US, which was still supportive of this government.

When his five years were up, Michael asked the Catholic Church in the US if he could have another five years. His request was granted.

Over the course of his ten years in Chile his faith grew stronger, but in a new way. Here, he says, he saw that people didn't just speak the word of God. They lived it. The normal structure of the church, like any organisation, as he points out, is top-down. But here the people organised it from the bottom up. 'This was the grass-roots church. That was the gift of the theology of liberation, which today you can't talk about anymore. Because it challenged the church in Rome. But there we were all equal.'

He also began to understand what he had to offer, that his presence itself was a contribution. 'You were one with them in the struggle. The whole idea of solidarity is a word that became entrenched in my understanding. The people wanted you to be with them.'

After ten years, the Bishop in New York said it was time for Michael to come home. But he had come to the realisation that he wanted to be on mission for life – with Maryknoll. And he told the bishop this, even though Maryknoll had not yet formally accepted him. It was a risk. If he were to be released from the diocese, he would remain in a no-man's-land for the year of waiting. If Maryknoll rejected him, there was no way of knowing what he would do – strange indeed for a man who, more than most people, had seemingly chosen a secure vocation. He took the chance.

A year later, he was accepted into Maryknoll and asked where he wanted to go. The choice was Brazil or Thailand. Like Chile, Brazil was predominantly Catholic. Thailand was Buddhist, 'a country where they didn't need your preaching. They kicked out the Portuguese and the French, because they'd tried to convert the king hundreds of years ago.' So what would his presence offer there, where people weren't of his faith? Brazil was the obvious choice. He chose Thailand.

On arriving he worked with Burmese refugees or people who were detained because they didn't have visas, Sri Lankans or Africans caught in the drug trade. He and Maryknoll would do outreach work with them, or support the poor hill tribes in the north, in Chiang Rai and Chiang Mai. The only preaching Michael did was the occasional monthly mass in English in Bangkok. That was the least he could do, he points out, laughing, so people did realise he was indeed Catholic.

To communicate, he had to learn Thai. I can personally attest how difficult this can be for a westerner. Chinese, itself not an easy language, has four different tones for words; to top its northern neighbour, Thai has five. Spoken in one tone, suay, for example, can mean beautiful, and in another tone – bad luck. Luckily Michael was not tone deaf, and he managed to grasp the different intonations.

After a few years, he came to spend most of his time at the temple of Wat Prabat Nampu, the AIDS hospice in Lopburi, a few hours north of Bangkok. The hospice was founded by a Buddhist abbot, and since then 10,000 people have been cared for and treated there. Of those people, 7000 have died. Another number gives an idea of just how much stigma people with HIV/AIDS still face: only a thousand of those people's bodies have been taken by their families.

Wat Prabat Nampu is a sanctuary, where many of the monks too are HIV positive. It is also a place where visitors can come to learn more about HIV/AIDS in the hope of lessening the stigma, where the average Thai can learn how people are now able to survive with proper medication. For years, it has also served as Father Michael's base, as he goes to and from his small quarters on an old black bicycle.

'First, I introduce myself to the patients as a volunteer, never as a priest. And I am just one among many others who are here to be with them.' What he does are what he calls the simple things, whether it's changing a diaper or getting people to drink or to walk, or taking them out to the store near the temple. 'It's encouraging them to keep living. And that's what we do for each other; we keep encouraging each other that today is what's most important.

'It may be called a hospice for the dying, but I call it a temple of life. We try to encourage people to keep living. I'm not here to take away their pain; I can't. But I can be with them in it. And through that, find a way to keep going, keep living. We have a famous saying up there, "Stay in the struggle." It's like the days in Chile, the struggle with power.'

Though a foreigner, Father Michael has found that a sense of compassion could unite the other volunteers, the patients and himself. 'Compassion is a call to be among the most discriminated against, the neglected, the poor, the most needy. But it's never what you say; it's who you are. What people want is for you to be present, being with everyone in their suffering as well as their joys. What I do at the temple is just go there and let them know I care about them.'

But Father Michael also found his own faith reinforced by the people at the hospice. Rather than reinforcing the conflict between East and

West that has dominated dialogue post-9/11, he grew to see how much the various faiths have in common. 'All religions speak of compassion. For the Muslims, one of the names of God is The Compassionate One. Buddhism is the compassionate path. For the Chinese, there is the goddess Kuan Yin, their example of a Bodhisattva, one who has not achieved Nirvana but stayed on Earth to bring compassion to people. And of course Jesus said, "Be compassionate as God is compassionate."'

My own first meeting with Father Michael was some years back when I was making a film about children orphaned by AIDS. I had gone with my crew and a teenage boy to visit the hospice. At the time, Father Michael was sitting beside a young woman named Welaporn, who was then skin and bone, the disease gradually destroying her body. She still had beautiful, but weary, eyes. Father Michael sat beside her and encouraged her to sing to the boy. Welaporn gently sang an old Chinese pop song directly to the teenager. Though weak, her voice had passion, and he and our entire crew were moved to tears.

I was moved again as Father Michael talked about Welaporn as the person who had touched him most over the years. She had no one to be with but the volunteers; her family had abandoned her, frightened of AIDS. 'But she was always so gentle and kind. Every morning when I came in, when I said hello to her, she would always open her eyes and just be so grateful and gracious.

'The day before she died, she looked at me and said, "Will you be here tomorrow?" I said, "I will always be here with you." And there was a peaceful smile on her face that day.

'It wasn't anything we did for her. All we did was be there with her when she had no one else. We were able to say, "I want to be here with you. You may be neglected, but there are others who still care, who know your life has value and dignity." I'm not saying I made much difference. But in the end, she knew someone was there for her.

'Little did I know she would die two hours later.'

Father Michael stays quiet, remembering the young woman. Then he continues. There are stories too of people who survive – because of the small things that Father Michael speaks about.

'We have one woman, Manasawee. She's 28 years old. When she first came to the temple, her family had also rejected her. She was so traumatised that she would just grind her teeth endlessly. She felt that she had no one and nothing left. We couldn't get any food into her for three weeks. It took us a while to get her to know that she was accepted by us.

'In the last six months, not only did she eat and put on weight. But where she used to stay in bed, now she wants to get up and go to the store every day. She's heavier now,' he says, smiling, 'when I lift her into the wheelchair. She goes into this little store and buys a little can of Coke. Every day. If there's any food that's there, she takes it back to her bed. That's five minutes every day. She has no money, so I pay for that.

'So the money I receive from people in the States goes to help people like her find a little bit of enjoyment. At least she knows that around 11.30, she's getting up out of that bed to buy something. And so that's where this money goes, to someone who has no one, totally rejected, discriminated against. And she hasn't just come back to life, but to a renewed sense that her life has value and dignity. So that's what I tell people when they send me money; your money goes to buy food for Manasawee.'

To Father Michael, that is the point: all of us can contribute, even if it is just by being present for someone like Manasawee. 'I would encourage people to volunteer at the temple, but not just in Thailand. Anywhere. Volunteer to something that brings you out of yourself, so you're not just worried about your own or your family problems.

'My brother lives in Reading, Pennsylvania. His wife died of cancer two years ago. But now every Sunday, he goes to the same hospital where she died and volunteers, helping the nurses. His life did not end with his wife's death. He finds a sense of happiness in giving.'

Father Michael calls it the happiness of giving; Siri calls it the contentment of giving. But eerily, they seem to have reached the same conclusions.

'It doesn't mean one should sacrifice oneself. It just means what can I do today in a simple way to brighten up the life of another. If that means giving someone a sandwich, volunteering at a soup kitchen or being with someone and making their day because you stopped to see them, that's what makes the difference. The simple acts of compassion.

'What you get is a sense of happiness; there's an interchange. We touch each other's lives, but at significant points in our lives. That's what drew me to the church in the first place. I was with people at significant moments in their lives – marriage, death, baptism. But this goes beyond ritual, beyond language, culture, and all that.

'We all need to go beyond our work and our family to contribute to a larger picture. So that it affects me what happens in Iraq, Thailand or Africa. Not that it depresses or discourages us. Some people see pictures of our temple and they say, oh how terrible. But they don't see the other side, that we're trying to help them live. That it enriches you and brings you a greater sense of fulfilment within.'

Father Michael dunks the last of his donut into his coffee at, appropriately, Dunkin Donuts, opposite the Siam Center and the endless Bangkok traffic, suggesting that I try the same with my donut. I feel as if I were Manasawee; his presence is indeed comforting.

After ten years in Thailand, Father Michael will have to leave. He is being sent to the place he heard about when he first went to Maryknoll: Tanzania. Where he will have to learn, as he says, how to be all over again.

We talk about Africa. I mention Idris, the rebel from Sudan, and how he is trying to solve a crisis that at times seems overwhelming. Michael nods. 'You can't solve a whole issue, but you can do one small thing for someone right now, the eternal now. All you have to do is open your eyes, and you'll see what needs to be done. If it's someone on the corner, in your own home or down the street who has just had a terrible tragedy, or in the hospital, it's the simple things that make a difference. Like getting someone a drink of water.

'It's the simple things.'

Chapter 6

Have patience

All human wisdom is contained in these two words: 'wait' and 'hope'!

Alexandre Dumas, *The Count of Monte Cristo*

The best example of waiting and hoping comes from dealing with children. They will grow in the time it takes them to grow, regardless of whether institutions or governments want them to grow faster. The same may be said for the time it takes to build up organisations dealing with children. It took Siri at least ten years to build her network of schools, and now she has been working with children for nigh on 30 years. And Siri had an advantage: nepotism. Her school principal was her husband. On the many afternoons and nights when she had to travel to do her unpaid work, he also acted as her chauffeur.

In each district, Siri would coax the teachers to spend their time learning more about the lives of the children they taught. Normally, every teacher followed the same routine, only seeing children in the classroom. So one by one, Siri would go with them to the home of a child who was having difficulty in school.

When they saw the problems in the children's homes, the teachers began to see their students differently, just as we might notice something different about a building we pass every day if we vary our route. 'One of the teachers said that she never knew that some of the children she had seen every day were in such great difficulty,' Siri says.

Then, once each teacher came on board, they started out by doing simple things, as Siri and Father Michael had done. 'At the outset, they started the same as me. I took my son's clothes and unneeded personal effects to help out. And the network members did the same. Food and clothes came from the teachers in the network first. We didn't get any materials or support elsewhere.'

Siri did not search for outside funding. She says that came about by accident. 'I didn't know anything about non-governmental organisations. Most were based in Bangkok, in the big cities, but we teachers had been here for 20 years.

'It took ten years, all this time, in order for the teachers' network to talk and understand the same things. But one day some undergraduate students from a university in Bangkok came to do academic counselling at our school. And on a particular day when I had a break, I took off to visit a boy, Prakop. When I returned to school, some university students asked me where I had gone.

'Once they learned of my visit, they wanted to come with me. When they found out the whole story, they wanted to take the information to one of their teachers, and a member of the Foundation for Child Development.' The foundation started to provide support, and after that came another charitable organisation, AFXB (Association François-Xavier Bagnoud), which saw the value of Siri's example. As she points out, it is a simple model really to help the community: it's getting teachers, who already want to help, to see, listen, use their skills and, most importantly, take as much time as necessary – even years, if that's what it takes.

Fighting for Destiny's Child

Supagon Noja

I've seen a certain amount of horror in my life, but none of it prepared me for what I was shown by Supagon Noja. Supagon is a 39-year-old man, normally with a smiling face and cheerful eyes. But when, in his meagre office, he brought up a photo to show me on his computer screen, his dark eyes were sternly focused and his lips were drawn in a grimace.

It is a picture of a white Norwegian man in a dingy motel room with orange plastic furnishings. He is naked on a bed. Two Thai boys lie on either side of him. They are seven and nine years old. Naked too, they are caressing the man. He is smiling at the camera.

With grim satisfaction, Supagon notes that this is one of the men he has helped to have arrested. Over the last 20 years, he has rescued many children like this from life on the street and sexual molestation; he has also helped arrest around 200 people. He has files on at least 50 more paedophiles and agents, whom he intends to get no matter how long it takes, even though his own life is in danger.

Where we are is Pattaya, which has a few different reputations. One is as a beach vacation area close to Bangkok, where Thai locals and foreigners can take a break quickly and cheaply. Another is as a sex 'R&R' spot used by American servicemen during the Vietnam War. The third, sadly, is as a place where paedophiles migrate from around the world.

Here, too, in an old concrete building in a narrow compound, is where Supagon Noja runs his rescue centre for street children. It's a former home for the blind. Supagon wears a button-down shirt to work, as if he were going to an insurance job, using the degree he got in business management. But the computer on his worn formica desk is grey and old, in stark contrast to the fixtures in the many cheap but flashy resorts nearby.

Supagon first came to Pattaya in response to its reputation as a cheap vacation spot, needing a break from university and work. All he was looking for was a few days out. He certainly did not foresee that he would ever live here, rescuing children and getting their predators arrested. In a way, it is all due to a boy he might refer to as 'Destiny's Child'.

Like many of the children he helps, Supagon came from a rural area. He was born into a poor family in a village far further north, near Chiang Mai. It was a rice-growing area, like Siri's. Supagon says proudly, 'My family did not have a problem except for the fact that we were poor.' They were farmers, with enough land for crops but little else.

Supagon Noja

'My parents, though poor, wanted me to have an education. Thai people believe that if you get more education, then you will have a good future. In the future, my parents said, "You won't have to be like us."'

The local rural school was small, but with his parents' encouragement Supagon studied hard and did well. Knowing he could only go so far in the country, his parents applied for a scholarship for him to study in a city in the next province. It was one of the Assumption schools, a well-respected Catholic school chain across Thailand.

Supagon was awarded a scholarship, and went to the city to attend boarding school. 'That taught me about the schools in the country and the schools in the city, how different they are. And it's a lot better in the city,' he says.

Even at a young age, he had a sense of injustice at the lot of rural people, especially the poor and younger children who, unlike him, wouldn't be able to attend a good school. 'I learned then how people in the country were basically kept down by people in the city,' he says, but always with his courteous and warm smile. 'The people in the country had no chance. It was not fair that they got help from no one.'

On finishing secondary school Supagon gained entrance to Chiang Mai University, but he didn't have the money for the tuition fees. So he decided instead to come to Bangkok and attend the Open University there. Like other poor but driven students, his idea was to study part-time over several years, while working to support himself. He worked as a waiter, then as a salesman in a department store. At university, he studied management, intending to go into business and, as his parents had intended, make a better future life for himself.

One day at university, he saw a notice asking for volunteers. It was for an organisation that helped people who were sick and unable to take care of themselves. Feeling he had been given a chance to work in the city and escape his parents' life, Supagon decided to contribute his time. Along with other volunteers from the university, he began to visit some of the patients that the organisation worked with. Like Father Michael, he began with simply offering his presence, comfort and some food.

But this group was also connected to an organisation that helped street children. Many were originally from the rural areas; some were now using drugs. Imagining how easily he could have been in their place if he had not got a scholarship to secondary school, Supagon became a 'street teacher' for the group.

Many of the children were found in places like Hua Lampong train station or Lumpini Park, home to the then-famous night market, where they begged or hustled for bits of food. Supagon would counsel the children, earning their trust by taking their sides against the police and government when necessary.

'At that time,' he points out, 'if a representative from the government found the abandoned children, they would just arrest them. Not to put them in jail, but in an institution.' Fearing a prison-like existence, the children were terrified of the government officials and would just run away from them.

At the Open University, Supagon did so well that he was on track to get his degree in three and a half years, in contrast to the other working students like him who often took five to seven years. Just a few months away from graduating, he decided to go to Pattaya for a few days, to take a break from the stresses of working and studying.

He found a reasonable motel, and went out to take a walk along the beach, the soothing sound of the ocean a balm after the roar of traffic in the city. As he continued strolling, looking out at the water, a child greeted Supagon. Shocked, Supagon turned around. It was a street boy he knew from his project in Bangkok. He asked the boy, 'Why are you here? How did you get here?' And the boy said, 'Oh, it's not only me. There's a whole group of us here.'

Supagon could have just continued his walk on the beach. He could have savoured his few days in the sun then gone home. But he decided to accompany the boy to where the children were hiding.

'First, the boy took me to see his group. Then he took me to see even more groups of children. Each group had about twenty or thirty children.' Some of them had come, like the boy, directly from Bangkok, escaping the government agents, and some from as far as Chiang Mai, as Supagon had.

'I just came to Pattaya to have fun,' he says. 'But when I met the young boy, I wanted to know why he was here. And in talking with his group, I found out how those children had been hurt by people with power in the area. The people gave them money, to sell drugs for them, or sell their bodies for sex. These were children from about six to twelve or thirteen years of age.'

Supagon was horrified. Prostitution, or sex work, is a well-known fact of life for adults in Bangkok and Pattaya, but to see children this age forced into committing sexual acts with adults for money enraged him. 'I asked the children if they had people to help them, or some organisation here. There was no organisation to help them. Just the government, which would only arrest them. So the children would always continue to hide. Even when they had problems with their health, or got hurt and bruised.

'The only help they got was from a small organisation run by someone called Father Ray. He was an American guy, Raymond Brennan.'

The late Father Ray, who was originally from Chicago's South Side, spent 30 years devoted to children and the poor here. He was lauded by US President Ronald Reagan, and had been surprised to find that even the Dalai Lama knew of his work when they met.

'Father Ray helped abandoned children, but had a very small organisation then,' Supagon continues. 'So the next day I went to meet him. Father Ray said that he wanted to help those children, but didn't have the staff or people to do so. So after I talked to Father Ray, I was interested. At the time, I had half a year to finish at school. But on my days off, I came here to do research.'

Over the next six months Supagon did as he had promised Father Ray, while continuing to study. Ever diligent, he finished his degree on track. At this point, Supagon could still have begun a career in business, which would have enabled him to better help his own family. His voice grows serious and quiet as he speaks about his decision in regard to the children, and his thoughts echo those of Chung To, who had been drawn to help the orphaned children in China. 'I thought these children had no chance. They were not going to school. What would happen when they grew up? What would Thai society be like with this generation when they grew up?

'These children needed help. Because they didn't have any power. They couldn't just go to the government and say, "Hey, I need help." The government would say, "Who are you?" I thought that if I came to start this organisation, I could help the children talk with the government, companies or organisations to help them.

'I looked at myself: I was born to a poor family in the country with no chance. But I got the opportunity to fight for myself. And with these children, they were the worst-off children in Thailand. They would not get another chance because they'd done all these bad things, the drugs and so on. So I wanted to fight for them. For them to have a possibility for their lives, to make them better.'

Though his choice would mean he could be of little help to them financially, his parents were supportive. Even now, when asked if he finally earns a significant salary, he laughs loudly, and points out it's more like a deficit.

Supagon returned to Pattaya. For good. 'I came and talked with Father Raymond. He gave me some money to rent this building, and some money to do this work, to help the children.'

The building he chose was the abandoned former school for the blind where I meet him. It was close enough to the downtown area for wayward children to drop in, yet far enough that they were removed from the bars of the beach.

He went and told the children that for the moment what he had for them was a place to stay. There was no staff, and no programme. It was just the building and Supagon.

But Supagon was not alone for long; in fact it was only a matter of hours before the kids trundled in. 'The first day there were 36 kids who came here,' he remembers, smiling. 'I had nothing to begin with, no beds, nothing. Just the building. But the children thought at least here they could sleep. At least it was not on the street. It was in a building. When it was raining, they wouldn't get wet.'

To make food, all they had to begin with was a rice cooker. 'We would cook rice and then buy other food, and we also got donations. People who saw us here gave us noodles to cook. I would go walk around and tell people what we were doing, and they would donate clothes or food for abandoned children.'

That was how he began his programme. As he slowly built up a small staff, he knew the most important thing was that he would have to invest his time. It had taken time to gain the original children's trust, and more time would be needed for those he did not yet know.

Once that trust was gained, Supagon would first try to get the children's original communities to care for them. But even if this solution was successful, it necessitated more time for follow-up. For the children whose families refused to help them, the staff needed to find which they could put into proper schools or, like Friends in Cambodia, which ones wanted simple vocational training.

Supagon's investment of time was especially important in developing enough trust with the children to build evidence against those who did them damage on the streets: the sexual predators and their agents. Wary at first, the children who sought refuge at the centre would eventually confide in the staff. Once certain they were no longer in danger of being beaten by the adults who had sold them, Supagon says, 'They'd tell our street teacher, "Those people made me go with that foreigner. And he stays in such and such building, and they made me have sex with him." So the street teacher could find out more information. "Who made you go? Which hotel, which place?"'

Equally importantly, Supagon and his staff also made connections with the community, the government, and the police. 'The thing that works is connection. We've worked for a long time, and we know these organisations for the children or the government. So when we speak, they listen and send someone to look at the situation.'

Another connection they built was with the local schools. Children in the schools would know to contact Supagon's centre if they saw something suspicious in the area, like a girl on the street who seemed hurt.

But it wasn't only the children who could be in danger. As Supagon went after the individuals and groups engaged in the child sex trade, some of them went after him. 'They've shot at me three times, and at my car. The last time, a few years back, bullets came through the window of my office,' Supagon says, laughing. Luckily, he's never been hit.

What he doesn't find funny is the abuse, evidence of which he shows me in some of the hundreds of photos his team have gathered. There are plenty of others besides the Norwegian man and the two boys. Some of the pictures are of local Thai predators and agents.

One, whom Supagon and the team are still building evidence against, is a gaunt man in his early twenties. In the photo Supagon shows me, he is flaunting a small moustache and wearing a black and orange striped shirt, and he is glaring at the camera. Supagon says the worry is not only that this agent traffics in the children, but he is HIV-positive and he 'tries the children out sexually', boys and girls, without protection.

Other photos show physical abuse on girls as young as two, inflicted on them by their own families.

Though Supagon has helped to have over 200 people involved in child trafficking arrested, the 50 he is still after gall him. Though he laughs about being shot at, he admits to being disheartened at times. 'Sometimes I feel like giving up. I make the connections with the police or the government, but they often work so slowly. But if I give up and do nothing, it is not going to make anything better.

'So,' he points out, 'I'm still here.'

At his centre there are now 40 children. Over the course of a year about 150 will come through, the rest either going back to their families or into schools. There are new young people coming in all the time.

I meet one boy whom the street teachers rescued from the bars only the week before. A skinny 15-year-old, he had been brought as a child by his grandfather from Malaysia to beg for money for him in Bangkok. As he spoke no Thai, when he was caught by the police he was repatriated to where they thought he had come from: Burma. After living with a poor family there for a few years he escaped the country, driven by the promise of fast money in Pattaya. Here, the teenager told me, he had had no choice but to work in the bars and be sold for sex – until he had been rescued by Supagon. Now, smiling shyly, he proudly said he was about to begin vocational school. To learn English.

As for the boy Supagon encountered on the beach all those years ago, 'He finished high school. Then he applied to the navy, where he got a job. Today, he's still in the navy. When I met him, he was ten years old. Now he's 27, and married with his own children. But he always comes back. He comes and buys things for the young people here.'

Supagon too is married now. His wife is an insurance broker. Like his parents, she is proud of the work he does, and she too supports it. In fact, on her days off, she works at the centre as well, in it for the long haul.

As for the insignificance of his salary, 'My wife understands,' Supagon says, 'that I work for my heart, not for money.'

Wasting time with glue-sniffing street children

Alphonce Omolu

Like Supagon, Alphonce has spent his adult career dealing with children from the streets. But in Kenya, where he lives, by conservative estimates there are 250,000 of them. I saw them in Nairobi sniffing glue and living in cardboard boxes; to me, they looked like victims of war. When I first encountered these children, I would have been satisfied if even a Dickensian orphanage had taken them off the streets and put them into schools.

But Alphonce differs. As much as anyone, Alphonce wants the children to grow up in a safe, comfortable and nurturing environment. Yet he also wants to listen to the children, to find out why they are on the streets. If a child wants to live in the street, one should leave them there, he says. Further, the child has a *right* to live on the street, until they themselves want to leave. Though Alphonce's method may seem agonisingly slow, he says the only thing that works in the long term is what no corporate efficiency expert would suggest: 'We should be willing to waste time.'

Alphonce understands the difficulties first-hand, as his own brother and sister-in-law contracted HIV/AIDS. At the time, Alphonce was director of an organisation fighting the local stigmas and taboos around the disease. He offered his close relatives free life-saving medication. Instead, frightened of the stigma, they refused to admit to having the disease. Sadly, their choice killed them, leaving their children to be brought up by Alphonce and his wife Pamela.

But his work has led to happier endings too – for example, with a boy named for a fruit – Mango. Alphonce's willingness to waste 20 years of time changed Mango's life.

Alphonce grew up near Lake Victoria and Kisumu. Like many in the community, his family had traditionally been farmers. But in 1962, heavy rains drove water levels in Lake Victoria up over two metres, flooding the land. Afterwards, people were forced to depend on fishing or selling fish to middlemen. That was what Alphonce's mother did. His father continued to raise a few cattle, and the family eked out a living as well through subsistence farming and by taking reconstruction jobs in the area.

Even though the family struggled, just as Supagon's had, Alphonce's parents made sure he went to school. 'When I was in primary school, the fees were 25 shillings per year. That was difficult for people to afford. But in those days, the school provided the textbooks and other expenses. By the time I went to secondary school, it was almost three times that. But the school provided all the facilities, so there was no other burden on the parents. Those fees changed later on.'

In the 1980s, under the structural adjustment programmes instituted by the International Monetary Fund and the World Bank, the Kenyan government put higher school fees in place. Poor families were

Alphonce Omolu

unable to afford such fees, so their children were forced out of school. Many were left to fend for themselves, part of the reason growing numbers of them ended up on the street.

Growing up, Alphonce was involved in local youth groups within the Catholic Church. 'Although my parents never pushed religion on me, they did give me an example of how we could help the poorest among us. They were very good people and assisted others, especially my mother. We had many relatives staying in our home, her tenth cousin and such.'

Although his parents weren't well off, Alphonce felt he could afford to help others even as a teen because he had been taught to become self-sufficient. His parents told him he knew best what he wanted and needed to do. This set his internal model for dealing with the street children down the line – the idea that they too knew best what they needed.

'I was determined to do whatever I wanted to do to the best of my capacity. That put me in a lot of leadership positions, because when I did things, I did them well. But it was my parents who created an environment that allowed me to be self-sufficient. I learned to believe in doing things for myself. I bought my own clothes. I bought my own shoes. I even built my own house with some assistance from my parents. So I believed in being able to do for myself.

'And early on, I did counselling for young people who had challenges in their lives. I encouraged them to do for themselves too, as opposed to waiting. Some of those younger people really prospered, far better than me economically and academically. So that was a motivation for me later on, that I was able to help desperate young people achieve better living conditions for themselves.'

But his career goal at the time was to do something that would involve machines and technology. 'When I left school, I wasn't going to work with people. I wanted to do medical work, lab tech, doing research and analysing things in the lab.' Though his grades were excellent, his attempt to go on to higher education left him facing the corrupt system head on. 'You could only get a chance at a very few colleges; either you had to bribe yourself through, or pay somebody to make way for you.

'So I decided to do teaching. I was admitted to teachers' college. But again I didn't have the money to bribe people to attend, even though I qualified. At that point, I kind of lost hope.'

Discouraged, Alphonce took what jobs he could get, mainly as a manual labourer. He worked on his uncle's rice farm. He did construction work. He went mining for gold. Sometimes, digging the soil and washing the ore, he could make good money.

But his teenage years helping young people had not gone unnoticed. Some community members were now working at the Pandipieri Centre, which had been begun by a Dutch priest named Father Hans in a Kisumu slum. There was a position in their street children programme. 'It wasn't my intention to work with street children,' Alphonce says. 'But due to my work with youth when I was young, they invited me to go for the interview. So that is how I ended up at Pandipieri in 1987.'

He began as an informal educator for the children, what Supagon calls a 'street teacher'. 'Twenty years ago, when I started, the number fluctuated between 15 and 20 street children that I worked with. Apart from basic literacy and numeracy, I also did some garden work with them to enhance job discipline in their lives. Because when they came in from the street, their lives had become chaotic from glue sniffing. As I was the one who would be with them for a long time, my focus was to bring them back into a normal and somehow organised life. Where they would be able to start thinking at least what they wanted their life to be.'

As the centre expanded, the number of children the team tried to place back in their communities grew to around 250. Sometimes they were successful; other times the children would run back to the street.

'It was very fulfilling most of the time. Though there were parents who were not happy to see their children, you'd feel good when you'd go to the homes where parents *were* happy to take them back. And when you followed up and the children wanted to stay at home, it was quite rewarding. Because then you had influenced the living conditions of the overall family, to be more concerned with each child.'

Pandipieri could have gone the traditional route of building orphanages. But they realised that 'rescuing' children from their community would just create more children who would head to the street in the long run. 'We did not believe in orphanages. We believed in communities taking responsibility. That was the only way we could reduce the number of children coming to the street, because then the communities would ensure better living conditions for their children.

'Our approach was re-integration with the family or relatives. If that was not possible, we would approach any member of the community willing to assist the child. Then as an organisation, we would support them in the ways that we could. And our 70 per cent success rate encouraged us that this was the right way.'

Over time, Alphonce gained ever more responsibility. Six years on, he was elevated to programme co-ordinator, in charge of staff, fundraising, documenting and further developing their work. Part of what Alphonce and his team did was to try to understand what drove the children to the streets in the first place. But they used a child's logic, not an adult's.

'In most cases,' Alphonce says, 'there are simple things which put children into a situation. A parent might tell a child, if they didn't do a chore or errand, "If I see you here when you never did what I told you, I will kill you." Now, the parents didn't mean to kill them. But children might really think they'd be killed. If the situation is not handled properly, then children end up in the street.

'When we met them in the street, for me normally the best thing to do was remember they were not born there. Unless they *were* born in the street,' he says, and smiles wistfully. Because these days, some are.

'You'd always ask them why are they on the street in the first place. And it's very important that you listen to their story. It's on that basis that you discuss things with the child. Then the child can start thinking about their future life and the best place to tackle it, especially when they are assured we would handle the problem in the home. Or if the issue was the school, we would talk to the teacher. Most of the time, the child would decide that they want to go home.

'But we never forced them to go home. Some children we left on the streets for years, because they really did not want to go back home.'

It sounds callous at first, the idea of letting them stay on the street, begging or sniffing glue. But, says Alphonce, 'They were still our friends. We still offered counselling and helped them. But the only thing we could promise the child was our friendship. "This is your situation. If you want to improve it, we are here as a friend to assist you in any way we can." The children were never brought to the centre. They were invited to come by themselves.'

The child had to take the initiative. Because to the child, the street was the solution to their problems. According to grown-up thinking, the street is of course not a place for children, or adults. But there were things the children enjoyed, even if they sometimes didn't have enough to eat. The most important of these was their freedom – to do what they liked. 'So when you approach them there, you don't trash their life in the street. You appreciate the fact that they are living there. The question is, why would they choose that chaotic life? It is only when we know the thoughts of the children that we are able to help them.

'It is not your situation you are trying to address. The ownership is with the children. So the problem has to be defined by the children. You can only help them to see it clearly. So you must be prepared to take your time to listen to them, work along with them, and support them in every step that they're taking in life.'

Alphonce is very aware that this is antithetical to normal practice in modern society. 'In our current mindset, we want to see results here and now. As such, we do not consider whether processes we are putting in place to improve the living conditions of a child are sustainable. But if they are to be sustainable, a child should be part and parcel of the process, able to continue even without direct assistance. This is why if one chooses to support them, it is important to put time into it. And we should not be dejected when it takes so long to happen.'

Alphonce became the manager of the entire institution of Pandipieri until, after three years, he felt it was time to further his own skills. In 2006, with a scholarship provided by a Pandipieri donor, he attended a master's programme in London to hone his findings on street children over 20-plus years. Now he is applying his knowledge to children in Tanzania, in an organisation that deals with over one thousand children.

But he still applies the same principles, especially concerning patience and the wasting of time. 'One of the children I started with at the organisation was Charles. His second name was Mango, like the fruit. He was initially living on the streets of Nairobi and ended up in Kisumu. He lived in the street for three or four years.

'Then he came into our centre. He had a mother who had a paralysed leg and was working as a house help in Nairobi but not earning enough. So when he wanted to go to secondary school, we paid for him to be in a boarding school in Nairobi, to be near her. But he dropped out. For a while, he did all sorts of odd jobs including a stint as a security watchman. Then, he disappeared.'

Alphonce was saddened; this boy had started in the programme at the same time as he had. When they saw each other again, in the streets of Kisumu, the boy was in his twenties. 'When I met him again, seven years later, I challenged him, asking if he still wanted to go back to school. And still, he told me no.'

Alphonce let him be, willing even after all these years to offer his friendship and 'waste time'. 'Shortly afterwards, he wrote me a letter to say that he'd finally decided he needed school. I went to meet him, to support him with school fees. He was already 25 years old when he joined secondary school again in Form 9, with students almost half his age.'

Mango finished school this time, in a disciplined fashion. His dream was the same one that Alphonce had once had – to be a teacher. With help from Alphonce and Pandipieri, he got into the training course. 'He is now a teacher, of mainly English and Swahili. The reason his main subject is English is because he likes poetry. He has written some hundred or so poems. Now quite ambitious, he is even thinking of publishing those poems.'

Alphonce 'wastes' a moment of time to reflect. 'What people need is encouragement,' he says, whether it is in getting rid of the stigma of AIDS, which claimed the lives of some of his own family, or supporting a drop-out for over 20 years until he could stand before a blackboard in front his own class. 'Encouragement.'

Chapter 7

Encourage the dream

Some men see things as they are and say why ... I dream of things that never were and say why not.

George Bernard Shaw, *Back to Methuselah*

At her house, Siri tends first to her elderly aunt, who stays with her, to make sure she is comfortable. Lying down, the aunt nods and motions her off with a toothy smile. Siri then waters the numerous orchids she has planted in her extraordinary garden. It is the flower of which she is most fond. As she walks through the plants in this almost fairytale setting, Siri says, 'Obviously without money, one cannot live. But without the dream, one also cannot live.'

When Siri's teachers' network eventually began to get funding from non-profit organisations, they ran into a problem. The people in these organisations were so impressed by Siri's notions of encouragement that they seemed to see that as a way forward in and of itself. They would fund people only once they saw that they were already taking steps on their own.

But though Siri believes in dreams, she is firmly rooted in reality. 'At first the NGOs said there had to be some "developments" while they gave some very small allowances. We disagreed. We said, if someone was about to die, how can any development come about? They must first have something to eat.

'As time went on, these newcomer organisations finally understood that the focus had to be on both parts. You could give sustainable assistance, and some ideas of how to live after and develop one's life.

After someone feels good, after they have food, clothes, and a little money to live, then you help them to find an idea. To inspire, we must help first and give them a will to live. Then give them the dream.'

The dream of a fish pond

Yai Aom

On a small patch of land in another village is a single-storey concrete house. In front of it, a seemingly feeble old woman sits on a low stone wall. She has creased dark skin, deep-set eyes, white hair that almost glows, and she wears an orange patterned robe over her traditional checked tube skirt. Beside her are two girls. The older one has a white and black striped shirt with the word 'Zero' on it, and the other a dark tee-shirt.

When she first had to care for her granddaughters on her own, the old woman despaired. She had no idea how to realise her wish to keep them in school. An even more immediate problem was how she could feed them something more than rice and plarah, the cheap fermented fish sauce used to flavour the soup Siri had seen in the home of the young girl many years ago.

The woman's name is Yai Aom. Yai is a Thai word of respect, meaning grandmother. Aom is a nickname, and can also mean a money-box in the form of a doll. But Yai Aom has lived a reality far from a rich doll's life.

Born in Buriram, she came from a family too poor to send her to school. Instead, Aom went to work at a young age in a limestone quarry for a cement factory in Saraburi, in central Thailand. This is where she met her husband, who was also working there. They continued to labour for five years, until Aom had her first and only child, a daughter.

After that their little family moved closer to her home area near

Buriram to grow rice and raise the child. When the little girl was old enough that Aom could work again, she joined her husband in their rented rice field. The system was similar to the old sharecropping system in the US, where a large percentage of the money from one's crops went to the owner. The couple worked the paddies for a year, but when the harvest was bad it was difficult to avoid getting into debt. So they moved again.

This time they moved into the city, living away from the land they knew, taking on whatever work they could. 'I went on to do some menial work in Buriram. I cleared grass away from gardens and houses, while my husband drove a tuk-tuk for hire in the town. After work in the evening, we used to go out to buy rice to eat.'

Their daughter grew up, left home and went to work in another city. She had two children of her own, both girls, by two different husbands. Years passed. Eventually Yai Aom's husband became too ill to drive the sputtering tuk-tuk and they could no longer afford to live in the city. So they moved back to this tiny plot of land and house about 20 kilometres from the city. At least, she thought, it was among villagers she knew.

Then, as hard as life had been, it got harder. Her husband's condition worsened so that he could barely move. Then her daughter got sick and was diagnosed with HIV/AIDS. So, now an old woman, Yai Aom took her weak daughter and two granddaughters in.

Her husband died in 2004.

Two years later, her daughter died.

Yai Aom was 75 years old. She had no education, a small plot of land, few skills and two granddaughters to support. The rural villagers she had known for so long now avoided her, terrified of the disease of which her daughter had died.

Yai Aom, who is illiterate, was scared to go to the government for assistance. She thought she was getting the only money to which she was entitled, and she didn't want to jeopardise that by bothering the bureaucrats. When her husband was ill, she had been getting his welfare benefits as well as her own. But now, with his death, she only got her monthly share. That was 500 baht, about US$18. 'Not since my husband passed away had I received anything from the provincial agency. In the past, I received blankets, and shirts, but then nothing.'

The family subsisted on the few vegetables she grew, none of which she could sell to the other villagers, who avoided her, as the saying goes, like the plague.

Yai Aom, a small old woman with very big responsibilities, didn't know where to turn. But she had heard of Siri and her teachers' network when the girls were in school. The organisation had also held seminars in the village. So she took some local transport, asking strangers for directions to Siri until she eventually found her. She wanted help with her dream of an education for her granddaughters, no matter what happened to her. 'When I went to ask for help from her, I gave her the traditional Thai greeting, and said, "Help my granddaughters go to school until the sixth grade." I told her, "I might not make it; I am not gonna last." But Khun Siri replied, "Don't worry. We'll get your daughters to go as far as they can."'

'Khun Yai Aom came to see me at school,' Siri says. 'She was in agony, because she was so very poor. She came in search of help. So we gave her a hand-out, some little money, to keep her going. Then I followed up with a visit.'

The money Siri gave her as a start, from her own pocket, was about 2000 baht. It's not much, as she says, but it was about four months' normal income for Yai Aom, and would enable her to meet her family's basic needs.

The next thing to deal with was the stigma surrounding her because of her daughter's illness. Yai Aom was ashamed of the cause of her daughter's death, and this was another reason she had not asked for more help from the government or the community. 'But,' as Siri points out, 'if she wouldn't reveal her ordeal, she would not get anything.'

Siri and the teachers in the area dealt with the villagers directly. 'Her neighbours were secretive and worried about what had happened,' she says. 'So when a family is HIV-infected, our teachers' group quickly move in to help them or get acquainted. And when the people around see the teachers visit them, they realise it is not so dangerous for them. And it begins to get better.'

Siri also appealed to the non-profit organisations, asking them to work together. They organised a scholarship fund for Yai Aom's granddaughters, enabling them to continue their schooling.

The next thing Siri did was to pass on one of her skills to Yai Aom

Yai Aom with her granddaughters.

– her gardening. This is one of the most valuable skills in such rural communities. Though the villagers are experts at growing rice, Siri's skill with a variety of vegetables is something many don't have. So when they fall on hard times like Yai Aom, or the price of rice goes down, they really have nothing.

Yai Aom was a quick learner. She took on Siri's vision of a beautiful garden as her own dream, and her vegetable patch quickly became something that her neighbours envied.

With funding from the NGOs, Siri also showed Yai Aom a simple but clever way to get protein – specifically fish. Not just fermented fish sauce, but something special: fresh catfish. They built a very small pond on Yai Aom's land and put in young catfish, which could live off almost anything. In only three months they grew to a large size, and in time produced more fish.

'Now she has a fish pond, a small vegetable garden, and two pigs, one of which is pregnant,' Siri points out. 'In Yai Aom's case, if we just gave her money and food and then left, that would be useless. She would not survive once we were gone. You have to help her with her idea: to live life, take care of her family, send the children to school, and have something good to eat.'

Yai Aom is proud now. The family eat what fish they don't sell, then they wait another month for the next fish to grow. When I visit, her granddaughters are busy playing with two black puppies, which are licking at their faces. The girls also delight in showing off the large pregnant pig. Next, the puppies snuggled in their arms, they show off the thriving garden. Some neighbours now buy Yai Aom's vegetables, even though the fear of HIV/AIDS still keeps others away. 'At present, it is better,' she says. 'Now, people will buy bunches of fresh vegetables or fresh fruits.' Some also come to Yai Aom for advice, to teach them how to plant as well. She is no longer a figure to fear or demean, but someone to respect.

There is a light in Yai Aom's eyes as she poses for a photo with her granddaughters and the puppies. Her dream was to keep going, get her grandchildren through school, and have something a bit better for them to eat. She began with the help of Siri, the network, and the other organisations. Now she is doing it herself.

Notes from the 'usual suspect'

Mustafa Akka

'The last time the police got me I was 21. The accusation was attempted murder. All the witnesses said my name was first. And the next morning the police got me. I got into the cell, and I was wondering, is this what I want? I started thinking, if I get out, I'm going to make something of my life.

''Cause I'd always said to myself, "Moose, don't give up. When one door closes, there's always a door that can open somewhere else."'

Ironically, this arrest was for a crime Mustafa did not commit. But, as an admitted gang leader and felon, it gave him the chance to work for his own redemption. His childhood dream had been to be a soccer player, but he did not get any support. So now he encourages the dreams of kids like him, who come from the school of hard knocks.

Mustafa had his own share of hard knocks, growing up in the middle of Europe, in Amsterdam. He lives in a place that stands in stark contrast to the tourist images of the Netherlands – of tulips, clogs and quaint buildings – another reality, in a neighbourhood called Slotervaart which has become a self-titled Dutch Moroccan ghetto.

This is the neighbourhood of the notoriously unrepentant Mohammed Bouyeri, the murderer of Theo van Gogh, who had made a film which projected quotes from the Koran onto women's naked bodies, in protest at women's treatment in Islam. This is the neighbourhood, Mustafa claims, that politicians come to when they hold press conferences about the problems of immigration and integration in the Netherlands. It is often cited as the flashpoint for the conflict between the Islamic community and the Dutch.

Mustafa walks the street where Bouyeri was raised. It comes off Piet Mondrianstraat, named for the Dutch painter who did grid-like portraits of nature. Only here are grids with thousands of people stuffed into flats. This is not the centre of Amsterdam, with its exquisite old buildings on the canals, dating back to the time when Rembrandt wandered about. And it is not where you see the modern, bold steel and glass Dutch architecture. Here, drab might be the word.

Yet a new condominium is being built in the one section of grass left where the boys previously played soccer. These are boys, like the young Mustafa, who dream of life in a professional football club, in Spain perhaps, or even with the local beloved Ajax! On the construction site, a billboard shows a smiling blond Dutch couple in their new flat. It stands amidst the graffiti written on the buildings, women with their heads covered, and kids who bounce their black and white balls off the walls of the buildings.

Yet, strangely, Slotervaart borders Rembrandt Park, which is large, green and empty in comparison. On the other side is the Dutch community. The gap between the two areas seems similar to the one Mustafa says exists between the Moroccans and the Dutch. This is a gap that many in the Netherlands claim is impossible to bridge, especially the politicians on the far right.

Mustafa too feels hopeless sometimes, listening to the 'same problems, the same song they've been playing every day for the last ten years'. Unlike many of the well-meaning Dutch people who come to assist from outside, he says he understands what the young men and boys in the area feel like. 'I used to be a problem child. I have seen this prison and that prison. I know the system from inside and outside. So I know what these guys feel, what they think, why they make problems. I know because I used to be one of them. And ten years ago, I was much worse.'

A little over ten years ago, in 1998, after an altercation between a Moroccan teen and a police officer, there were violent clashes between the young men and boys in the area and the police. The issues of integration and the failures of Muslims within the Netherlands became the hot issue in the country. Mustafa, the leader of a well-known criminal gang, was involved in these violent incidents.

Years later, in October 2007, Mustafa would be involved in similar events, but now it was as a social worker trying to release the younger neighbourhood kids from their own mental jails before they ended up needlessly in real prisons.

The first time I met him, he was sporting a bald head, as if to look like the arch-criminal. A few months later he had a full head of dark curly hair, a far softer look. He is a wiry, intense young man with sharp features who walks and talks quickly, as if he has too much to accomplish and too little time. This quality could also be called enthusiasm.

We first met on an evening late after Ramadan Iftar, breaking the fast of the day. It was at a local café, over cakes and the special Moroccan sweet mint tea that is taken particularly by the older men and women of the area. Mustafa began to tell his story, which I got to know in further detail over the next couple of years.

Born in the Netherlands into a Moroccan immigrant family, Mustafa felt he belonged to neither society. 'Here in this neighbourhood, and all of Holland,' he says, 'it felt and feels like "we are we and you are you".'

The Moroccans and Turks first came to the Netherlands in the 1960s and 1970s, as 'guest workers'. Unlike their schooled, French-speaking counterparts from the cities, most of the Moroccans who emigrated here were Berbers, indigenous mountain people from the

Mustafa Akka

north and south. This was also true of Mustafa's parents, who first lived on the other side of Amsterdam, in the east. But they soon migrated to Slotervaart.

At that time, it was a middle-class and mixed neighbourhood. 'I came here when I was six or seven years old. But it felt like I was born here, because I was so young when we came. Then the area was very mixed – Dutch people, Moroccan people, Surinam people and everything. And it was nice to grow up here.'

But as Mustafa grew up, the area became a Moroccan enclave as the other communities moved out. Ironically, it was among his own ethnic group that his difficulties began. It wasn't the Dutch or the Surinamese who bullied Mustafa. They were gone. 'It was my own people,' he points out with a laugh.

The one thing that could have saved him from the bullying was his dream. As a boy his ambition was to play football professionally, and he would go out on the streets to learn what he could. But he had to do it on the sly. 'I didn't go to a club because my parents didn't want me to. I was asthmatic, and they were afraid I would get an attack. So they didn't stimulate me to play because they didn't have the knowledge that there were a lot of medical things that could let you play.'

Unable to display his football prowess publicly, and because of his family's poverty, Mustafa got picked on quite heavily. 'When I was being raised here, they judged you on your appearance, what clothes you had, what shoes you had, what your hair was like. It started when I was really small that they began to bully me, the guys who were with me in the same class.'

Isolated from the wider Dutch community yet bombarded with the same advertisements, it was even more crucial to have the right brand of clothes or sneakers. 'I was different. I used to wear second-hand clothes. My father, always at work, was a concierge at a hospital. He tried his best, but he had eight children. So it was not possible for him to buy the best of the best.

'I didn't lack love. But I didn't want to tell him those things about bullying. I had three sisters. But you cannot take your sisters to fight for you. And I didn't have a bigger brother who could protect me. I didn't have any back-up.

'What I learned was always to stand up. For me still, there is no turning back. There is always forward. So I started fighting with the bullies. Usually there were two, three or four of them, and I was one. They made fun of me, and they laughed at me. From first to sixth grade, the bullies beat me. For six years, it was really hell.'

And at the beginning of his teenage years, life didn't get any easier. 'When I was 12, or 13, I went to a bigger school. I learned a lot of things. I learned what love is. I fell in love with a girl. But she didn't love me back. I didn't have the clothes that she wanted to see. Or the shoes.'

At this point, even without the right shoes, Mustafa was a decent student, but he was still being bullied. 'My first and second year I was really good. I had good numbers.'

He continued to improve his skills as a soccer player too. 'The street and older boys from the neighbourhood taught me. There was a neighbour who used to play for Ajax and used to teach us skills. We used to play street against street. We'd buy a bottle of Coca Cola, and the winning team would get that.'

At 13 or 14, Mustafa even joined an amateur football club and, against his parents' wishes, improved his skills even further. But the conflict between Mustafa the good student/soccer dreamer and the bad boy lured by the streets grew.

'The third year I spent more time on the street and got to know some neighbourhood boys. Then it was finito. From then on I was going only backwards, not forwards.'

He quit school and embarked on a life on the streets. Because finally he was able to get his own back: he got his own gang.

'From 15 till 20, I lived on the street. For me, the gang was my life. I think it was the feeling they gave me, because I was with five, six boys. We were unstoppable. There was no fear. All the guys who bullied me before, when I got older and crazier, I got them each, one at a time. I really made it hell for them in the area. They paid me, and now I wanted it back with interest.'

As a 'bully banker', Mustafa became a notorious tough guy in the neighbourhood. 'In no time, I was really respected. When you've got status, a lot of people want to hang with you, girls, you know what I mean? I became a lover boy. I experienced drugs, alcohol, women.' Yet his religious parents stayed by him, even as he strayed from their Islamic values. 'When I got fucked up, they still tried to help me or reach out.'

As he hit 16 and then 17, he drank more and more alcohol and got into marijuana and hash, though he claims he wasn't into anything harder. Most importantly for him, he was always one of the leaders of the gang as it grew. He made sure he maintained that position, and that his gang had 'respect'. He still played soccer in the amateur club, but that dream now came second most of the time.

'We had to defend the street, to defend our honour. When we went out, if somebody made jokes or tried to be bigger than me, I had to be bigger than them. It was really important nobody was ever going to bully me again. So when I saw it was going to escalate, I was always the first one to punch. Why? If he punched me, maybe I would bleed in my nose or get a bad eye, but I would teach the guys, "Be the first one. Don't back off. If they are 30 and you are five, you back up and you come back with 30, no problem."

'We didn't use knives or pistols. We had the old book – "mano a mano", with the hands, no weapons. When somebody picked up a gun and pointed it at us, we just laughed. It was confirmation that he was chicken shit. Because if you're a man, you don't fight with a gun or knife. You fight with your hands.'

But it wasn't just getting drunk, high, getting back at bullies or fighting with others on the street that Mustafa got into. 'I had no work. So I started criminal activities. I began with small things like car radios. Then I began to do bigger things, motorcycles, cars. And after cars, even bigger things. I ended up between the buyer and the supplier, the middleman. And I was really making big bucks, as a middleman.

'There was nothing that could stop us. We didn't fear the police. We had good contact with the police. Because they wanted to know who we are? No, because we wanted to know who *they* are. We wanted to know what car they were driving. We wanted to know everything. Because when we were doing things, we had to beware.

'Now these youngsters, they want to do criminal activities, but they don't do research. We weren't like that. We sometimes spent two, three months observing and preparing for the day. And we did big things. We didn't do things for 50 or 100 euro. We were a big group. What were we going to do with so little money? We did things for ten, fifteen, twenty thousand.

'We broke into people's houses. We broke into big companies. But,' Mustafa claims, 'we didn't steal from the poor.

'There was a moment that I wanted to stop. But my problems were still running close behind me. And any time there was something happening in these areas, because I had a reputation, the police'd always come to me. "You had to be there, because you are one of the leaders of the gang. So you had to be responsible." And a lot of times they'd fine me or keep me in custody for a week or five days. They said, "If we can get you on a single thing, we're going to lock you up for years."'

At the age of 18, he did get a chance to leave the life he was leading, to fulfil his dream of playing football. 'When I was 18 years old, I was still a good soccer player. I wanted to get out of this world. And I got the chance. Even though my mother worried these places were too far, I went to Spain and Belgium, to do professional trials. I got accepted to both clubs. So I was going to earn a lot of money.

'But my mother got breast cancer. And it spread through other parts of her body. At the club where I did the try-outs, there were two players, me and another guy. And they chose me. But the position had to be filled. And there was only a certain amount for one player. So I went and saw my mother, who had just been operated on. I stayed with her three months, and I went back to the club. And they told me, "I'm sorry, maybe next year. You're a very good player, but we don't have the money."

'So I went back and I played with amateur clubs. And my mother went every day to the hospital. I left football outside, and I spent time with my mother because I was afraid she would die. She was my mother. But I didn't leave the gang. I was still in the group. After a year, I was 19, almost 20. I wanted to play soccer again but then I got an injury.'

As he points out now, keeping his soccer skills up by going out until seven o'clock in the morning on a Saturday night and then trying to play his best at noon on Sunday didn't work too well. His dreams of getting out through football remained unsupported – even by him. He retreated to the gang. They at least listened to him.

'I could tell the group what I feel, that the opportunity I had was gone, and my mother was very sick. Maybe I should have talked about it to somebody who was much older than me. But it got only worse, because I started to do more alcohol, sometimes drugs, and marijuana.'

The worse it got with his mother, the worse it got with Mustafa. He used the gang as a crutch. And contrary to his Islamic upbringing, alcohol became a mainstay of his life. 'I was really an addict. Twenty years old and I had to drink. When I woke up, it was first a cigarette, then it was outside, and we started drinking. All day every day. For me, alcohol was an object to forget all the problems I had on the streets, at home and with my mother. And I had a girlfriend who also was crazy.

'At this point, I had given up on life. With all my feelings and problems, I thought, if death comes, thank you. For me, it was till 6 am outside, and then go home, sleep and wake up at 5 pm. I thought, "You don't have nothing. Football is gone. Education, gone. The police have got you, so you have a record, so you cannot work."'

At this point, Mustafa might have ended up just another troubled young Moroccan man who the politicians could point to as the problem with *those people*, who contribute to the crime and the high unemployment rates in the community. But then two things happened. The first was that a friend of his died from a drug overdose.

'The friend of mine who overdosed, he overdosed on the same problems as me but he couldn't handle them. Me, I have always been a fighter. And the spirit I have inside tells me, "Moose, don't give up. There's always a door that can open somewhere else." He'd begun with drugs and booze. But then he took pills and cocaine. But there was one day where he mixed a lot of pills with booze. And also cocaine, very dangerous. When my friend died, I was tired. And I had seen the whole process.'

At this point Mustafa felt, like his friend, that he had little to live for. Yet seeing his friend die affected him. 'I started to hate myself. And I saw all the guys in the area who were doing great – car, driver's licence, some of them married – and I thought, I want to achieve those things. But that was very difficult because the group was always leaning on me. I was the engine.'

The second thing that happened was an arrest charge that could have kept him in prison for a good long while. Yet of all the crimes he was accused of, this was one of the only ones he hadn't committed.

'I was 21, the last time the police got me. And the accusation was attempted murder. There was a guy who got a beating. He got a beating from maybe a hundred youngsters in our area. I was there, but I did not touch him with one finger. I was there, because it was people from my area, area against area. But all the witnesses said my name was the first. Luckily, he lived. But he was in the hospital. All the bones were broken. He was in a coma. So maybe that was lucky for me.

'At six o'clock, I was still asleep. And the police came to get me. The neighbours were looking. My mother was very angry. And my father. I got into the prison cell, and I thought, "Is this what I want?" I thought, "When I get out, I'm going to make something of my life." Although I had a lot of things that I learned from the gang and things we did together – we cried, we laughed, like we were one person – I had to give it up. And the police file on me was like this.' Mustafa holds his hands far apart. 'They had 20 dossiers on me.'

When the police released him a week or two later, he couldn't believe he was free to go. 'They said, "You can go home." I went, "What?" They said, "Yeah, you may go home." I thought they were joking. So when they let me out, I ran to the tram. I was afraid they would tell me they had made a mistake.

'And I thought, "I won't go home. They'll go there and pick me up." So I went to my uncle's. I sat there two or three hours, and I phoned home. Nothing. So then I went home.

'From that moment, I chose to back out from the gang. After I made the decision to leave, the group came every day to my house. When I was on the street, they came to me. When I was at work. I told them, "This life is not for us. What do you want? To be a crack addict, eventually end up in prison or die? Let's make something of our life."

'And out of the gang, there are two people from the group who really made it. The other guys are still alcoholic, still using, still damaged. And if I see the youngsters we used to be and the talents we had, we did nothing with that talent.'

Mustafa's discipline of only looking forward stayed with him. He began to work. He got a job, a job helping others.

'I got an opportunity to work where I could drive sick people to the hospital. For six years, I worked only with old people and youngsters who had AIDS, cancer, or need dialysis for the kidney. And I really began to appreciate life. Because me, I had been really fucking up my body. I saw babies born with cancer to a young woman who had no breasts. But when I saw that somebody was praying to God every day, or Allah, for a month more, because his kidney or his heart or the cancer was spreading out, that made me another man.

'I got really satisfied because I was paying back. I was not only driving the person to the hospital but was talking about the problems. Many of the old people were in care houses. And their children came only one time in a year to see if they were alive or dead. When I came to pick them up, they would tell me this was the first time in three or four months they'd even gone outside. So I'd go and make extra rounds. I tried to be better – for them. I took my work very seriously. And did not forget I could be the last one who had meaning in their life for them.'

But on his own time, he began trying to help local youngsters. He didn't want them to make the same mistakes he had made.

After getting some training as a social worker, he got a job with one of the Stichtings – non-profit organisations. In the past he has criticised them for bringing in too many outsiders with no experience of the community to work with the Moroccan youth. But because he was of the community, Mustafa could really listen to what it was the youth needed. That was his special skill.

Even now as he walks around the neighbourhood, it's noticeable how many young boys greet him, speaking to him about this problem or that, wanting his attention, as if he were their older brother – unlike many who made it. 'What I always see when a girl or guy of my own roots makes it in the world, they don't look back. And I always look back where I started. I will never forget where I come from. And I will always pay back to the person who's standing beneath, behind, at the top or the bottom where I was.'

He even began to feel sorry about having gone after the bullies who had made his life hell when he was growing up. He tried to make peace with them, even though bullying is something he still gets angry about – especially now he has children of his own. But most importantly, he felt he understood why the young boys would join a gang.

'The gang made me realise how vulnerable we are. I went to the group because they satisfied my needs. And my needs were that I was lonely. So I chose the wrong things, the fast and easy things.'

In response to the question of why people become criminals, he says, 'Criminal activities are very easy. And to join a gang is not hard.'

The riots of October 2007 began with a 14-year-old Turk who stabbed a 16-year-old Moroccan in the neck at school, killing him. Then a 20-year-old Moroccan boy jumped over the desk in the Slotervaart police station and stabbed a policewoman three times. Soon, neighbourhood boys were throwing stones at the police station, and at journalists as a media circus ensued.

Mustafa didn't take part in the riots of 2007, but did what he could to prevent them escalating. The police who used to come after him for every crime now came to him for assistance. 'Everybody was really nervous and hoping that it was not somebody from the neighbourhood who had got killed. But the next day the police came out, and they said it was a boy from Moroccan roots who got killed. So that was really like a bomb in the neighbourhood again.

'For me, it was important that it wouldn't get bigger. And through my job, I tried to do something. I talked with the mosque and other organisations in the neighbourhood. We worked together to calm down the people. We gave a press conference with the police to tell what happened, and someone from the government came and told what happened. And someone from the mosque translated for the people who don't understand Dutch. But people were allowed to ask questions; we said now is the moment to ask. So we wouldn't get a lot of untrue stories.

'I worked the whole day here and then went on the streets from 6 pm till 4 am talking with the lads to calm them down. Four cars got burned, and yes, they threw the rocks at the police station, but from there that was it.'

However, as in 1998 the press did point out that the riots re-affirmed the problem with Moroccan youth. But the problem as Mustafa sees it has to do with not just the youth, but how they and the whole neighbourhood are seen.

'This is an area where 20,000 people live. And yet we'll see the area like it's nothing, because there are 50 bad youngsters. It was an accident that happened and some boys use it to do their thing. They don't know how to control their emotions. And for a lot, they're just going with the gang. They don't know how to identify themselves. Are we Dutch? Are we Moroccan? Are we Amsterdammers? Are we Muslim? And then these kids hear, oh it's a Moroccan boy *bom bom bom* ... But he has born here. He lives here. The roots may be from Morocco. But he could not even live in Morocco. He's a Dutch boy.'

When asked if what he does is effective with young people, and why, Mustafa says, 'I think my strength is that I used to be one of them. So I can talk easily about the problem with them. And they know my background, which is also for them an icebreaker. For them it's easy to start talking.'

And for Mustafa to listen, and use whatever skills he has to help. More importantly, as he says, he's there for the long haul. 'When I promise something, I always commit on the promise. When I say I'll do something for you, I'll do it. But it's a process. How I work, it's five years sometimes.

'What I experienced when I was young was that most organisations fail because they have a project, they help the boy or the girl for a year and then it ends. When I help, I help you until you don't want the help anymore. Until you don't need it. If you want me to help you until you're married, no problem. I will help you. And after that, I'll still be your friend.

'A lot of these youngsters don't have somebody who they can lean on. If you see the parents, sometimes they don't have contact with them, even though they live at the house. I try not only to be a professional but a friend. And what I see, and the years I have worked with youngsters has proved it, when you give confidence to a youngster and show that you are always prepared to help him, eventually it gets better. Because you don't only confront them with the help but with a better life.'

Now, to encourage youngsters in their dreams, Mustafa has started an organisation called Ara Cora. He is taking his soccer skills and sharing them with the young people in the neighbourhood. 'I have a guys' team and a girls' team. A lot of youngsters have a dream to be a professional. Some of them make it, and some of them don't. Some of them make it and also fall down because they don't have the mentality.'

But Mustafa's programme comes with a caveat. 'If you're good, we put you in some team and eventually what you have to do back is you have to do community service. That's the price you have to pay back for us.

'We're going to help you. If you have problems, we're going to solve them for you. Because we work with the organisations that have the things that can help them – money, school, things – and we're going to use football to pull them with us, and teach them about mentality, team building, discipline and respect. We're going to show them if your trainer says you have to do that, you do it. Without giving a big mouth.' Something Mustafa claims he knows all about. 'And *we* can say that, but the trainer can't say that. Because our guy acts very *great;* he's going to say, fuck you man. I can play everywhere. This is the ego they have.

'So we're going to help them and also try to get them to give back.

The organisation keeps growing rapidly, and two players have already made it to professional teams. More importantly, Ara Cora is a place to learn life skills as well. The youth have to clean up the neighbourhood, among other tasks.

'For me, the young lads here in this neighbourhood are much more important than even my life. They are the roots of our society. Maybe there's even a mayor here between these guys, or a pilot or a lawyer. You don't know. Because 15 years ago, everybody was saying Mustafa was going to die or go to prison. And now, 15 years later, I have a good job, a good reputation, and I'm still climbing the stairs. So everything can happen.'

We go out for lunch at a local eatery with a friend of Mustafa's, a young man with whom he works, who founded the Ramadan festival that takes place every year trying to reach out to the wider Dutch community. This is the festival at which an orchestra made up of Arabs and Israelis played on stage. It is the festival through which I met Mustafa in the first place. The two of these young men and I share mint tea and they treat me to lunch, in between talking enthusiastically about their projects. They are not concerned about my being Jewish and their being Muslim. Mustafa's only concern is that my belly is getting a bit bigger than necessary. He says that, given time, he could design a work-out for a flat stomach for me. He points out that for the time being, to make a good impression on a woman, it's a good idea if I suck in my stomach so that at least it seems flatter.

Today it's not only the young people that Mustafa continues to work with, but also the elderly from his first days of doing social work. He helps them achieve their goals as well. One group of elderly Moroccans in the community wanted to see for themselves what had happened during the Holocaust, having heard so much about it both in the European and their own world. They also wanted to make a conciliatory gesture after so much bad will between Jews and Muslims. They took a trip to the concentration camp in Auschwitz, and Mustafa was the sole young person accompanying them. What they saw shook them, and him. They met Jewish survivors and visitors from all over the world. Mustafa says the experience opened him and the older generation in ways he could not have foreseen. And it gave him even more impetus to work with the young people, to help them achieve a worthwhile future.

When asked what he gets out of the work he does with youth outside of his job, he says, 'Materially, nothing. But what I get emotionally – you know what pays me off? When I see the boy or the girl that I helped is doing great in society. That is for me the pay-off. For me, there is no greater feeling than to see that the guy or the girl that I help are doing good. When I see somebody has a good place in society that is my pay-off and my greatest achievement.'

The same is true with regard to his own aspirations of a career in soccer; creating the kind of support for others that he didn't have is like getting his own dream fulfilled. 'It was not about a lack of soccer skills, because if I had the opportunity or chance I would have made it. The only problem was that I was not being stimulated or encouraged to reach the level I could have. So I know with these youngsters what the traps are for them. So with my experience, I tell them if you don't do this, you can end up like a lot of players who don't make it. I didn't make it. But if I see youngsters who have the skills, if they make it, it's like the missing puzzle in my life. It's like I'm getting my professional career.

'Until 20, I was still dreaming like everybody. But now I'm 30. So if these kids can do it, it will be like my dream too.'

From nightmares to dreams in a dying town

Brenda Gregg

When she was in her mid-thirties, Brenda Gregg seemed to have everything she had wanted since childhood: she had a full life in her Baptist church, a minister for a husband, a son, and a good job. Then, as her marriage turned more abusive, she discovered her spouse of 17 years was having numerous sexual affairs – with men, and her son's life descended into a hell of addiction. 'I went through disbelief, wondering, "Why am I having to experience this craziness?" And God just said, "Why not?"'

Now 59, Brenda has been an ordained minister for 25 years, and is a pastor in an African Methodist Church in inner-city Pittsburgh. For many years she was also a manager at Children's Hospital. In these two positions, she focuses on encouraging a community rendered hopeless in an economic wasteland. 'People come into the hospital under stress. And you see the same thing in the church. What I do is link with people at their weakest times, because people are hungry for something other than what their daily lives lead us into.'

A striking, light-brown-skinned woman with a big smile and long locks, Brenda lives in a two-storey red brick house near where she grew up in the Braddock area in Pittsburgh. It's in a well-kept neighbourhood on a hill, only blocks from the boarded-up buildings on the main street below.

An example of her work is on that desolate street, where all the doors of the shops have long been shut. But inside one of them is a warm room filled with children playing with handcrafted educational toys. It's a Montessori preschool she has created, a system normally available only to the rich. 'Poor people should have choices,' says Brenda. 'I think we'd all be surprised at how strong people are with the right support and encouragement.'

Brenda Gregg was born in 1949 in Newport, Tennessee. Her family moved to Braddock, Pittsburgh just before her sister was born three years later. The town in the fifties was booming, just like the steel industry it served. For years, Main Street teemed with busy stores, and the elegant old stone banks did a solid business. Braddock even featured the first public library ever built in Pennsylvania, paid for by the 19th-century steel baron Andrew Carnegie.

Although segregation was firmly in place across the United States, the community here was mixed. 'This was the fifties. Pittsburgh was a mill town. So African-Americans did pretty well, because they all worked in the mill.'

The mix gave her a unique perspective, she says, that people had more similarities than differences. 'My next-door-neighbour was a Navajo Indian. We called her Granny and spent a lot of time at Granny's house eating rolls. Her granddaughter became my best friend. Then there was an African-American family where they had 13 children. In our family, it was just my sister and I. So we'd love to go there. And there were white families all over the street.'

Brenda Gregg

Brenda's father continued to work in the steel industry, even as it began to fade. 'My father worked in the steel mill some 30-odd years. And my mother worked in what was then called Westinghouse Electric in a factory, then ended up in healthcare. But every Saturday morning, my mother went to the thrift shop. She came home with bags of clothes. And she sewed and made us dresses. We all lived that way, not trying to be rich but having a comfortable place to lay our heads and be happy on the inside.'

What Brenda loved growing up was going to church, especially with her maternal grandfather. A Baptist preacher, he was Brenda's role model, along with her grandmother, who 'walked in ministry with him'.

'We always travelled to church with him, because he always had very small congregations out in the rural areas. It would take us hours to get to church. I just learned to do almost everything. You'd have to sing in the choir. You'd have to usher, collect the offering, and read the announcements. So I always knew I wanted to do something in ministry.'

As he grew older, her grandfather's preaching days grew fewer in number, but Brenda continued to go to the church nearby where he was a member. Every week, back home, she would watch through the large picture window to see when he would come down to the house with the church lesson in his back pocket. 'Now that we were older and we weren't going to church with him, he would test us. "What was the Sunday school lesson? Luke 15? What did it say?" That was the beginning of my loving the scriptures and wanting to share it or share the faith with someone else.

'At that time, church was our whole life. If you were going to have friends, they came either from your neighbourhood or from the church. If you were going to date, you dated somebody from the church.' She laughs. 'Or you weren't going to be able to see them.'

Times grew harder as she grew into a teenager. 'That's when the poverty happened. They began closing the mills. Everything changed in Pittsburgh. People felt like they didn't know what to do. They were used to making top dollar. But they had no education. So then there was a lot of drinking, a lot of addiction. A lot of that came from the depression of just not being able to take care of your family anymore.

'By the time I got out of high school, the mills were closed, '68. It was bleak.

'I was fortunate. My dad could at least always build something, as his family were architects. So he would leave and go to Tennessee and send money home so we could live.'

Fortunate or not, she began her first revolt, not understanding why her dad's word was law just because he was a man. 'Dad was the chief, and my mom treated him that way. Nobody talked back to him. Nobody challenged him at the dinner table.

'But I did. My dad would look shocked that anyone would go up against him, like, "Who are you not to agree with me?"'

In church, Brenda got to know a young minister named William Ernest, and she continued to date him after graduating from high school. 'I didn't think that I was going to preach from the pulpit. I always thought my ministry was going to be connected to the person I was married to. And because I had seen my grandfather and grandmother walk in agreement in ministry, I always thought I would marry a preacher.

'In fact, I probably married my husband because he was a minister,' she says, laughing loudly. 'Growing up in the same church, there was an expectation that he and I would get married. I married two weeks from being 20.'

However, over the early years of their life together she began to realise how little income her minister husband made. 'So I needed employment. I had worked in a supermarket in high school but was looking for a full-time job. Because my mom and sister had worked in a hospital, I was intrigued by Children's Hospital. My first job at Children's was in the library, medical records. But I found out that I'd rather work with people and ended up in finance, then years later, eventually, management. While I was working there, I went to college. I stayed two and a half years at the hospital, until I had my son.'

Meanwhile, William Ernest, or Will, went from job to job, with no salary from the church. As times had become worse, the community could not afford to pay their minister. So Brenda began working again at Children's Hospital.

Several years into their marriage, as their son was growing, she felt she too had the call to become a preacher. Though their marriage was troubled, she acknowledges that Will was supportive of the idea – at first. 'I said, "I think I'm to preach." And he said, "I'm not surprised." He was supportive. I think he saw me doing it anyhow, as I was helping him in the ministry.

'But he didn't expect that I would then want to be ordained. So when I said to him, "I need to be ordained," he said, "For what?" He had been brought up that way. And one uncle, who was also a minister, told my husband, "*I* wouldn't license her." But Will said to him, "Well, I will, because I think she really does have a call."'

As a woman, Brenda found it hard to find role models for her work as a pastor. She remembers hosting a women's conference and being chastised by the other women for 'shaking her body' to Amy Grant pop songs while wearing an aerobics outfit. It seemed she had to give up her femininity if she wanted to be a pastor.

But her feelings about her desirability came under attack closer to home, in her own marriage. 'It was always something in terms of Will's job and what he liked and what he didn't like. Then he got mean because he couldn't get settled within himself.'

He began to abuse her and their son. At first, it was just verbally, but then it became physical. 'That affected my son. He had a real hard time. And my husband, when I would challenge him on anything, couldn't handle that. Like my father, except my dad was a good provider.'

Will started going out in the evenings. Where to, she didn't know. What she didn't realise was that he was staying out during the day as well. 'I'd thought he was working. So then I was waiting for a check to come in. And guess what? The check wouldn't be there. But he'd still get up and take me to Children's, and say he's going to work.

'It got so crazy at the end, I did not know where he was going. And that got scary for me. But it turned out he didn't have a type of drug or drinking problem. He had a sexuality problem.'

The Baptist minister was out having multiple affairs with men.

Having been told homosexuality was wrong in her faith, and having no experience with the gay community, Brenda thought that she was responsible for the decline of her marriage. She wrestled with whether to stay.

'I was home one evening, thinking I don't know where Will is, what he's doing, who he's with. My son was about 14. Finally I had a road to Damascus experience: that it was time to go. I made a decision that it would be easier for me to go than for Will to find a life. And this way, my son would not have to leave his school.

'So I left. I was very much ashamed that my marriage was not making it. Though I had told my sister about our problems, I didn't even tell my mom until I showed up at her door and said, "I need a place to stay today."

It was only seven years later, after far more turbulence with her son, that she dared to ask for a divorce. She was still ashamed; no one in her family had ever had a divorce, and Will still would not admit to being homosexual. 'Until he left Pittsburgh and moved in with a man.'

Brenda says her instinct to leave proved to be a lifesaver. 'For me, that Damascus appearance had been, "You must leave and you must do it now." But why, I didn't know until later, when he got AIDS. If I had not have left when I did, I might have gotten it too.'

When Will died in Virginia, it was his male lover who had been caring for him. At the memorial service, the attending pastor did not even know who Brenda was. He only realised that her name was related to William's. The stigma was such that, later, when her ex-husband was buried in Pittsburgh, this pastor pretended Will and Brenda were still married. This was when Brenda discovered her church community would not discuss the epidemic that had taken her ex-husband's life.

Back when she had left her husband, the cumulative effects of the abuse and the separation had taken a toll on her son. He became addicted to crack cocaine at the age of 15. 'The thing that I regret most is not being able to help my son in all this. I oftentimes wonder if I had've stayed longer in the marriage, if I could have gotten him through school. At that time, I knew nothing about drugs or alcohol. And because of his addiction, he never went to college or university. And my son is still struggling. He really is.

'It's probably one of my motivators. And that motivates me with all the kids that I work with. Because I know my son in both states. I know what kind of kid he is when he's okay. But a lot of people only see drug users in their addicted state. If you actually knew who they were, you wouldn't see them that way. So it's given me a hope to be able to see people whole rather than just addicted.'

When her son got his girlfriend pregnant, twice, Brenda adopted his daughters. 'I got Alicia before she was a year old. And Brianna I adopted when she was 16 months old. The mother had addiction issues as well, and had eight children.'

At the time, Brenda found herself anything but encouraged. 'I'd never expected to be a divorced woman. I struggled with a son who had addiction. And then I adopted two children. Sometimes I felt like I needed personal support.' She sometimes even doubted the one thing that had kept her going through all her earlier troubles: her own faith.

But Brenda says, 'Life goes on. Always the issue is, when you go through a crisis, can you get back up on your feet?'

She left the Baptists and joined the African Methodist Episcopalian movement, where she was also ordained. 'I stumbled across the African Methodist church. Then eventually I was asked to pastor.

'My first church was in a very small community outside the city. The second was the suburbs. Then I was appointed to a church in the inner city on the north side of Pittsburgh with lots of issues.'

To add to her own difficulties, she had taken over a church with seemingly insurmountable problems. 'It was in a little place called Manchester. The first few weeks I was there, there was gang violence, a killing up the street. And houses were torn all around. It was chaos, and people were afraid.

'And here was this little brick church in the middle of the park. When I got there, I ended up preaching to 15 people sitting there. The only young person was someone's grandchild. I thought this was crazy. I was in a community where there are kids all around. And I asked myself, "What was I doing here?"' She laughs.

But it was here that she began to find her own calling and a new way of approaching hope. 'Was I going to go in and do church as usual? What was the reason I was sent there? I began learning that doing for others could take my eyes off myself and my own situation.'

She began to ask what the families in the neighbourhood needed. What were they looking for? What should the church be doing? And the first response was that they wanted a safe place for their children to play after school. There was none in the neighbourhood.

'We listened. We didn't want to just be a church that I call "Sunday Morning Live". You know, a church that's alive Sunday morning and then you close your doors.

'So I opened up our church and said, "This is a place your children can come." And one of the first things we did was begin an after-school programme. Then we did a Saturday service, where kids could come and do untraditional things as well. Like let's push the tables out of here,' she says with a smile, 'and let's dance down in the church basement.'

As her congregation began to grow, she took the issues that had killed her own husband – about sexuality, and condoms for young people – into her church. And she began to wrestle with authorities. 'The first time I brought somebody in to teach the kids about AIDS and safe sex, I was told, "People are not dying of AIDS in this community." They said, "So why are you talking to young people and young adults about sexual issues? And is that the church's place?"

'Soon after, a young man came to our church and started talking about his own life; we found out that he had been brought up in Manchester. He had left for years and came back when he was very sick, and eventually he died of AIDS. His name was Greg. We became very close.

'And he taught us more in his short period of time of what a church should be and what I should be doing than anyone else. He taught us that we should be there as support to people, to encourage them, no matter what the issues are. If we say the church is a hospital for people's issues, then we've got to be ready when they come to us.'

Brenda's church began to reach out even to the people who caused the violence in the community. People who had served time in prison found a home there. In turn, Brenda mentored their children. There were people struggling with drug addiction, 'I mean really struggling with it. I have no doctors in my congregation. I have no attorneys, but I do have teachers, social workers.

'And now,' she says proudly, 'the congregation on the roll is about eleven hundred.' From a starting point of 15.

Her new way of looking at things from her church affected her work at Children's Hospital too. She no longer just played the role of a manager. 'I didn't set out to be a trailblazer, but I do ministry a little differently. And with my healthcare background, I'd always seen the tie with healthcare, wholeness and spirituality. At the hospital, people took care of your body but not your mental issues. So it was almost my gift to do this kind of work.'

Beyond being part of the community and African-American, unlike most of the management, she had a more important gift. 'I listened. And poor people often either don't have a voice or no one listens to them.' In very poor areas the authorities, she believes, think they know what everybody needs without listening. To save money, for example, they don't want to replicate any services, and they offer only one option to those in the community. But, says Brenda, 'Why couldn't poor people have choices?'

If they were given options, then they would have more possibilities from which to create their best education, their best healthcare system, their best job, or their best home – in other words, their dream.

Brenda says that at one point she and a doctor at Children's Hospital, Heidi Feldman, were concerned that mothers were not getting good early healthcare for their children in the main hospital. Sometimes they would bring the children in late for their appointments, and the doctors would take them to task. But, Brenda points out, the mothers were coming from far away, and often had to take two buses; if they missed one, they would wait an hour for the next. In the meantime, it was the health of the children that suffered.

Some of the mothers were also dealing with addiction. But, Brenda says, allowing that issue to define their lives runs contrary to her way of thinking. 'One issue shouldn't define your whole life and whole being. For example in Alcoholics Anonymous, they stand up and say, "I am an alcoholic."

'Well, I disagree with that. Say "I am a human being that has struggled with alcohol. But I don't define myself by my weakness. My strength is that I've been clean for four years."'

Brenda knew that each mother, even if she was addicted, still wished the best for her children. She and Dr Feldman came up with a different approach to the parenting problem. 'We thought, what if we started helping parents when kids were little? What if we went to the neighbourhoods where there were the no-shows? Let's get a mother who is newly pregnant connected to healthcare and support, tying the psychosocial and the health needs. If you could tie parents in early to what was right for their kids, the teenage years would be better.'

They began creating Family Care Connection sites, support centres in the areas of need. Like those of the Aboriginal Medical Service in Australia, they are community-run. 'The parents take ownership of the centres and really provide leadership and mentorship to each other.'

Brenda points out how difficult it still is to find funding for these forms of prevention, or encouragement. Yet they are cheap compared to the costs of keeping people in prison or in emergency care in hospital. Echoing the thoughts of Siri and Alphonce, Brenda says that encouragement takes money, but it takes even more of something else.

'Encouragement takes time.

'So we determined we've got to stop and listen to some of these kids and mothers. In traditional healthcare, doctors give you five minutes. You come in; they read your chart. "What's the matter?" The workers that we have in these communities don't get paid a whole lot but, boy, are they worth what they do get paid.'

The Family Care Connection site closest to Brenda's heart is the one in Braddock, on that once-thriving main street that now lies empty. Literally every store appears closed. The only place where one can buy food is blocks away, a 'Dollar Store'. In it, there is no fresh produce, only processed food and frozen vegetables.

But in Brenda's centre, in a room to the side, a nurse shows a parenting-skills video to a group of women. These mothers seem young but weathered. They are single, and have come from a refuge to learn parenting techniques. Afterwards, they sit at a table together and share stories. Though the ravages of drugs and hard living are clear on their faces, there is a tangible warmth in the room. But as Brenda and her colleagues point out, today they are just young single mothers with the dream of raising their children better than they would otherwise be raised. That is why they are here.

Giving the place even more warmth, in a large room in the back, children play with various handmade wooden blocks. This is the new preschool, to get the kids ready for kindergarten. But it's not the sort of preschool one normally finds in a slum or beaten down area. It's that other dream of Brenda's, to enable the poor parents in this community to have the best choice for their children: a Montessori programme normally reserved for the rich.

Ironically, just as Brenda broke ground in her community as a female minister, Maria Montessori, the programme's founder, was one of Italy's first female doctors. The Italian physician started her programme with children labelled 'deficient and insane' and unfit for schooling. Yet within two years, they passed all the standard tests. She next put her ideas into practice for preschool children in the slums of San Lorenzo, on the outskirts of Rome, in 1908. A hundred years later, Brenda Gregg decided to do the same – in Braddock.

'I tried to find out what difference it can make in a kid's life. One example I liked was the peace rose. When I give you the rose, it's your turn to talk, and when you give it back to me it's my turn. And this flower could make a tremendous difference because there's so much violence around here.

'I was impressed with how kids were taught, and the inner strength they were trying to pull from kids rather than what's normally done, which is all about testing. And I thought, what if we took that into the inner city?'

Brenda has had to fight the city's ambivalence about 'duplicating services', as well as convince parents to pay just a little something towards the school. She says, 'I believe with freebies people don't appreciate it. If your child comes part-time and it's a hundred dollars a week, then pay 25. Cut out a few cups of coffee, cut down the cigarettes for a week.'

Since children now fill the room, parents must be switching to tea or improving their lungs.

Just as her dreams for her own church fed into her work with the community at Children's Hospital, so her role there fed right back into her community in Manchester. Her after-school venture, named Project Destiny, grew, and it mentored teenagers, especially teen mothers who didn't believe they could get into school. Through Children's Hospital, she developed a closer relationship with the Harber Charitable Foundation (HCF), an organisation focused on youth development worldwide and one of the funders of Family Care sites.

HCF had been looking for a place for inner-city children to get a break from their own situations for a while and grow by experiencing nature. The more Brenda and HCF worked together, the more they found they had in common. Together, they found an old farm which could be made into a camp.

But as Brenda has learned, nothing is that easy, and it all does take time. The legalities involved with that property were too extensive. However, subsequent conversations with HCF over time have improved the situation.

Together, they bought a warehouse in the midst of a troubled neighbourhood in the city, to take Project Destiny out of the basement and into the open air. Opened in February 2008, it is a space where neighbourhood children can learn art and dance, and about computers. And there is also some greenery nearby. 'This place wasn't cheap, but it was a small amount compared to what governments put into things like stadiums. And this will give more hope.'

With HCF, Brenda also created a partnership with the Pittsburgh Zoo, her sentiments echoing those of Wil and Flor with their animal farm. 'What would it mean if kids had a love for animals? Since people disregard life so much now, what would that mean? We've been looking at the African Painted Dog and how they care for each other and their family model, for instance. And the zoo will come here and do education about animals.'

Finally, together, the zoo, HCF and Project Destiny did find the right site for a nature reserve. Now the children will have the opportunity not just to get away but to see animals in the wild. The cabins are built now. 'We're taking the kids into a different environment. Even though it's only an hour and a half away, they're almost in a new world.'

When asked what people really get at Project Destiny, the Family Care Connection, and its Montessori programme, Brenda is clear. 'What are they getting? Hope. People need somebody in their lives that encourages them, who says you really can do something. It's a lonely place when you don't have anyone around you that says, "You're a pretty neat person." Who says, "No matter what your issues are, I like you. I may not like some stuff that you do, but I like you. And we can get through it."

'It's a long haul. The heart of mentoring is to be there, on your good days and bad days.'

Brenda no longer works with Children's Hospital; she spends more time developing Project Destiny as the need for its work continues to grow. But her own growth continues as well, with encouragement from unlikely places. 'I sit on the AIDS Task Force now. I have gotten to know so many people who have a lifestyle of homosexuality. And I think sometimes, "God, you have a real sense of humour. You're going to take a crazy experience that I've had and give me friends dealing with this stuff."'

Brenda enjoys her own lifestyle in her lovely home, a life where she is able to cook a pleasant breakfast for friends with plenty of sausages and biscuits to go around, while still being able to help others. 'I can't be in poverty and help. You can't be unhappy and expect people to be drawn to you or to what you do. Because there's no hope in that. But when you help others, you get a better life too.

'I am stronger than I would have ever imagined. Because I know that, I know people are a lot stronger than they can imagine. And I encourage people to let them know, no matter what, life goes on. Life goes on.'

Brenda's best example of encouragement comes from a very difficult case. A mother who had no connection to her own parents was living in endless temporary situations with two young daughters, aged five and six, and battling drug addiction. Then, to top it off, she and her children had seen a local taxi driver murdered. As a key witness, the mother was put into protective custody.

Though this woman's dream was that her two girls should be able to read, she had never even got them to school. Neither child could read at all. Brenda took the two children into her home. She got them into remedial school, and took the older one to a reading specialist. The children ended up staying with her for ten months.

In less than a year, the first-grader had learnt to read. Her favourite book is *Inside Mouse, Outside Mouse*. 'And,' Brenda says, 'even in the midst of her mom's craziness, when her mom saw her, she said, "My baby can read," and there were tears in her eyes.'

Brenda's eyes grow misty as well, as the phone rings. It is the two girls. They call every week now, a good year later, to let her know exactly what they are doing, encouraging her too.

Chapter 8

Why not just let government do it – or, what's wrong with Big Brother?

Which government is the best? The one that teaches
us to govern ourselves.
Johann Wolfgang von Goethe

Even after hearing these people's stories, you still might reasonably ask: why do individuals like Brenda, Siri, Alphonce or Paul need to help? Shouldn't we leave that to the government? Isn't taking care of people the government's job?

After all, in most countries, we pay taxes in varying forms: income tax, GST and VAT, sales tax, unemployment tax, social security tax, import duty, environmental taxes, export duty, petrol tax, airport taxes, and all the other taxes too numerous to mention. The money raised in this way should be enough to take care of everyone, certainly in developed economies.

So, if we notice a problem in society, can't we just notify the government and leave it at that?

When I put that question to the people whose stories I've told in this book, the answer was universal: laughter.

No one advocates anarchy. Even the rebel from Sudan, Idris, would just like a government that didn't kill its own people for a start. He agrees, with hope, that there are things government is good for, such as building roads and infrastructure, providing schools, police, courts, and yes, even collecting taxes. But there are things government cannot do. Especially, as is the case in Darfur, when the very people in power are the problem.

Government 101: Problems don't fix themselves

When Chung To discovered AIDS in China was killing villagers and orphaning their children in the tens of thousands, he didn't need to notify the authorities. They were already spying on him, and on the elderly doctor who was trying to help. It was the government that was trying to keep the issue quiet, because it had caused the problem in the first place by getting those very same villagers to donate blood and then accidentally infecting them.

When Supagon Noja first tried to help the street children, he found they were more scared of the government than the flesh peddlers trafficking and entrapping them. It took his organisation and others in the country to build trust between the kids and the authorities. They also had to help the authorities change their institutions so that they served the children's needs as opposed to just getting them off the street.

Alphonce Omolu's experience with the Kenyan government's handling of street children in Nairobi was even worse. Though the administration did establish a new outreach programme, Alphonce saw 'when you went to the ground, it was not practised the same way that it was talked. There was a lot of caning in the children's institutions. There was a lot of mistreatment of street children by the government security; sometimes they beat street children indiscriminately. Even while a senior officer was telling me that such acts are against the law. So a lot is said, but nothing happens.'

Wherever people's rights are violated by the authorities, whether in Kenya, the US, Australia, France, the UK, the Netherlands or Thailand, governments don't seem to act in accord with the people's needs, especially minorities. As Idris points out, the Sudanese government still claims no genocide is occurring in his country. During the years of apartheid in South Africa, the regime never highlighted its own crimes against its citizens.

Rather, as Rachel Wotton and Paul Pholeros point out, those in power mostly accuse the people they govern of being the problem. Aboriginal leader Naomi Mayers and her co-worker Dr John Daniels say, 'We keep hearing that Aboriginal people aren't ready for self-determination. But these things are slogans, perspectives from a self-fulfilling right-wing prophecy. But if we look at the Aboriginal Medical Service, we're the longest running aboriginal medical service in Australia. It's also the oldest generalist primary care service in the world. I don't think we have to prove the argument that Aboriginal people can manage our own affairs.'

In Pittsburgh, as Brenda Gregg points out, 'The city closed down a lot of the city pools. So where are the children going to go? It's not that the government doesn't have money. The question is where do they put it? In Pittsburgh, they put their dollars into stadiums.

'As a society, we invest in bricks and mortar. We don't invest in our kids. We don't invest in our people. Or else the jails wouldn't be filled with them. The whole issue in our neighbourhood with drugs has to do with economics. And we have not done anything about it, from the street level.'

Contradicting the oft-repeated US government claim to be waging a war on drugs, Brenda says, 'We don't have a war on drugs. We have a war on those who are addicted to drugs. We have a war on poor people.'

Government 102: Governments can be corrupt, self-serving, or at best slow ...

In Kenya, as in other areas of the developing world, the average wage is between one and two US dollars a day. An average Member of Parliament gets an annual salary of US$140,000 – that's US$383 a day, if he or she worked every day of the year without taking off weekends or holidays. So the people who govern the country make between 191 and 383 times the amount the average individual makes, without even taking into account the rorts that regularly make the front pages of the scandal sheets.

When such generous sums of money are available to pay the politicians, pleas for foreign aid may seem odd.

Alphonce comments, 'In our country, the MPs don't do much to improve people's lives. The economy is improving but only for the elite, who have the businesses, but not for the ordinary people. In a country where the economy is said to be growing by 7 per cent, the price of essential commodities continues to rise. So with the little money people do get, they are not able to buy the essential goods that they need for their daily life.'

He points out that it's a matter of taking the long view and, most importantly, helping the people to help themselves more directly. 'Any assistance given should not be to solving the problem of today, but establishing an environment where marginalised people are able to ask for their rights from the government. Over decades, people have voted along tribal lines, to the benefit of these same MPs. But once they become educated, are able to articulate their views and wield some power, governments may have to actually provide services.'

Sandra Meihubers reflects on the situation in Nepal, where she shares her dentistry skills. 'We normally come with our gear, and a local health post or school opens up a room. We deal with the local government health post. And they don't have a lot of resources and are not well funded.'

But in one village of 60 homes, the government official found his funding a different way. 'The guy took us into a little room out the back where there was a foul smell coming in the window. Outside was a terrific view, but it was the filthiest room I've ever worked in. There were rat droppings on the cupboards. He hadn't made any effort at all to prepare the room, even knowing we'd be coming to offer free care where people can't get access.

'But then I found out that this government guy was charging five rupees to each person coming in, for his office kitty!'

You might wonder, then, whether people like Sandra and Alphonce and the organisations they work with are in fact allowing bad governance to continue by taking on the responsibilities of governments, and lessening the fallout from their corruption. 'Are we taking over the responsibilities of government? We are in a way,' Sandra says. 'I don't know how we can get around that where I work, in remote areas. Because once you get to remote areas, everything just dries up. I don't know how we can overcome the inability of a lot of governments to distribute resources. And that's common around the world.'

Mel Young points out that governments aren't tackling the problems of the homeless, for example, as many are elected on a policy of low taxation. But then they claim they don't have the money to spend. 'And what gets cut? Welfare. Look no further than the United States of America for that. The United States of America, richest country in the world, three million homeless people on the street. Every major city in the US has people on the street. Where is the government?

'It has money. It's spending it elsewhere,' and he can't help but laugh. 'It's interesting now what's happening. If you look back over history, pre-World War II, the church looked after the poor people. And then post-war, you had the welfare state in many countries in the world. And it was government. But then it seems like we're going into another age where government is saying it's not us; we can't handle it.

'And they're not particularly good at it. Because the governments say, we'd never have done something like the Homeless World Cup. We'd have taken four years to think about it and then not done it very well. So other people are coming in, social entrepreneurs or even corporations. You can see individuals like Bill Gates who take the view that we can deal with some of these more intractable problems. And we'll get on with it. And we'll be more efficient.'

To add to Mel's point, patience is not a quality in the treasury of most governments and big institutions. Politicians campaign in the US, Russia and even Western Samoa on platforms that they will get rid of crime or solve the crises of the environment, healthcare, education or any other issue. But the electorate wants to hear about results, which is difficult when, for example, those in the US Congress have a term of two years, and the President four. The kind of time needed to effect real change, as we have seen, is often a lot longer than that – give or take, it may be 20-odd years.

As Wil and Flor discovered on their small farm in Amsterdam, big non-governmental organisations have procedures to follow, reports to read and write, and practices to study, like any big corporation. Patience is required on the part of any individuals who are dealing with them.

Even when big institutions contribute to the smaller organisations, as Sébastien Marot from Friends points out, 'Time is one of those things donors do not understand. Even though the people usually have kids themselves, they forget that. Money! Numbers. They want to see numbers.' Luckily for him, he has kept his group running over 14 years. 'So after a while you have the numbers, because of the sheer time involved in the ongoing operation.'

Government 103: Right-wing, left-wing – it makes no difference

The good news, or the bad if you were hoping government was the answer, is that whether one is a fundamentalist Muslim or Christian or even a social atheist, the issue of whether governments work is not a matter of left or right. Both come under criticism. Naomi Mayers says inefficiencies are 'to do with the mentality of bureaucrats and the change of governments, what a friend of mine calls "The Follies". We sit here waiting, and the bureaucrats do this dance on the stage. Then they leave off, and another lot comes on. They do their little thing, with a report. And the next lot comes on. While we're still sitting there waiting for something to be done. How many reports do they have to spend millions on that no one takes any notice of?'

Paul Pholeros agrees, having been frustrated by Labor then Liberal then Labor governments in the seemingly obvious task of making bathrooms work across Australia. 'An organisational anthropologist is writing a book on the work we do, and she's flabbergasted. She's talked to the so-called left of politics and the right, and the key bit is neither really are interested in the content. Whether it be taps or toilets. People in Canberra will say, "That's just tedious. What's your grand vision? What's the ideal house?"

'I say, "If you can get a tap up the right way, then I'd start to think more grandly." I never ask a person about their ideal house when there's sewage in the lounge room.'

One recent proposal particularly incensed Paul. In 2007, the government minister in charge of Aboriginal Affairs suggested his own solution to housing: yurts.

Originally found in Mongolia, a yurt is a simple five-sided tent with one door and one window. In Australia they've often been modified and built in wood, and used as children's playhouses. The government's preferred version was a plywood yurt, about five by five metres, with one door and one window – basically a bare wooden room.

'He wanted to build 18,000 of them. This way they'd solve the Aboriginal housing problem. And his staff said, "You have to admit that the minister's point is correct. Your own data shows that the biggest problem is in the houses with a shower, laundry, toilet and kitchen. So we'd be better off *not building them*."

'The particular model the minister preferred was called the "Aussie Battler". A stripped-back yurt that has no insulation or lining, basically a box.

'My test,' says Paul, 'is this: would you put your mother in an Aussie Battler in central Australia in summer?'

When he put that question, Paul did not receive a reply.

Government corruption, inefficiency – or having not Yoda-like but yurt-like answers – is not restricted to any one country. Ronni Kahn says, 'We have slack government in every bloody country. Very few governments do what they're supposed to be doing, which is look after the people. And I don't blame the people. I blame the system for making it so hard for people.'

Government 104: Government is self-preserving – that is its nature

An old fable tells of the sad relationship between a scorpion and a frog. The scorpion begs the frog to take it across the river to the other side. The frog demurs, saying the scorpion would just sting it to death. The scorpion promises it won't, pointing out that if it killed the frog, it would only drown and kill itself. So with that promise, the frog begins to swim across the river with the scorpion on its back. Midway, the scorpion stings the frog. The frog cries out, 'But why?' And the scorpion shrugs, if scorpions can shrug, and says, 'It's my nature.'

According to the US Constitution, government is meant to be 'of the people, by the people, for the people'. Other governments lay claim to those ideals. However, Rachel Wotton's community of sex workers, also people, remain unprotected. She points out that 'the people that are running government and their decisions are so far removed from the grass-roots level of the people who are affected by the policies they're writing, that I think the politicians lose their humanity sometimes.

'For example, with American presidential elections, how many millions of dollars are given to potential candidates for the presidency? I'd rather them say, this year what we've decided to do is fund a group of organisations so that everyone has a place to live.'

In the Netherlands, Mustafa points out that the government doesn't bring in obvious solutions to local problems; that is, local people. So in Slotervaart they bring in people from outside who have learned academically about the situation of the Moroccans. 'They haven't put the trust in us. The government is busy with a lot of things but not the real problem. A lot of Stichtings – government-funded non-profit organisations – when there's a vacancy, they give it to someone who comes from elsewhere. He comes here, and he has never seen a Moroccan.'

Father Michael sees the problem as the distance governments keep from their own people. He also sees it within his own Church. 'Our big institutions lose the importance of the simple things of life. They're so involved in how things are organised, with meetings or gatherings. And yes, there has to be planning and organisation. But it's the individual before you that makes the difference. What are you doing for that person who sits before you, stands before you or is in a bed before you? How does what you're doing relate to them?

'Today, for example, the Thai Prime Minister is going to the temple. Will he ever come back? It has to be more than that. It has to be a willingness to spend time.'

Politicians may seek to fix problems by appearing, like the Thai

Prime Minister, at temples or churches, or where homes have been destroyed, such as in New Orleans after Hurricane Katrina. But their visits are fleeting, and they don't have the staying power of the many dedicated servants of the community who try to fight the system, knowing first-hand its ineffectiveness.

Brenda Gregg, in Pittsburgh, expands on the notion of why society and its members have to be responsible when their own governments fail. 'We may have the finest healthcare facilities, but many won't meet the people where they're at.

'If government *could* do it, they would have done it. People change people's lives. Not institutions. It's those one-on-one relationships, whether it's with a physician or with a worker. That's really what's going to make the difference in people's lives. If you don't have a friendly place to walk through the door, if it's intimidating, if it's not sensitive to the cultures people live in, it won't meet their needs.'

Siri points out why individuals still have to get involved, even if one has a positive view of government. 'Some governments try to help. And having been involved with children on numerous occasions, I see sometimes government agencies can't reach them all. They are short of staff. And many of these cases need person-to-person counselling.'

The issue of trust, especially in sensitive issues, is something that government cannot overcome, full stop. 'They try to set up in communities everywhere,' says Siri, 'but those infected with HIV/AIDS, for example, will not reveal themselves. They remain anonymous. Only those who are close to them know. The government can't help, because they can't know. But people like the teachers know, because they are locals here.'

What the people described in these pages agree on is that because government does not and cannot solve the problems, it is up to the people – those who make up the 'governed' – to create change. It is what each individual has to offer that makes all the difference.

To create change is a matter of being flexible. But think of how hard it is for each one of us to change when we want to. Then think how it must be for government, an organism made up of many individuals under layers of rules. As Sandra Meihubers says, 'Government is about compartmentalising. And you need to be open.'

And as Sandra points out, for individuals, there is a pay-back. One of her greatest joys is in sponsoring one student in the village in Nepal where she works. Making a difference in just one human being's life, as the old Jewish philosopher Maimonides pointed out, is worthwhile: 'To save a life is to save a universe.'

Chapter 9

The moral imperative

We make a living by what we get,
but we make a life by what we give.

Winston Churchill

If the consensus is that government can't change society one individual at a time, that still begs the question: what is the moral imperative to help others?

Why is your problem my problem? Or my problem yours?

Ronni Kahn says a traditional starting point is the notion of 'There but for the grace of ... name your deity or belief ... go I', or, 'Do unto others as you would have them do unto you'.

Sébastien Marot, who found himself caring for children in Cambodia, says, 'Why Cambodia? Our work will eventually be in France as well. It will eventually be in the US. In our countries too we say no no, we don't have the same problems as these poor countries with children and their safety. But we have exactly the same problems. And that's what our organisation Child Safe is about also, now starting in the West. So I'm coming back to my roots. It's a global problem. Everyone needs to be involved. I do believe that.'

But shouldn't the Cambodians do this work themselves? Sébastien says they do. 'That's why Mitt Samlanh is run by Cambodians. We from overseas start the project, because we have the experience and the access to money, but the objective is for them to run it. That's why we train people. It's so they can train their children. It's their responsibility. They have to do it. I will help them to do it, but I will not do it for them.'

As to the question of why one can't just focus on one's own prosperity, and not worry about others' problems, Sébastien is more forceful: 'If you have a lot of people that are unhappy and miserable, and you're happy and rich and sitting on your beach, they're going to target you first. If you're a rich person that did well, great. But think about the others that are behind you.

'I was trained in politics. Prosperity now is in the hands of a smaller group of people, and increasingly so. While you have a bigger group of people getting frustrated. That will bite back one way or the other. Cambodia is the perfect example. I say to the local people we work with, "You have to do this because otherwise you will have the same situation as 1975. The cities were rich. The countryside was starving. They came and took the city and killed all your people in the city because you didn't share." And that's what '75 was about. It was triggered by Vietnam and other things. But globally, peasants get roused up by people that take advantage of them.'

The violence that occurred in 2008 from Haiti to the Philippines over the escalating price of rice and the shortage of other foods illustrates Sébastien's point. Mel Young, now working with homeless people in over 70 countries via the game of football, shares Sébastien's view. His point is that the situation is unsustainable with or without the 'revolution'. 'You can't have a situation where the rich get richer to such an extent that some people are richer than whole countries. And where you've got a level of poverty where people can't even get to water. Some of our teams haven't got shoes. It's just not sustainable. People say, oh well, there'll be an uprising. Well, maybe there will and maybe there won't. People in politics wait for the revolution, but it never happens.

'But other things happen that are unsustainable. One example is that you're much more likely, if you're homeless and living in poverty, to get sick. And now they're talking about this multi-resistant TB. They cough, it goes through the air, and I get it. So if nothing else, it's in everyone's interest to make sure that you guard against that sort of thing. How do you do that? You lift people out of poverty.'

Father Michael Bassano says he learned he couldn't remain isolated when he left his small Italian-American community in Binghamton to learn about his own church in Chile and Buddhist Thailand. 'We need to be connected to what's going on in the world,' he says. 'Not just to be focused on challenges in our own family lives. We need to see that there are many people suffering worse than we are. It can be Darfur or anywhere. We are connected far beyond our boundaries and need to try and alleviate some of that suffering. You're not just located in your family and your city, but to other people, whether it's in another state or in a hospice somewhere.'

Paul Pholeros, working with the Aboriginal community in Australia, is angered by the fact that so many of the friends he's made have already died. 'Most of the mates I've had have all died in their forties or early fifties. There's no reason why that should happen. No technical reason. Why do Aboriginal people put up with that? Why do we put up with that?'

To Paul, the moral imperative comes with the privilege of being better off than others by the very nature of one's birth. 'You have to accept that you have power, and the power is the education and health you've got. We live longer than people in a lot of parts of the world. And we've got wealth. Even if you are poor in Western terms, you're still much better off than most of the rest of the planet.

'The next bit of that is to say, "How do I use it?" It may be just a drop in the bucket, but you need the drop to begin. Then you start filling the bucket slowly. If you don't start the first step, then you're never going to go on the long march.'

This doesn't mean you need to live in a shack and have no food yourself; you just need to do something. 'Maybe Gandhi and a few great leaders would disagree. But I think that a lot of people in the middle of the road can do it and have a bit of fun.'

Father Michael concurs. 'I certainly at times feel sad and tired when I see so much need at the temple. This past week, we had four people die. It makes you wonder, "Can I keep doing this heavy work?" And when a new person comes in that new bed, there's that hesitancy: do I get to know this person who's not going to get better?

'But sometimes courage is the quiet voice at the end of the day saying, "Try again tomorrow." So I get up each day to go to the temple. I keep from that sense of despair by knowing I'll do whatever I can each day, knowing that that's enough.'

Though technically a missionary, Father Michael's own moral

imperative has nothing to do with converting anyone to Catholicism. He refers again to Mother Teresa who, when asked if she was converting Hindus in Calcutta, said that converting was God's business. A dear friend who is a Buddhist monk told him that they are on the same journey together, like Buddha and Jesus being brothers.

'I'm still rooted in the Christian tradition, but I've learned so much from Buddhism. Because exposure to every religion helps us to become better in our own tradition, to see the unity in the diversity. To see that there are differences with the Other, but that's the diversity. It's not to condemn the Other. Not to divide people into we and they. We are all family.'

Father Michael says the most prejudice he experienced in Thailand came from his own community. When he was working with the hill tribe people in the north, he would make a reverent bow to their sculpture of the Buddha. A few Catholics who witnessed this complained that he was abandoning his faith. Father Michael told them he was not recognising a god in the Buddha, only another teacher. He was being respectful to the Other, the Thai, who he was caring for, and who were, like his Buddhist friends, caring for him.

As he sees the moral imperative, it goes beyond what is actually of benefit to other people. And this is the crux of the matter. Through getting to know different human beings across the planet, *he* has benefited. 'My life has changed,' he says. 'All I have to do is be open. I don't know what to expect. I only know that I want to be open to whatever they have to give to me, to the interchange, the sharing.'

Chapter 10

What one gets – the contentment of giving

> I slept and dreamt that life was joy. I awoke and saw that life was service. I acted and behold, service was joy.
>
> Rabindranath Tagore

I learned the word and the concept of sharing in kindergarten so far as I can remember, though I'm sure my mother tried to get me to share my toys with my brother earlier than that. At my school, we came to class and shared our experiences and things, even a toy, in the American childhood ritual called 'Show and Tell'. At one time I believe I showed my garbage truck, which was then my most prized possession. (Another time I shared – i.e. gave away – my mother's silver comb, which of course wasn't mine to share in the first place!)

Parents try to teach their children about sharing at an early age; it is considered one of our communal values. And a value implicitly has worth. Why? What does one get from sharing?

The first thing everyone whose stories I've touched on in this book will tell you is that it's not as if some miracle happens when you share, and money just leaps into your pockets. But what they do say is that they see money differently. What they appreciate is that money becomes secondary. It's not their first waking thought.

More importantly, they feel useful. Anyone who has ever felt that they are worthless or of no use will understand this. Feelings of 'uselessness' can result from being unemployed, being undervalued, left out of decision making or even ignored in the office. But feeling wanted or even needed is crucial to well-being. That means being connected, whether it's with one's spouse, friends or new or old communities.

For Alphonce Omolu, the feelings of connection he has with his spouse and with his community are strongly linked. 'Am I happy in my marriage? Excellently happy,' he says. 'Both of us have taken upon ourselves to help others, other children, other young people, and other families. We both focus on the same direction. She does it on her own level with relatives, and she also works with women's groups working with HIV/AIDS orphans.'

Alphonce talks about one of the things his wife's group does at Christmas, which sounds similar to Siri's network. 'In December, they put together their own clothing and buy foodstuffs and distribute this to the poorest of the poor within the area. So she and I have similar ideas and aspirations of what we want from life.

'The fact that we are many people in this world is not by accident. It gives us the opportunity to live with one another, to support one another. That's why people are so different, with such different skills and capabilities. We need one another to actualise our lives, to share these different skills and capabilities.

'For me, it has to be two ways. You are given, and you give too. It can't be only one direction. If it is only in one direction, then that loses meaning,' he says, echoing the Buddhists. 'It has to be two ways, in that you give and you receive in one way or another. You may not receive what you give, but you receive in different ways.

'I feel self-fulfilled when I see people happy, when they achieve their life objectives. So that's the way I get back.'

What Mel Young received from his years publishing *The Big Issue*, and now in realising his own childhood dream of a football league through the Homeless World Cup, is pleasure from the work itself. 'What do I get out of it? I think you have to be honest. People say they do it all for the common good. It's not true. You get something out of it. I get a tremendous sense of satisfaction personally. It's very hard. We work incredibly hard here with very little resources. But it's almost like not a job. It's like we're part of a movement. We're change-makers. And I love coming to work. I love it. The biggest problem is getting me not to stay at work. And so in that sense it's not work, or not a traditional form of employment if you like.'

And with his wife doing social work, his marriage hasn't suffered in the slightest, but rather has been buoyed. And as Mel points out, his children, who are all grown now, also get immense pride from the Cup.

When asked about her work and her relationships, Sandra Meihubers says she couldn't wish for a different scenario. 'Paul and I are independent people who live together and love each other. A lot of people call us soulmates because when we're together we're emotionally wrapped around each other. Yet we can be apart for several weeks, and that's fine because we're immersed in our work. And there's a health to it, because we're not threatened by what the other person might be doing.

'If anything, I'm energised when I meet up with him, because I hear what he's been doing. And then hopefully,' she says with a Mona Lisa smile, 'he listens to what I've been doing too. And we pick up bits and pieces, and we grow. Because we do overlap in our work, we can talk about the same kinds of programmes and communities. I develop my intimacy with my work, he develops his, and we share the overlaps.'

And of her work in Nepal, with people far removed from her own ethnic group or social circle, she says, 'I like going into a place where you see how a programme can be developed. I enjoy the process of starting from nothing and seeing how we can put all the pieces together. It gives me the satisfaction of seeing something where there was nothing before.'

When I suggest that she and Paul could make a lot more money, Sandra says, 'That's the accepted wisdom, to focus on money. But that doesn't mean the accepted wisdom is right. Paul and I live very simply. I charge reasonable consultancy fees. People pay me. Every time I chuck out an invoice, I get paid. That's the good thing about my clients in the Aboriginal community.

'But personally, on one level, I do find it hard when I see the sick children in Nepal and their lack of access to medicines. There was one young boy I met last year whose mother died between then and now, because she fell in the village. She injured herself, she couldn't get care, and she died. Life can be tough and brutal.

'But if someone said to me you've got to stop the work you're doing and do private practice for the rest of your working career, and you're going to make a squillion dollars, I'd say give me the lethal injection now.

'Because now I have all sorts of experiences. I can work in a Nepalese village. I can also be dancing at three in the morning under a starry sky, music blaring from some ungodly sounding stereo system and everyone dancing, because it's a festival. And I get three hours' sleep and the next day I'm back to work.

'Then when one of those young fellas you're helping sees you're about to leave, and you've mainly had quite formal conversations, and he just jumps up and grabs you and walks away, that's pretty good.' Sandra's eyes fill with tears. 'He really values it. And I value him. And it becomes addictive, the feeling. Joy. Not joy. I don't know. Tears maybe. I work and play with the same people.' Including her own husband. 'It's seductive. It's really seductive.'

Paul speaks of Sandra with similar admiration and enthusiasm. Like her, he acknowledges that if they had had children it might have been slightly different. 'It's been a lot easier for Sandra and me to put enormous amounts of time and money into things that we would have had to put into kids. We've even worked together in Nepal. She knew the villagers and had the relationships, and I had another technical skill.

'It's a fantastic life. I get a huge amount out of it. The mythology is that somehow I'm being noble. But I'm doing the work I was trained to do, and enjoying it. If I wasn't enjoying it, I wouldn't be doing it. So it's not an act of sacrifice. It's an act of doing stuff I was trained to do.'

Paul, who says he learned to see from blind Yami Lester, also learned a different way of perception from other Aboriginal elders in the desert. This is one of the experiences that affirms for him that he has gained as much as he has given, if not more.

'To students, I say, don't worry about getting involved; just jump in. The people will sort you out.

'I remember one of the first groups that was key to me was two old blokes. This was after we'd done a bit at the base of the Rock. They took me under their wing, very polite people, very formal. We were sitting on the ground, and one of them says, "Just look over there." Not at Uluru, the famous rock, but just a bit of country. They said, "What do you see?"

'I remember saying, "There's a tree, and a bush and a rock." They looked at each other and put their heads in their hands and said, "Oh. This must be horrendous for you, if you can see nothing. So the way we live and what we do and the way we talk, this must be all a complete bloody mystery to you." I remember thinking, yeah, you're right. It is a complete mystery.

'So then I used to say to these people, "So you'll teach me?" And they'd say, "Yeah." And I was ready with a notebook. Then there'd be nothing. Until they'd say, "Anyway, let's go for a walk." So I'd put my teaching pad back. And this went on for ages and ages and ages.'

Later, as Aboriginal activists, younger men in their forties, negotiated the title of Ayers Rock back to traditional ownership, renaming it Uluru, Paul's old men said, 'Oh, those young blokes. That's a waste of time, all that.'

Paul asked why, since Aboriginals were indeed the traditional owners. 'They answered that they didn't own the rock; it would always be there. So what was the drama?' The old men said that if the activists had problems with the politicians, all they had to do was just bring them out there. Paul asked if then they would teach the politicians. The old men just looked at him and said, 'No. The country will get into them.'

'All of a sudden, the penny dropped,' Paul says, visibly moved. 'The literal translation of what they said in Pinjara was, "The country gets into you". You don't have a choice 20 years on. You just drive the country, sleep in the country. You're in the place. Your head isn't over there or back there, thinking about the next thing. You're happy to sit in the place. And it may sound guru-ish, and I don't think there is a metaphysical and a physical.

'I think they just had a physical, which became metaphysical. Their message was just bloody stop. Just bloody sit down.

'Then you see all the stories from over the last 20 years, and all the people who've driven with you when you've driven it, when you've broken down, when it's been raining. You see the country has a million faces. It has rain. It has animals. It has incidents. And their argument is there's a reason why those incidents occurred. Which is building the country to you. And you can't be separate from it.

'And if you sleep by yourself in a swag in the central desert 100 km from any settlement, even as a white fella, if you go through that and think you're a big person as opposed to absolutely insignificant, then I reckon you're better than I am. In the middle of the night, you can hear your heart beating, it's so quiet. There's a star and you're on the plain. And that to me is a great thing. These people there led me to those experiences. How can I ever repay them?'

As moved as Paul is by the life to which he's been introduced, he's not a sentimentalist. He knows exactly why he went there, and the bottom line of what he gives – and gets.

'I didn't go out there to be liked. There are people who want to become Aboriginal. I didn't. I'm a white person. I was there because they got me to do a job. To make the houses work better so their kids weren't as crook. So their kids didn't live less than if I'd had kids. And every waking hour I was out there, that was my main intent.

'Some people say, "Oh, you want to change the world?" I say, "Yeah, but one little bit of it." And it's good to know we made a dent working with a lot of good people, black and white.'

In the United States, Brenda Gregg is more softly spoken, but her view about investing in other human beings is similar to Paul's, or even Brak Sareth's, the young Buddhist monk in Cambodia. 'You get a better life,' she says. 'Because you're only as safe as those around you; you're only as happy as those who are in your path.

'And I love seeing someone's life change. It's a very selfish feeling of being able to pride yourself to see someone do better for themselves. It's the little things.'

Having dealt with so much need in China, Chung To says, 'I get more happiness and more strength. And there's the dark side of it. I became more depressed sometimes. I have seen horrible things, which I was not trained to see. I saw a lot of people dying of AIDS, literally in my arms.

'And in the beginning my parents were very sceptical. Because I'm the only son. They didn't want me to suffer. But my goal is to empower the children to help themselves. If I help 5000 kids, it's a great thing. But what I want is those 5000 kids to become a Chung To, to help more people. That has a rippling effect.

'It's not just about us helping a group of underprivileged kids, but it's about empowering them to help themselves. Now there are a lot at university who come back to help us. Some have even graduated university and decided to work for us full-time as paid staff. Others got very good jobs and work for us as volunteers on weekends.

'This year, three university students we sponsored came to Hong Kong, and ran the marathon. They stood in front of the public and said, "Although I came from a family where my parents had AIDS, I'm not ashamed of my family situation. I made it through university, and I'm proud."

'It took a lot of courage and breaks a lot of stigma, for the younger AIDS orphans behind too. It makes me feel proud, because we must have done something right by these children, so that they have the courage to tell other people.'

The horrors Chung To witnessed may have made him less religious, as he says, wondering why the God he believed in would let them happen. On the other hand, he also has gained a belief in hope, on a larger scale.

'I think everybody can do what I do. Because I don't want people to think this is about me. It's about how everyone can do something great.

'I have learned that there's a lot of hope in life. I have faced a lot of obstacles. And a lot of people came to help us, wonderful volunteers, great people. I might be the front, but behind there are a lot of people who believe in our philosophy and work and have given support. It makes me feel the world is a hopeful place.'

Then there's Ronni Kahn, the event planner, connecting hungry people to food that those who paid for it no longer need. When asked what she gets, she first smiles. Then her eyes begin to fill with tears. She echoes the same deep physical response given by each person I have asked.

She says, 'I get to feel special. That I've done something more than just wake up in the morning and worry about me. That I've shown my children there's more to life than just worrying about ourselves. I just feel blessed that I got that message. It came late, but hey!

'Someone said to me, "You started your charitable life too early; you should have waited till you had enough money." But nobody ever thinks they've got enough. Even the richest. He'll never believe he has enough.

'What you get is what money can't buy you. You get to know that you have made a difference to people who you don't even know.

'There's one venue where our van goes, where the people all live individually. And they didn't know each other before. But our Oz Harvest van now has created a community. People come together to wait for it. They talk, sit around, then share their food.

'And those who work for us love working for us and feel they're working for a family. Dozens of like-minded people, because of what we do. So knowing that I have made a difference in my little element, that I've touched indirectly people who are hungry every day, it's a luxury that will stay with me forever.' She smiles. 'This is winning the lottery and keeping it every day.'

Sébastien Marot too has found a version of happiness. It's come after time and patience. 'I know that I am much more efficient if I'm happy. So I try to make sure that everyone that I work with is not struggling, is comfortable and can concentrate on the work. You don't need to be miserable to do great stuff. There are some people who had to, for example the Mandelas, absolutely amazing. But they were fighting an entire system. And they were devoted to that.

'I sacrificed a lot in the beginning. It was hard. I spent all the money that I had. I worked at night in order to make money during the day, because our training programme didn't have funding for two and a half years. I translated newspapers and things. All that money went into the service, and I lived very basically. Not miserably, but basically.

'My private life became a super-mess, because I got involved and I couldn't leave. My partner and I divorced. It wasn't something I wanted at all. But I'm now very happy and more efficient than I was before. I have another baby coming, a two-and-a-half-year-old and my lovely wife. I'm not rich, and for retirement I have nothing. So the future looks bleak, but at the same time I'm building knowledge and experience and eventually will find a way to make money with that.

'I'm here. I can drink and eat. I have a good life. I have a nice house, a beautiful garden, and wonderful weather all the time. That's not bad. It was fascinating in Japan and I loved it, and Paris is a great city, but this is such a great life.

'I'm very lucky actually. I'm getting upset and fighting for the children, but I'm not suffering. Because I'm happy, and I sleep at night. Though I have some frustrations, I see all these people around me who ask, "What do I do with my life? Where am I going? And why am I doing this?"

'I don't have that issue. Because I have a passion. I'm lucky.'

Being lucky, grateful, and having a sense of purpose is universal among these people – whether it's Brak Sareth, the Buddhist monk turned teacher, also in Cambodia, or Mustafa with his soccer training in Amsterdam, or Rachel Wotton fighting for sex workers' and disabled people's rights in Australia.

They express little in the way of self-flagellation or self-doubt, but they also don't proselytise. None of them are trying to convince anyone else of anything. None are asking anyone else to do anything unless they want to. They have each found what they needed, to quote St Francis again, preaching the gospel of the contentment of giving – without words.

Here and now.

Even those who might push the reward of a hereafter prefer to speak about this life. Father Michael, the 'monk from Christian', as his Buddhist friends call him, doesn't think about the rewards he might receive in heaven later. 'The point is to make a little heaven for us now,' he says. 'The eternal is now, not after.

'I don't think they'd throw me out of the church for that. That's not heretical. Where is this idea that we have to wait to bring some sense of heaven?

'These states of being, we have to see them as a way of experiencing heaven now. Jesus says the Kingdom of Heaven is in your midst now. It's not something you wait for. Some mystics say if we're waiting to reach heaven in the future, we're missing something – now – or as the Buddhists would say, the present moment. This is where if we can bring love and compassion to people that brings them to life, it brings us to life.

'So if I give of myself, I get so much more.'

What he gets is a sense that one's life has meaning.

'I remember a guy, Chayanat,' recalls Father Michael, his voice faltering at times. 'He was a chef for ten years in Tokyo. He got HIV/

AIDS and came back to our hospice. His family rejected him, except for his daughter who was a soldier; she alone would visit him.

'But in the temple, he was very demanding. I had to wash his dishes twice. If he didn't like the food, he'd tell me I had to go to the supermarket and buy this ingredient or that. He was a real test of patience.

'But one day out of the blue, he calls me over and says, "I want to tell you, I look at you, Michael. And I see in you the eyes of compassion. I want you to be here at the moment of my death, so that I can die together with you."

'So he wouldn't be alone when he died.

'It was at that moment that I knew that's what makes life meaningful for me. That we can touch each other, when we least recognise or know it.

'We were there with him when he died. And there with him in his cremation. So if I can, I call that a blessing, that I was there for that moment. That's what makes life fulfilling for me. Does it happen all the time? No, but it's those moments that we remember. And if each of us can have those moments from time to time where we touch each other, we know that our lives have meaning.

'It brings a sense of what's most important, what makes an impression that lasts forever, which is the eternal. Heaven on earth is here, where we're helping each other, not distinguishing boundaries and nations. Where we come together as one family. Where I am a part of everyone. I do not exist alone. That's when heaven becomes real; when no man is an island.'

Father Michael and I parted. He was going back to the United States for a few weeks, and then onto Tanzania, for the next ten years of his life. His handshake was strong, and his eyes literally twinkled through those thick black glasses of his. Then he disappeared into the crowd.

I make another visit to Siri's garden. It feels as if it is indeed a tropical, peaceful island, a piece of heaven on earth. Here she grows her ghost-like orchids, breathing in their nutrients through the air as they do.

Further away is her vegetable patch where she includes other things not usually found in Thailand, like zucchini, plants she has discovered can round out her garden.

By her pond is a small resthouse with a lovely teak covered porch. Here her aunt is taking a nap. Her husband breaks out a bottle of wine that they made themselves. It is from three years back, when they decided to grow grapes. We nickname it Chateau Siri. The taste is definitely of alcohol and yeast; the sense of the grapes, though, is mysteriously gone.

Still, it is an enjoyable afternoon in the sun. Once in a while, a fish jumps out of the pond. Yet out of this place of tranquillity and apparent luxury, which costs so little really, thousands of children have benefited. Their families now have little ponds where catfish scour the bottoms (the sour-faced things are not prone to jumping for joy) and gardens where zucchini are planted as well. It expands their possibilities for food, exposing them to other ideas on diet, another example of the Other, or the variation that allows real growth.

As her husband, partner in her operations, and former chauffeur, pours round two of Chateau Siri, and she serves sun-dried fish, Siri says, 'When you help others, it is like a picnic. Like when you go on vacation. And you will feel happy, when you see the people who are suffering get better. Then, in terms of helping, it is solely happiness to help. Then helping brings about contentment. And that's why I help, because it makes me happy.'

Then she turns the tables on the author, as he sips his wine in the sun. 'Do you feel that coming to work here is like coming to a picnic or coming here is hard?'

I have to admit, it is enjoyable.

'Right, it does look like a picnic,' she smiles. 'We are having wine. I don't wait for happiness in the next life. It comes about in the present.'

As we make a toast with the last glasses from this bottle of Chateau Siri, echoing Father Michael and his 'eternal now', Siri says, 'Because when help is given now, happiness comes now also.'

Epilogue

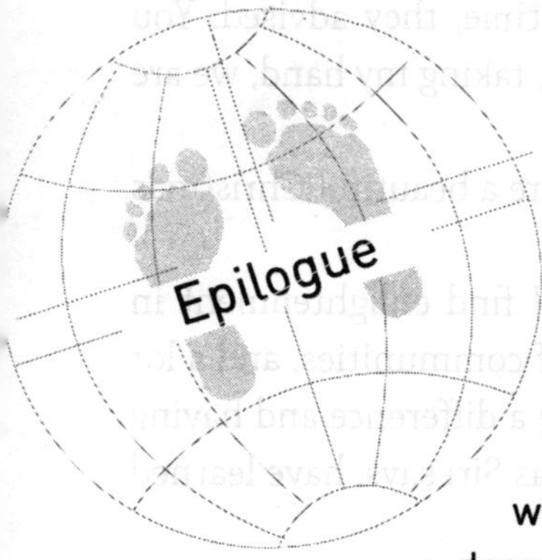

> **Love thy neighbour as thyself.**
>
> Leviticus 19:18

> **Thousands of candles can be lighted from a single candle, and the life of the candle will not be shortened. Happiness never decreases by being shared.**
>
> Buddha

Many of the people who have most impressed me as balanced, happy human beings are those in this book, people who work individually and at a grass-roots level. With the help of friends and colleagues worldwide, I was fortunate to find these architects, dentists, teachers, farmers, sex workers, priests, event planners, investment bankers and monks. They are a motley crew, ranging from former criminals to former saints, some with three-act stories that rival any Hollywood thriller. They live across many continents, from Africa to Asia and Australia, Europe and the US. But what they all have in common is a dream, a commitment to working hard to help others, and joy.

So – why help others? Because we're told to by our parents, by political or religious leaders or by society? These people would say no. We help others because it makes our own lives happier, healthier and more rewarding, sometimes even financially.

Strangely, the ultimate form of self-help, as it's popularly called, is to aid 'selves' other than our own. Purely and selfishly.

People who believe that greed is healthy have been shown to be wrong, and those who believe, like the Beatles, in the power of love, seem to be right.

This last was made evident to me when I went to visit two of the people in this book, Wil and Flor, one Christmas at their children's farm. In their cosy little house, where they had even adopted a little orphaned lamb as a household pet, they stopped me when I went to leave on my busy visiting schedule. Take time, they advised. You need to enjoy life. More importantly, Wil said, taking my hand, we are worried about you. Because we love you.

Though the words cost no money, they were a beautiful Christmas gift.

No need to be worried, my friends. Did I find enlightenment in writing this book? I don't know. I met a lot of communities, and a lot of individuals within them, that were making a difference and having the time of their lives. These are people who, as Siri says, have learned the 'contentment of giving'.

That contentment is something we all know from childhood. We know that the joy of gifts is in the giving. We are all excited when we see the look on our beloved's face when they open our present to them. It is the giving that feels important.

That is at the heart of having the courage to dream and to make one's dreams into realities for ourselves and everyone around us. This courage is the antidote to a whole world of ills. Over the course of such a life, we lose financial worry, have extraordinary adventures, create a lot of friendships and gain – yes, love.

As this book ends, we might realise we knew about these ideas all along. Of course that's the great thing about truths; once we know them, we realise we always did know them – like Dorothy in *The Wizard of Oz*, with *her* shoes, which could always take her home if she only knew how to use them.

The journey, as Father Michael and Siri say, can start with as simple an act as a smile. That takes even less effort than clicking one's shoes in Oz. And it is even more rewarding.

Useful websites

You can discover more about the work of some of the people and organisations profiled in this book through these websites:

Brak Sareth
Raise and Support the Poor
www.rspngo.org

Brenda Gregg
Project Destiny
www.projectdestiny.org

Chung To
Chi Heng Foundation
www.chfaidsorphans.com

Idris Azraq
Democratic Justice and Equality Movement
www.sudanjem.info

Mel Young
Homeless World Cup
www.homelessworldcup.org

Father Michael Bassano
Maryknoll
www.maryknoll.org

Mustafa Akka
info@aracora.nl

Naomi Mayers and Sol Bellear
Aboriginal Medical Service, Redfern, Sydney
www.ahmrc.org.au

Paul Pholeros
Healthabitat
www.healthabitat.com

Rachel Wotton
Scarlet Alliance
www.scarletalliance.org.au
Touching Base
www.touchingbase.org

Ronni Kahn
Oz Harvest
www.ozharvest.org

Sébastien Marot
Friends International
www.friends-international.org

Acknowledgements

Thank you to everyone who shared their stories in these pages. They gave their time, trust and commitment with warm hearts and generosity. I'd also like to thank all the people whom I interviewed who could not be included in this book for reasons of space and time.

Thanks too to the many people who don't get publicly celebrated for what they do. I know one who, as a young woman of 17, adopted two orphans and never wavered in her devotion to creating the best life for them. Others include staff at Monash University who quietly give their time and efforts to students in need, and helped fulfil one of my own dreams. Another is an old man who, with only his bottom teeth left, sells flowers to taxi drivers: whether the people buy or not, day after day he gives everyone the free blossom of his smile. Unsung heroes abound everywhere, and their praises should be shouted from the rooftops.

Gratitude as well to my publishers and editors; they have been steadfast supporters of this work. Also, my appreciation to those who have read drafts and given feedback during the whole writing process.

Thanks especially to Chris Hennessy: without his invaluable support, kindness and friendship, this book would not have been possible.

I am endlessly moved by the heights of human compassion that I have been privileged to witness everywhere in the world. In what I'm convinced is our true economy, these are the acts that make us all the richer.

Gratefully yours,
Miles Roston